THE MAKING OF THE TEST BAN TREATY

# THE MAKING OF THE TEST BAN TREATY

*by*

RONALD J. TERCHEK

MARTINUS NIJHOFF / THE HAGUE / 1970

ISBN 978-94-011-8689-6 ISBN 978-94-011-9502-7 (eBook)
DOI 10.1007/978-94-011-9502-7

*To My Mother and the*
*Memory of My Father*

## TABLE OF CONTENTS

## TABLES

# ACKNOWLEDGMENT

I am greatly indebted to the many individuals who gave freely of their time and talents. Several Senators, senatorial assistants, officials in the executive branch, and officers in nongovernmental organizations provided me with information with the understanding that their names would not be used but without their help the book would have never been completed.

I would especially like to thank the Society for the Study of Social Issues and the University of Maryland for assistance in completing the manuscript. Professor Elmer Plischke read an earlier draft of the work and offered several helpful suggestions. It is to my wife Mary, however, to whom I owe my greatest debt for her encouragement, editorial assistance, and patience.

CHAPTER I

# INTRODUCTION

Eighteen years after the United States presented its plan for the international control of atomic energy to the United Nations, the first major arms control agreement was signed between the United States and the Soviet Union. Including Great Britain, the three major nuclear powers pledged to refrain from nuclear tests in the atmosphere, outer space, and underwater in a treaty negotiated in Moscow within two weeks during the summer of 1963. It was hoped that the treaty would at least discourage those phases of the arms race which required large-yield nuclear explosions in the atmosphere or outer space as well as eliminate further radioactive pollution of the atmosphere. In addition, the test ban would discourage, though not eliminate, the development of nuclear weapons by other treaty adherents because the underground testing allowed under the terms of the document would escalate already heavy costs for countries intending to conduct their first nuclear tests. The Kennedy administration expected other agreements to follow the test ban treaty, particularly an agreement to keep outer space free from nuclear warheads and to outlaw underground tests in the near future.[1] But one of the most important anticipated benefits of the treaty was the expected improvement of relations between the United States and the Soviet Union.

The treaty was important not only because it was a tangible breakthrough in East-West arms-control negotiations but also because of its implications for domestic and international politics. To many Americans, agreements with the Soviet Union had inevitably favored the communists who, according to this argument, would break their word whenever it served their convenience. Focusing on the Yalta and Potsdam agreements, skeptics saw the test ban as another instrument to serve Soviet interests but endanger American security. To the opponents of the treaty, any gain for the Soviet Union would inevitably lead to commensurate losses for the United States.

[1] See, for example, his speech to the United Nations, September 20, 1963.

However, a substantial segment of the public, press, interest groups, the Senate, and the executive branch believed that the two great nuclear superpowers shared mutual interests and that the United States could safely enter into agreement with the Soviets without endangering American security. The U.S.S.R. had not disappeared as the major threat to American security after the treaty had been signed, but the treaty indicated that each was prepared to accept concretely the principle that they could seek agreements on substantive issues when they shared interests. Coincident with improved relations with the United States, the Soviet Union was finding itself increasingly, and at times belligerently, disagreeing with the People's Republic of China. American policy-makers hoped to exploit this ripening Sino-Soviet split and reach new agreements with the Kremlin.

The test ban also marked a shift in the reaction and behavior of American decision-makers. One of the major stumbling blocks between the United States and the Soviet Union had been the American insistence that on-site monitors were necessary to insure compliance with the terms of an arms control agreement. But technological advances enabled identification from remote stations of any clandestine testing in the atmosphere. Although there had been notable improvements in monitoring devices to detect underground tests, they were not yet sophisticated enough at that time to be placed outside of the Soviet Union and still detect all illegal tests. Given the new spirit of cooperation, hints by Premier Khrushchev that he was willing to accept a small number of monitors on Soviet territory, and improved detection techniques by the United States, it did not seem unreasonable to many officials in the administration that a new round of negotiations would lead to a comprehensive ban on all nuclear tests. Although the Soviets must bear much of the onus for previous failure to reach arms-control agreements, domestic opponents were often able to thwart the presentation of a negotiable American position to the Soviet Union. Opponents had not disappeared in 1963, but they had declined in numbers and influence, and many who remained were adroitly isolated by President John Kennedy.

Previous administrations had often been skeptical of Soviet motives. President Harry Truman had sponsored the Baruch plan which he considered eminently fair but which had been rejected by the Soviet Union. Soon embroiled in the cold war and then the shooting war in Korea, the Truman administration placed its emphasis on building Western security, not in negotiating arms control. The Eisenhower administration pursued disarmament discussions, and for awhile in 1955 it appeared an agreement was near; but American misgivings about the dangers of possible clandestine nuclear stockpiles terminated the negotiations. Mr Eisenhower's

Secretary of State and his Director of the Atomic Energy Commission were continually opposed to a formal agreement. John Foster Dulles was particularly insistent on the need for on-site inspections while Lewis Strauss appeared to oppose any possible agreement.[2] Nevertheless the great powers voluntarily agreed to suspend nuclear tests in the atmosphere in 1958 for one year, and the moratorium was informally extended in 1959. Following the 1959 Camp David talks between President Eisenhower and Premier Khrushchev, prospects for disarmament brightened with a proposed summit meeting in Paris; but in the interval the Soviet Union shot down an American U-2 plane spying over Soviet territory and prospects for negotiations dimmed.

However sincere the Kennedy administration might have been in achieving an agreement with the Soviet Union on arms control, the administration appeared to be bargaining from a position of weakness during its first two years in office with the lackluster Vienna summit talks between the American President and Soviet Premier making the United States look unsure of itself. Accompanied by the West's toleration of the construction of the Berlin wall and the ill-fated Bay of Pigs invasion of Cuba, the administration began to fear that its own image suggested weakness and indecision in foreign affairs to both domestic and foreign constituencies. Moreover, the Soviets appeared in no rush to compromise with the United States. President Kennedy's dramatic and dangerous confrontation of Soviet missile power in Cuba marked a turning point in the self-confidence of the administration and quieted domestic complaints that the President was too naive and weak to deal effectively with the Soviets. Having increased the sense of danger of nuclear war in both Washington and Moscow, the crisis also accelerated written and informal contacts between the two world leaders.

However, not all Americans believed that arms control agreements with the Soviet Union, including a limited test ban, would serve American interests. Not only members of the military services and Senators who had consistently opposed a *rapprochement* with the Soviets opposed an agreement, but a large segment of the administration remained suspicious as well. Some pockets of opposition assessed the treaty by its effects on their primary goals. For example, some in the Department of State were appre-

[2] For the position of those opposed to arms control or skeptical of it, see Earl H. Voss, *Nuclear Ambush* (Chicago: Regnery, 1963). For a history of arms control during the Eisenhower administration, see Bernard G. Bechhoefer, *Postwar Negotiations for Arms Control* (Washington: The Brookings Institution, 1961) and Saville R. Davis, "Recent Policy Making in the United States Government," in Donald G. Brennan (ed.) *Arms Control, Disarmament, and National Security* (New York: Braziller, 1961), pp. 379–390.

hensive about adverse effects in the Federal Republic of Germany and France while scientists in the Atomic Energy Commission feared that their laboratories would become moribund. However, much of the opposition feared the Soviet Union had disproportionately advanced a series of high megaton tests in the atmosphere in 1961, and the technical knowledge it had collected enabled the Soviets to develop an anti-missile system. The Kennedy administration's unwillingness to test at very high megaton levels, they believed, put the United States in an inferior defense position since this country allegedly did not possess the requisite data to proceed on an adequate missile defense. The treaty, they argued, would freeze technical capabilities and consequently keep the United States in an inferior defensive position. One of the primary concerns of the opposition was the blackout effect of high nuclear explosions. During high megaton blasts, radar was ineffective, and many scientists desired to know the extent and duration of radar impotency and its effect on the guidance systems of missiles.

Several ideologically based arguments were mounted against the treaty as well. Some felt it was premature to reach any settlement with the Soviets until they had demonstrated to the satisfaction of the United States that they would not abrogate the treaty. They argued that the Soviets should withdraw from Cuba or pay their outstanding debts to the United Nations. A *quid pro quo* was necessary to test Soviet sincerity. According to them, the Soviets would lose nothing by signing the treaty while the United States would surrender its ability to test in the atmosphere.

The treaty was thus a controversial issue which involved a variety of participants. In the following chapters, each of the major components which helped to influence or make American foreign policy is analyzed. The behavior of the interest groups, the mass media, public opinion, the office of the President, the several departments and agencies, Senate committees, and the Senate at large are all examined. No single component was responsible for the success of the treaty's negotiation, much less its ratification. The contest characterizing the making of public policy is not due to one component pitted against another component. Rather broad coalitions are formed, with some elements in the press, interest groups, the executive branch, the public, and the Senate contending against others in a counter-coalition.

Not only do the participants differ in influence, they also vary in the number and kinds of roles they occupy in the system. The President's role is not exhausted by submitting proposals; he is also an important decoder in the public opinion system, a supplier of information and recommendations in the mass media, a stimulator of interest group activity, a coordinator of administration policy often privately settling controversies within his own house to minimize the public coalition against him, and a lobbyist with Congress. In his dealings with the Senate, John Kennedy, like other presidents, formed alliances with favorably disposed legislators and together they worked with interest groups and members of the general public to persuade other senators to support the administration's policy. Many of the roles the President occupied were shared with several other individuals. The President, groups, Senators, and the media were all part of the lobbying system.

There was no simple causal chain in which the behavior of one participant determined the behavior of another in the latter's reaction to the treaty. Individuals were the objects of a succession of pressures and counter-pressures and the accumulated effect of one set often cancelled out the impact of other, potent counter-pressures. That Senator Dirksen, for example, announced his support for the treaty after he met with the President hardly means that John Kennedy was the decisive factor in this case. The minority leader in the Senate received calls from other Senators, including members of his own party, was urged to support the treaty by leading newspapers in his own state, received letters from average as well as influential citizens, and was the object of attention of several interest groups. The opponents of the treaty also attempted to bring the Senator to their side and mustered an impressive arsenal in their campaign. It is difficult to argue that any single individual or group was the most important one in bringing the minority leader, or any other senator, to support the treaty because many of the activities directed towards Senators had an accumulative effect. It is also important to emphasize that many of the participants, although they were intensely interested in the outcome and extremely energetic in their lobbying, were relatively ineffective. Often the hard word of some potential influencers went unnoticed by their intended recipients.

If it is often misleading to identify the sole individual or group responsible for directing most decision-makers, it is also unrewarding to attempt to determine behavior by simply examining the intensity of various pressures and allotting victory to the side which exerted the greatest numerical value. Not only is it difficult to assess appropriate numerical values to each activity with a high degree of confidence, but four other problems also preclude a simple cause-effect analysis. In analyzing the effect of the lobbying on an individual, the impact of feedback loops is inevitably overlooked. The more one side works, the harder the other side may be induced to work. Furthermore, blatant lobbying may stiffen positions because many decision-makers resent pressure. In addition the messages of some senders may be blocked and never have an impact. Assessment of strength is often made a function of activity and resources expended, but if the messages do not enter the system, their effects are lost. For example, many of the peace and rightwing groups were exceedingly active; but for all of their work, most of them were often ignored by decision-makers who were more attentive to recognized specialists such as scientists. A third consideration is that many messages associated with lobbying are accompanied by a high level of noise or distortion and the intended impact is lost.[3] Senator Margaret Chase Smith, for example, believed that people on vacation in Maine were responsible for most of her mail before Labor Day, minimizing the impact of citizens of her state who supported the treaty and wrote her about it before early September.

Finally, Senators, like everyone else, have their own values and perceptions. The behavior of the Senate and other decision-making units must be understood on the basis of their constituent members; and each of them is subject to a different set of influences, is vulnerable to different pressures, and has his own framework for judging issues. Nevertheless, these values are not usually embedded in immovable rock. It is beyond the scope of this study to identify and assess all the pressures on each participant and then analyze the vulnerability of each decision-maker.

[3] See Chapters 5 and 8 below.

CHAPTER II

# THE PRESIDENT AND THE TREATY

The President is the principal policy-maker for the United States in foreign affairs, but his program does not automatically become the foreign policy of the nation. He cannot dictate to his major competitors or allies abroad; he cannot enforce his will on all of his opponents; and his ability to secure agreement among the diverse offices of the federal bureaucracy is at best restricted. The President's constituencies can both strengthen and weaken his position; his dependency on others to supply him with information and to carry out his directives may severely limit him; competition within the executive branch may dilute his policies or require him to expend limited resources to consolidate his position; and attention devoted to one issue diverts him from other issues.

While the President does not totally control every situation, he is not a cork tossed in a wild current. His strategic location in the political system enables him to shape outcomes; he can select options to enhance his chances for success; he occupies several roles in the system which, if effectively used, can influence the conduct of other participants. In the making of the test ban treaty, John Kennedy occupied most of the roles customarily associated with the Chief Executive: he initiated policy; he helped to mold public opinion; he worked closely with interest groups; he lobbied in Congress; he consolidated the diverse elements and interests in his administration; and he negotiated with foreign governments.[1]

President Kennedy's role in the treaty-making process cannot be adequately explained by a catalogue of his activities between May and September, 1963. It is also important to know his goals, to relate them to his previous experiences, to identify his perception of the domestic and foreign environments, and to examine the ways in which he believed he could favorably alter the situation.

[1] Cf. Richard Neustadt, *Presidential Power: The Politics of Leadership* (New York: John Wiley & Sons, Inc., 1960), *passim.*

## *The President: Goals and Constraints*

President Kennedy desired to maintain a relatively stable international environment which would further American interests as he defined them, while minimizing the chances of nuclear war. He held that both the goals of peace and the integrity of the constitutional systems of the West could be achieved only if the apparent antithesis of peace, that is, military power, were sufficiently available.[2] When there was a conflict between the goals of peace and national security, the President usually opted for the application of force to assure security. This pattern is apparent in his addresses[3] and in administration responses to threats by the Soviet Union in the Berlin crisis in 1961, the Cuban missile crisis of 1962, and the commitment of the government to maintain a noncommunist South Vietnam. Kennedy held that if the will and resources to protect American interests were in doubt or inadequate, both peace and the possibility of a liberal democratic society would be threatened. The President desired to decelerate the arms race in order to decrease the probability of conflict while optimizing the probabilities of peace and security.

From his Inaugural Address in which he pledged that he would "pay any price, bear any burden, support any friend, oppose any foe to assure the survival and success of liberty," to his insistence during the test ban debate

[2] President Eisenhower devoted considerable time to a test ban treaty with the Soviet Union. On January 12, 1958, in a letter to Soviet Premier Nikolai Bulganin, the President urged the conclusion of a test ban agreement. In October of that year, Great Britain, the Soviet Union, and the United States began test ban negotiations in Geneva, and the three nuclear powers voluntarily suspended tests pending an agreement on a treaty. In April, 1959, the United States proposed a phased ban on nuclear testing. The American position, which called for the banning of atmospheric tests below 50 kilometers, was based on the ability of current technology to detect unauthorized tests only in this environment. Although the Soviet Union rejected the American position and insisted that on-site inspections were not necessary for a comprehensive ban, the three nuclear powers continued their unilateral suspensions of nuclear tests.

In the final year of the Eisenhower administration, the United States called for the banning of all nuclear tests except those which could not be monitored outside of the borders of the participating countries. In its February, 1960 proposal, the United States called for a ban on all tests except those below a 19-kiloton yield conducted underground. Within the next three months the French conducted their first atomic test, the Soviet Union conditionally accepted the Western proposal, the unilateral suspension of testing was expanded and extended, and an American U-2 plane was shot down over Soviet territory. The Summit Conference scheduled for Paris never materialized, and by late September, all test ban talks were suspended. For a discussion of earlier disarmament proposals, see Bernard G. Bechhoefer, *Postwar Negotiations for Arms Control* (Washington: The Brookings Institution, 1961), *passim*.

[3] See, for example, his Inaugural Address and the 1962 State of the Union Address.

that the treaty represented a step toward peace, Kennedy continued to balance these dichotomous goals. While insisting on the need for military preparedness, he also argued that steps should be taken to relieve the pressures of the arms race. In his 1962 State of the Union Message, he stressed an improved defense posture for the United States, but also pledged that his administration would pursue "a supreme effort to break the logjam of disarmament and nuclear tests, and we will persist until we prevail, until the rule of law has replaced the ever dangerous use of force."[4]

When the federal budget is used as a criterion, the Kennedy administration, like its predecessor, emphasized military power. However, there were two important institutional changes in the Kennedy administration from the practices of his predecessor. The doctrine of superior nuclear force was replaced by a strategy of flexible response which shifted attention to conventional forces and reduced the role of the Air Force which had previously been the almost exclusive custodian of American military power. This new division of labor among the armed services lessened the dependency of the nation on nuclear power to meet all foreign threats. Kennedy's notable innovation was the creation of the Arms Control and Disarmament Agency. When previous arms control policy had been formulated, it was proliferated among several departments, and there was no central office to represent the disarmament position within the administration except for a brief period when Harold Stassen acted as a special assistant on arms control to President Eisenhower. With the creation of the Agency, proposals continued to emanate from several offices; but a central office was given responsibility to conduct research and formulate programs.

According to Kennedy, nuclear proliferation, radioactive fallout, and the continued arms race were deleterious to national security. In the spring of 1963 he was "haunted by the feeling that by 1970 . . . there may be 10 nuclear powers instead of four, and by 1975, 15 or 20 . . . I regard that as the greatest possible danger and hazard."[5] Six weeks later, the President told reporters that if a test ban were not concluded soon, then "perhaps the genie is out of the bottle and we'll never get it back in again."[6] The President emphasized that time for effective action was rapidly running out.

Insisting that a number of factors impinged on a final policy position, Kennedy believed there were no easy or automatic solutions to political problems, and that each variable had to be judged and weighed before a choice was final. In discussing the office of the President, John Kennedy

[4] *New York Times*, January 12, 1962, p. 1.
[5] *Ibid.*, March 21, 1963, p. 1. (Press Conference).
[6] *Ibid.*, May 8, 1963, p. 1. (Press Conference).

insisted that "to govern is to choose," not blindly or mechanically, but on the basis of "what your estimate is of the great movements in history or the immediate movement, the security of your country, its well being, the prospects for peace, the dangers of war, and the hope that it is possible to make progress in this rather small globe."[7] Governing was the reconciling of conflicting demands which could leave considerable dissatisfaction among many constituencies in the country and abroad.

The President also had to consider legislative proposals which lingered in Congress and required his time, talents, and resources. Tax reform and revision, civil rights, social welfare, medicare, agricultural adjustments, and a battery of other administration proposals met moderate to determined opposition in Congress and among various interest groups. Kennedy cajoled, pressured, and compromised with the various political participants and built alliances with them. This did not guarantee his success, because, as Richard Neustadt observed, the "same conditions that promote his leadership in form preclude a guarantee of leadership in fact."[8] No president automatically succeeds: victory is related to the resources and options available to him and the way he exploits them to overcome an array of counter resources and pressures.

The President has the capacity to mobilize public opinion because of the legitimacy-provoking attributes of his office, including easy access to the mass media.[9] He can attract more attention on a broad spectrum of political issues than other participants, but the introduction of several issues into the public opinion system may overload its capacity to receive the President's several messages and follow all of them. When Kennedy proposed a new approach to arms control at American University in June, 1963, he received immediate media attention. Yet there was little sustained interest in that issue because he unexpectedly appeared on national television the next day to discuss the explosive issue of civil rights.[10] When political communication channels are overloaded because of mismanagement or because of the increase of unplanned announcements in response to unexpected but impor-

[7] From the transcript of remarks to participants in the White House Seminar in Government, August 27, 1963, as reported in *Congressional Quarterly* (September 6, 1963), p. 1551.

[8] Neustadt, *op. cit.*, p. 7.

[9] James Rosenau, among others, has discussed the uneven access different participants have to the press. See his *Public Opinion and Foreign Policy* (New York: Random House, 1961).

[10] More than any other issue, civil rights competed with the test ban, requiring the attention of the President, stimulating activity in the groups, and receiving considerable space in the mass media. Moreover, Senators were also receiving considerable mail

tant issues, the President will neutralize some of the messages he directs to the public.

As leader of his party, the President can press claims to partisan loyalty. However, when bipartisan support is desired, partisanship is not a tenable strategy. Adlai Stevenson, who had urged a test ban in the 1956 presidential campaign, next only to the President and Secretary of State, was the chief spokesman for American foreign policy. In the treaty signing ceremonies in Moscow, the Ambassador to the United Nations was not invited to participate because Kennedy did not wish to rekindle old partisan bitterness with the Republicans. This not only illustrates the President's strategy to build bipartisan support but also supports Theodore Sorensen's contention that "politics pervades the White House" and is "an ever present influence."[11]

As administrator of the federal bureaucracy, the President legally directs the policy and operations of the Executive Departments. However, the agencies are often linked with quasi-independent power centers and interest groups which can exert pressure on the administration to abandon or compromise its proposals. Agencies may also influence administration behavior because of the information they transmit to the executive branch. Decisions about language, what background data should be sent, and interpretations about its meaning continually confront administrators.

A significant factor in the President's handling of the test ban treaty was his control over information. Noise, distortion, and blockage of information[12] in communications channels within executive departments were lessened due to Kennedy's strategy of consciously witholding plans from several customary but unreliable participants, sending out messages under his own supervision and sharing information only at opportune times. By not pressuring his subordinates, the President avoided the debilitating side issue of "dictatorial" control as well as increased the credibility of other supporters within his administration.

As a policy initiator, the President is a critical gatekeeper for inputs into the political system. Although he commands the most strategic position in the system, he must be conscious of the possibility of overextending himself.

about this issue. On August 28, 1963, Martin Luther King, Jr. led 200,000 people in a march on Washington.

11 Theodore Sorensen, *Decision Making in the White House* (New York: Columbia University Press, 1963), p. 44.

12 Noise refers to unintended changes in a message, while distortion refers to intended alterations in a message.

If he submits proposals which are not apt to receive public support, he runs the risk of developing the reputation of a loser or of identifying himself with several unpopular causes. This does not mean that the President appreciably diminishes his reputation every time he introduces an unpopular issue into the political system. Although Neustadt speaks of a pattern of success, we can just as easily suggest that a President can sustain several defeats; but there is a threshold beyond which any additional failures reduce the President's bargaining power with particular political participants. Neustadt also observes that prestige is related to success.[13] The issue is not whether the President should support possibly unpopular programs when he believes in their correctness, but whether a President can propose too many unpopular issues and be blind to the eroding effects of successive defeats. The reputation of the President is not a series of discrete, unconnected evaluations, but a flow of evaluations which reflect, at any given moment, a composite of past and present behavior as well as predictions about his chances for future success. Forecasts about the future are based, in part, on historic patterns. The strategy for success would include a concern about how many and what kind of defeats can be sustained before prestige deterioration occurs, and what kind of victories can convert an unfavorable reputation into a favorable one.

Reputation is situational, and actions which diminish the President's standing with one group may increase it with another group. Because the relevant participants in the political system vary in their activities and interests from issue to issue, he must be concerned about the future effects of his policy on potentially interested and active groups. The discussion below indicates that Kennedy's reputation suffered because of his handling of the Bay of Pigs operation but that his stature increased because of the Cuban missile crisis for the public at large. His later success placed him in a stronger position for introducing the test ban into the political system.[14]

We have to emphasize the conflict between the President and his departments and his difficulty in sometimes exercising effective control over them.[15] However, the executive branch is not a loose confederation of Greek city states which enter and leave the alliance at their convenience. The

[13] Cf. Neustadt, *op. cit.*, p. 58–107.

[14] Whether or not the President actually increased his standing in the international community, particularly in Moscow, because of the missile crisis is not as important as his belief that his stature increased. Cf. Arthur M. Schlesinger, Jr., *A Thousand Days, John F. Kennedy in the White House* (Boston: Houghton Mifflin Co., 1965), p. 841.

[15] This problem of administrative control has been discussed by Peter Woll in *American Bureaucracy* (New York: Norton, 1963), pp. 142–171.

President can invoke symbols attached to his office to minimize conflict within the executive branch. In addition to several institutional constraints such as the budgetary process which reduced the domain of independence for the bureaucracy, legitimacy is an important cohesive element.[16] The office of President confers rights and responsibilities on him which his subordinates recognize and which often inhibit conflict between him and the agencies. This does not mean that whenever he does not attend to an agency's behavior, it will undermine his program. While some participants might be expected to oppose the President because they disagree with his goals or his interpretation of the situation, they respect the claims of the President as legitimate.

However, the President's claims to legitimacy may restrict him as well as help him. Even as he expects his subordinates to support him, they expect him to observe a pattern of behavior which is considered appropriate to his position. If he steps outside of these expected limits, his opponents will have an issue to use against him.[17] Consequently, President Kennedy was extremely cautious when he dealt with the military chiefs during the test ban debate, clearly informing them of his position but never directly pressuring them in a way that the opposition could claim indicated the President was abusing his powers. The President could have theoretically "ordered" his generals to support him, but he would have been exercising only a formal power which would probably have rebounded against him.

In his role of Commander-in-Chief, he must orchestrate strategic, military, diplomatic, economic, legislative, popular, and legal demands into a coherent policy. The bureaus under his jurisdiction have specific purposes assigned to them or which they have delegated to themselves. Because each of their purposes is not always compatible, and because they do not operate under the same constraints, conflict will periodically arise among the agencies or between one of them and the President.

[16] Legitimacy, as used here, is similar to William Mitchell's concept of authority. He observed that "the pattern of authority defines or specifies complementary obligations and rights: in the case of the leader, it is the *right to accept support* and the *right to regulate*." *Sociological Analysis and Politics* (Englewood Cliffs: Prentice Hall, 1967), p. 112. Mitchell notes that too often political analysis is based on pursuing the puzzle of who exerted power on whom, but that often "decisions may be made or accepted because authority is involved." (*Ibid.*)

[17] For a discussion of role, see Neal Gross, Ward Mason, and Alexander McEachern, *Explorations in Role Analysis* (New York: John Wiley, 1958), pp. 48–69.

### *Accumulated Experiences*

Although the President had desired a treaty earlier than 1963 when the test ban was signed, he did not devote the energy or the will in 1961 and 1962 to an agreement which he did in 1963. Several foreign policy experiences induced him to change his priorities, and some of these same factors, particularly the Cuban missile crisis, probably influenced the Kremlin to change its mind, accepting in 1963 what they declined in 1962. The President desired a nuclear understanding with the Russians throughout his administration; but after the Cuban missile crisis, it became a more important item on his agenda; and he had options available to him to ease the task of shepherding it through the maze of possible roadblocks. After the missile crisis, the environment had altered in important respects, and new experiences had been accumulated.

Kennedy had two notable diplomatic defeats and a series of standoffs in his first two years as President. His meeting with Khrushchev in Vienna in 1961 was irritating and unproductive, while the abortive Bay of Pigs invasion was politically frustrating and diplomatically disastrous. If the first was reminiscent of a confrontation between righteous innocence and righteous experience, the second defeat read like a scenario for the theater of the absurd. Chaos, confused goals, muddled communication, miscalculations, untimely publicity, and unclear lines of authority intruded on one another to compound the failure of the ill-conceived scheme. One of the lessons the President drew from was the need to control his lines of communication more effectively.

Two other events in 1961 were also important. His strong commitment to West Germany during the Berlin crisis helped to check his slippage as a resolute world leader, and resumption of Soviet testing forced him to examine the nuclear capacity of the United States. Each also had further ramifications. After France, the ally most unlikely to accept a test ban was Germany. The Federal Republic had developed a powerful constituency in this country, and its opposition to an agreement would stimulate opposition in America. Kennedy's action in Berlin gave him a line of credit with the Germans which he used when Chancellor Konrad Adenauer was reluctant to accede to the test ban in 1963. The Soviet atmospheric testing in 1961 required decisions about national defense which led to a full scale examination of nuclear policy within the administration. Many of the arguments which were advanced for an immediate series of high megaton atmospheric tests in 1961 were a rehearsal for the same brief against the treaty in 1963.

The President was generally unimpressed in 1961 with these points and increased his resolve through the spring and summer of 1963 that the arms race must come to a halt. The Defense Department was hardly united in its position on testing. Secretary of Defense Robert McNamara and others held that the Soviets would not appreciably benefit from their series of tests. The armed services, on the other hand, argued that a test ban would impose unacceptable risks on the United States. The proponents of testing in 1961 and opponents of the test ban in 1963 argued that the Kremlin had made important breakthroughs and that the Soviet Union would at least catch up with the United States, and, at worst, surpass it.

The most important foreign policy experience of all was the Cuban missile crisis in October, 1962. It increased Kennedy's stature and popularity among the American people and allies and, the administration believed, erased his image of indecision with the Soviets.[18] At least equally important, it fired his own determination to proceed with arms control as a necessary condition for international stability. According to Arthur Schlesinger, the President believed that the lessons of Cuba should not "bring about an increase in hostility but perhaps provide for an easing of relations."[19] Kennedy did not believe that the primary conclusion to be drawn from the confrontation was that a militant position would bring the collapse of the Soviets. What worked in Cuba might not be applicable in other circumstances. At its most elementary level, Cuba was a primer that taught Kennedy misjudgments could easily lead to nuclear war.[20]

The President also believed that Khrushchev and he were under many similar pressures. Although everyone agreed that the Premier was the dominant figure in his government, there was considerable speculation that he had to contend with a more militant group in the Kremlin. Averell Harriman's suggestion that the Cuban missile adventure was not Khrushchev's idea but had been pressed on him by hardliners was not uncommon in the administration.[21]

The President observed: "Mr. Khrushchev and I are in the same boat in the sense of both having this nuclear capacity and both wanting to protect our societies. He realizes how dangerous a world we live in."[22] This evaluation prompted Kennedy to continue his earlier correspondence with

18 Theodore C. Sorensen, *Kennedy* (New York: Harper and Row, 1965), pp. 727–725.

19 Schlesinger, *op. cit.*, p. 841.

20 *Ibid.*, pp. 832–833.

21 *Ibid.*, pp. 821–822.

22 Sorensen, *op. cit.*, p. 725.

Khrushchev. The frequency of their letters intensified during the Cuban crisis and continued afterwards. In October 1962, the President and Prime Minister Harold Macmillan urged the Soviet Union to join with them in a new endeavor to reach a test ban agreement.[23] The letters between Kennedy and Khrushchev, as well as informal probings from a stream of visitors, were designed to express and test the sincerity of each side and to explore whether there was some common ground for negotiations. After a slow start, optimism reached new heights when Khrushchev indicated he would accept monitors on Soviet territory. The Kremlin had previously refused to permit inspectors, holding that their national sovereignty would be violated and subversion would be facilitated. Although Washington considered the Soviet offer of two or three annual inspections woefully inadequate, the administration regarded this as an important shift. In his reply to Khrushchev, Kennedy asked him to accept a higher compromise figure. In rejecting the American offer, the Soviet leader argued that he had been led to believe that if he accepted the lower number, the Americans would consider the agreement satisfactory.[24] Khrushchev, who had based his conclusions on information received from Arthur Dean, implied that the President was bargaining in bad faith. Kennedy insisted that this was a misunderstanding and that his negotiators had never been empowered to give such an assurance to the Soviets.[25] The optimism of late winter faded with this new impasse.

The President persisted because he felt that an agreement was important and possible. The administration reasoned that the Sino-Soviet dispute provided opportunities which had not been previously present during the cold war.[26] Kennedy and his advisors also believed that the Cuban crisis had demonstrated American power and determination as well as the unity of the Western alliance, thereby enabling the United States to bargain from a position of strength.[27] The administration had been preoccupied with

[23] See *Documents on Disarmament, 1962,* Vol. II where both Khrushchev and Kennedy suggested a test ban treaty. (Arms Control and Disarmament Agency, 1963), pp. 991–994. Also see 1000–1001, 1239–1242, and 1277–1279; also see Schlesinger, *op. cit.,* 895–6. The administration had been asked to release these messages, but declined. However, Marquis Childs reported their contents, indicating that there were no secret agreements between the two world leaders which might compromise American security. Through Childs, the President was able to lessen the misgivings of some skeptics in the Senate without releasing his private correspondence. The Childs article appeared under the title, "Behind Moscow's Opening to the West," *Washington Post,* July 17, 1963, p. 18A.

[24] Schlesinger, *op. cit.,* p. 896.

[25] *Ibid.,* pp. 896–898.

[26] Sorensen, *op. cit.,* pp. 724–725.

[27] Schlesinger, *op. cit.,* p. 841.

fears of a vulnerable negotiating position, but the solution of the Cuban missile crisis not only diminished this fear, it also dampened the argument of Kennedy's critics who held that he did not appreciate the realities of power politics and did not understand Soviet foreign policy. Opposition would be forthcoming from some quarters regardless of his conduct in foreign policy, but the President worked to increase his prestige among marginal domestic allies and opponents, and the solution of the Cuban crisis served this goal.[28] His actions in the missile crisis discredited the complaint that he was selling security short. The President also thought it showed the Kremlin that the United States was prepared to use its power and would not accept any situation detrimental to American interests. Any residue of weakness from the Kennedy-Khrushchev meeting in Vienna and the Bay of Bigs incident had been dispelled to the administration's satisfaction, at least.[29]

Apart from these experiences, the history of Soviet-American disarmament negotiations is also relevant. Discussions between the United States and the Soviet Union for a limited test ban treaty had been futilely conducted for almost a decade. Most of the sessions were exercises in showmanship rather than statesmanship, as each side spoke to the uncommitted nations, its own citizens, and its allies before it addressed the other. Although the test ban treaty was similar to a Western proposal submitted at the Geneva Conference in the summer of 1962,[30] the sense of emergency and importance which characterized the 1963 negotiations had not been present at the earlier talks.[31] The later talks had been more carefully planned. The Soviets had shifted their position, and the President had been in regular contact with Khrushchev.

The President was also concerned about agencies in his own government. Several agencies and individuals had consistently depreciated the value of

[28] Prestige probably does not transform opponents to supporters, but prestige can make the journey from skepticism to acceptance less troublesome.

[29] The President, nevertheless, had to consider possible Republican opposition, which was potentially explosive. In early 1963, the Republican Conference Committee released a series of technical papers attacking a moratorium of atmosphere and underground tests. See Harold Karen Jackobson and Eric Stein, *Diplomats, Scientists, and Politicians: The United States and the Nuclear Test Ban Negotiations* (Ann Arbor: University of Michigan Press, 1966), p. 437.

[30] See Appendix 1.

[31] According to Sorensen, President Kennedy felt that the Sino-Soviet dispute "might increase the danger of desperation in Moscow or irresponsibility in Peking . . . But the new fluidity in the post-Cuban Communist camp, he recognized, presented opportunities which seventeen years of cold war rigidities had never made possible before." *op. cit.*, p. 726.

arms control, and a few energetically opposed such a policy. Two events brought these forces into the open: the Soviet resumption of atmospheric testing in 1961 and the formulation of the American position for the 1962 Geneva Disarmament talks. The first required an American response which finally resulted in a limited atmospheric testing. Kennedy's dilemma revolved around the possibility that future testing would lead to an acceleration of the arms race and that no testing would give the Soviets an appreciable lead over the United States while endangering international stability. As the debate within the executive branch raged, both the Atomic Energy Commission and the Joint Chiefs of Staff urged the resumption of atmospheric testing. Because Soviet testing persisted, Kennedy concluded that the "political and diplomatic" advantages required future atmospheric testing by the United States. The President was not impressed with the argument that the Russian tests gave the Soviets any substantial military benefits.[32] Many of the same military arguments were again advanced in 1962 and persisted in 1963,[33] and they were rejected as exaggerated statements.

### *Presidential Formulation of Policy*

Summit diplomacy is often understood as face-to-face meetings between heads of government. It also refers to letters between them and the dispatch of their personal representatives who are not incumbered by bureaucratic delays and departmental loyalties.[34] Kennedy used these secondary types of summit diplomacy throughout the test ban negotiations. His correspondence with the Soviet leader was supplemented with official and unofficial representatives to pursue matters with the Kremlin. The State Department continued to participate in its traditional foreign policy roles, but no longer exclusively. Unofficial representatives carrying messages from Kennedy to Khrushchev were often a more effective avenue in demonstrating American determination to reach an agreement than just another message relayed through the American embassy in Moscow.

The most notable instance of summit diplomacy, excepting the letters, was the selection of W. Averell Harriman to serve as the American repre-

[32] *Ibid.*, p. 728.

[33] See both *Ibid.* and Schlesinger, *op. cit.*, for a discussion of the President's growing skepticism of the foreign policy advice of some of the military officers.

[34] Elmer Plischke, *Summit Diplomacy* (College Park: Bureau of Governmental Research, 1958). Sorensen reports the President did not want a summit conference at that time but was willing to attend one if Khruschchev insisted on a meeting as a condition for accepting the treaty. *Op. cit.*, p. 735.

sentative to the negotiations. While he may have been the logical choice in retrospect, it was not an automatic appointment. Within twenty-four hours after Rusk suggested Harriman's name, the State Department had second thoughts, but the President preferred to have someone he considered loyal and capable.[35]

Another instance of summit diplomacy was the unofficial mission of Norman Cousins to Moscow in 1963. Traveling as a private citizen, he had been requested by the President to transmit a message to the Soviet leader clarifying several misunderstandings and to invite Khrushchev to reopen discussions. The President also relied on several visitors to the Soviet Union to relay his intentions to the Russians and provide him with information about their receptivity to a nuclear agreement. Through letters and visitors, he not only kept channels of communications open with the Kremlin but also had greater control of the process than if regular diplomatic channels had been used. The American University speech can also be understood as an example of summit diplomacy. As its principal architect, the President used it to address the Soviet leaders as well as the American people.

### *Preliminary to Success: The American University Speech*

In the American University Address on June 10, 1963, President Kennedy attempted to break the deadlock separating the nuclear powers. He not only revealed that Great Britain, the United States, and the Soviet Union would soon begin new discussions on a test ban treaty, but also that the United States was imposing a unilateral moratorium on the testing of American nuclear weapons in the atmosphere as long as the other nations did not test in that environment. The tone of the address was conciliatory but determined; it looked to the future and found two prospects – war with its tragedy for man, or peace with its hope for the human race.[36]

The American University speech was one of the major foreign policy declarations of the Kennedy administration with relatively little assistance requested or received from other agencies by the White House. While speed was one consideration which prompted the decision to bypass the slow-moving, cumbersome bureaucracy, more important was Kennedy's determination to make a strong plea for peace without contending with those

[35] Schlesinger, *op. cit.*, p. 903.
[36] *New York Times*, June 11, 1963, p. 1.

in the Departments of Defense and State who perpetually argued that qualifications must be added.[37]

Kennedy worked on his text for several weeks, and the decision to institute the unilateral moratorium on atmospheric testing was a "personal decision."[38] Sorensen, who wrote the draft of the speech, reported that the "President was determined to put forward a fundamentally new emphasis on the peaceful and positive in our relations with the Soviets. He did not want that new policy diluted by the usual threats of destruction, boasts of nuclear stockpiles, and lectures on Soviet treachery."[39] The interested agencies had intensively examined the problems and possibilities of arms control and a limited test ban in the summer of 1962. In previous negotiations several officials in the State Department objected to "false starts" which only disturbed some of our allies, particularly Germany, while not accomplishing the desired arms control results. Many military officers argued that arms control might circumscribe American military strength and lull the American people and allies into a false sense of security while the danger of nuclear attack remained. In order to preclude this internal debate as well as to forestall public attacks because of leaks to the press by disgruntled officials, the President worked with a limited number of close associates. He believed that the technological and military situations had not materially altered from 1962 when the United States supported a limited test ban. The important changes in the environment were the increasing danger of nuclear proliferation and more favorable climate for quiet diplomacy.[40]

The speech was already in its final form when the President was in Honolulu preparing to address the United States Conference of Mayors on race relations, a day before the American University speech was to be given. At that time, Khrushchev replied to an earlier letter from Kennedy and accepted a proposal for a new series of private meetings. Kennedy was reached in Honolulu by McGeorge Bundy who had received the Soviet message. A three-way conversation ensued among the President, Bundy in the White House, and Dean Rusk in the Department of State. Bundy had previously participated in drafting many of the earlier presidential letters to Khrushchev, and the three discussed the communication and whether it

[37] McGeorge Bundy, "The Presidency and Peace," *Foreign Affairs,* XLII (April, 1964), p. 363.

[38] *Ibid.*

[39] Sorensen, *op. cit.,* pp. 730–731.

[40] The success of arms control proposals is obviously not solely dependent on the will and skill of domestic participants but also on the readiness of other nations to enter into agreements.

should be acknowledged in the address the next day. The President decided to include reference to Khrushchev's acceptance by announcing toward the close of the address, that "high-level discussions will shortly begin in Moscow looking toward early agreement on a test-ban treaty."[41]

In early July, Khrushchev spoke in East Berlin and supported the idea of a limited nuclear test ban but tied this to a nonaggression pact with the West, a proposal which was unacceptable to the North Atlantic Treaty nations.[42] As early as three weeks before the negotiations began, there was no certainty that the conference would be successful.

### *The Harriman Mission*

Experienced in the art of negotiation, particularly with the Soviets, loyal to the President, and considered a realist in foreign policy, W. Averell Harriman was selected by the President to be the American representative to the Moscow negotiations. Harriman believed that the limited test ban proposal could be negotiated and would be mutually beneficial to the Soviets and Americans. He went to the Soviet Union with specific instructions from the President and reported directly to him daily. The office of the President supplied him amended or supplementary instructions when necessary. Harriman was specifically directed not to accept any linkage between the test ban treaty and a nonaggression pact between the North Atlantic Treaty and Warsaw Pact nations. He was to take the position that the United States could not negotiate on this matter until it was discussed with its North Atlantic Treaty allies and the United States received a mandate from them, although he was to listen to any suggestions the Soviet Union might make.[43] In the meantime, the North Atlantic Treaty nations were informed that the United States would not accept a nonaggression pact but would explore the means whereby the Soviets proposed to implement such an agreement. Harriman was also instructed to discuss the Laotian situation with Premier Khrushchev, but this topic did not receive much attention

[41] Schlesinger, *op. cit.*, p. 900.

[42] *New York Times*, July 3, 1963, pp. 1 & 4.

[43] See Dean Rusk's testimony, U.S. Senate, Committee on Foreign Relations, *Hearings, Nuclear Test Ban Treaty*, 88th Cong., 1st Sess., 1963, p. 52. For a discussion of the diplomacy involved and the negotiating history of the agreement, see Arthur H. Dean, *The Test Ban and Disarmament: The Path of Negotiation* (New York: Harper and Row, 1966), particularly pp. 1–106.

during the discussions, because the Soviet leader was preoccupied with the situation in Europe.[44]

The Harriman mission was much smaller than many of the postwar American delegations which negotiated with the Soviet Union on arms control. It included thirteen people, among whom were Adrian Fisher, Deputy Director of the Arms Control and Disarmament Agency, John McNaughton, General Counsel of the Department of Defense, Foy Kohler, United States Ambassador to the Soviet Union, William Tyler, Assistant Secretary of State for European Affairs, and Dr. Frank Press, an American expert on seismic studies.

The treaty itself was negotiated early. Discussions opened on July 16, and agreement was reached on the substance of the treaty six days later, at which time Press returned to Washington.[45] The remaining problem was whether a nonaggression treaty was to be a precondition for the test ban. The Western negotiators insisted that any such treaty must preclude the recognition of the East German Government and that it must be acceptable to the other North Atlantic Treaty member states. Assistant Secretary Tyler joined the negotiations for discussions on the nonaggression treaty. The West resisted the Soviet proposal, as well as a Soviet request for inclusion of a promise in the official communiqué which would bind the Western powers to seek a nonaggression agreement within their alliance. The test ban was then amended with only a few language changes and finally approved. The negotiations during the last four days appear to have been the most delicate phase because of the Soviet insistence that the agreement should be attached to a nonaggression pact.[46]

The Ambassador sent progress reports to Washington after each negotiating session and received new instructions before the next meeting. Harriman's message did not circulate within the government the way most incoming communications would. On receipt of the message telephoned from Moscow, nine copies were made; distribution was on a very limited short term basis, with no additional copies to be reproduced by the interested parties. Those persons who were not expressly included on the circulation roster were not shown copies, although some of them were briefed orally. For example, General Maxwell Taylor informed the members of the Joint Chiefs of Staff, who never saw the reports directly. The State De-

[44] "Rusk, Harriman and Martin Agronsky on NBC," *Bulletin of the Department of State,* XLIX, No. 1259 (August 12, 1963), p. 243.

[45] *New York Times,* July 19, 1963, p. 1 and July 21, 1963, p. 2.

[46] Based on press reports from the *New York Times,* July 15–26, 1963 and interviews, Washington, D.C., Spring, 1964.

partment prepared negotiating instructions for Harriman for the next day. The President, a few close advisers, the Secretaries of State and Defense, the Directors of the Arms Control and Disarmament Agency and the Central Intelligence Agency and two ranking officials from the Department of State reviewed the progress of the negotiations and discussed the daily instructions. The President frequently changed these instructions giving his negotiatiors considerable flexibility in Moscow but keeping responsibility and direction in his hands.[47]

Just as there are several places where a bill can be killed in Congress, there are many opportunities to dilute or kill foreign policy proposals in the administration. The special concerns of some of the agencies really dealt with demands for overprotection or manifested a suspicion of the Russians which precluded any meaningful agreement with the Soviets. Kennedy minimized the prospects for political opposition while the treaty was in its delicate negotiating phase. There was a real danger that some public leaders would support the treaty only on conditions which would probably dilute or sabotage its contents. Even if the President did not heed their suggestions, public statements by Senators and others during the negotiations might place them in a position from which they could not gracefully exit once the treaty had been negotiated. By sharing only a minimal amount of information, the President precluded this early opposition and dilution of the treaty.

### *The President and the Treaty*

The day after the treaty was initialed in Moscow, President Kennedy addressed the nation in hopeful, but sober terms. He recalled that during the past several years each acceleration in the arms race resulted in increased world tension. This spiral, and its unwelcome effects, had seemed unending, but now the treaty hopefully represented "a shaft of light cut into the darkness."[48]

The President identified four basic advantages to the treaty. First, it would provide an opportunity to reduce world tension and the possibility of nuclear war. Kennedy did not accept a complacent view of a future nuclear conflict, because he feared it would be more terrible than any other in history.

[47] Sorensen, *op. cit.*, p. 735.
[48] *Washington Post,* July 27, 1963, p. 8A.

A full scale nuclear exchange, lasting less than 60 minutes with the weapons now in existence, could wipe out more than 300 million Americans, Europeans, and Russians, as well as untold numbers elsewhere . . . So let us try to turn the world from war. Let us make the most of this opportunity, and every opportunity, to reduce tension, to slow down the perilous nuclear arms race, and to check the world's slide toward final annihilation.[49]

The test ban would also free the world from the fear of radioactive contamination which was a concern to all men. "This is not a natural health hazard, and it is not a statistical issue", he insisted as he rejected the assertions of those who argued that the dangers were small when compared to natural radiation and, in any event, would affect very few individuals. A third advantage of the treaty was its prevention of the spread of nuclear weapons to those countries which did not already possess them. The proliferation of these weapons "in the hands of countries large and small, stable and unstable, responsible and irresponsible" would provide neither stability nor security.[50]

Finally, the treaty would limit the nuclear arms race, which, on balance, will strengthen our nation's security far more than the continuation of unrestricted testing. For, in today's world, a nation's security does not always increase as its arms increase when its adversary is doing the same, and unlimited competition in the testing and development of new types of destructive nuclear weapons will not make the world safer for either side . . .

We have, and under this treaty we will continue to have, the nuclear strength that we need.[51]

The President believed national security was endangered most in militarily unstable and technologically fluid environments, where future increments in force levels or technical knowledge might adversely affect the uneasy military balance between the United States and the Soviet Union. The treaty reflected a common recognition by the participants of the dangers in furthering the arms race, and, consequently, advantage did not accrue from "concession either to or by the Soviet Union."[52]

The international environment was unstable and nuclear superiority over the Soviet Union was ephemeral. Stability and not superiority was the President's goal in the uncertain world of rapid and uncontrollable technological

[49] *Ibid.*
[50] *Ibid.*
[51] *Ibid.*
[52] *Ibid.*

and scientific discovery. This could best be achieved through a parity of strength and not by an overwhelming degree of nuclear superiority.

### *Linkage with Domestic Constituencies*

Kennedy accomplished only one of his objectives with the successful negotiation of the treaty. The advice and consent to the treaty by the Senate and adherence by a number of other nations were also essential. The President was conscious of the disastrous defeat of Woodrow Wilson in the Senate after his impressive accomplishments at Versailles. Part of the administration's strategy was to offer the treaty as the logical outgrowth of policies pursued by the Eisenhower administration. The President tried to present the approval of all executive agencies to Congress and the American people, but he was careful not to apply pressures which he considered to constitute "arm-twisting." The administration also made every effort to arouse public support for the treaty.

In his televised speech the President focused media attention on the negotiated treaty and acted as an input for the public opinion system. He also spoke to the agencies in the executive branch and clearly announced that he considered the treaty one of the important programs of his administration and implied that he expected their support and cooperation. The Senate was a third audience for the speech. Kennedy presented the test ban as a long awaited, bipartisan accomplishment and called on the Senate to approve the treaty. He attempted to build consensus rather than engender conflict.

A Citizens Committee worked closely with the executive branch, and together they attempted to build articulate support and coordinate group action. Through bipartisan Senatorial involvement in the signing ceremonies in Moscow and briefings with Senators before, during, and after the treaty had been negotiated, the administration hoped to build a climate for speedy approval. The treaty was a recurring topic at press conferences; administration officials provided background briefings; and at least one columnist was shown the Kennedy-Khrushchev correspondence. In addition, the President or his most trusted lieutenants coordinated the testimony of administrative witnesses.[53] As the next chapter will indicate, the President was linked to other participants transactionally. He did not simply send them directives and remain uninfluenced by their conduct. He initiated underground testing in order to win support and forestall criticism; he accepted

[53] According to Sorensen, the President "took pains also to coordinate the testimony of administration witnesses on Capitol Hill." *Op. cit.*, p. 738.

safeguards he considered unnecessary in order to diminish attacks from the military; he accepted the change in the direction of the debate as the Senate veered to military considerations and away from the treaty's political ramifications and did not insist that the treaty must be accepted only on his terms. Each of these adjustments by the President was designed to assist him as he pursued his major goal: the ratification of the test ban treaty.

### *Linkage with Foreign Constituencies*

Treaty supporters hoped to arrest the proliferation of nuclear weapons among the non-nuclear nations. If nations which did not possess their own nuclear weapons were prohibited from testing in the atmosphere, an important check was placed on proliferation. If most countries signed the treaty, this might act as a force on the non-signator states as well as give the treaty greater stature in the United States.

A Department of State survey conducted in early August, 1963, indicated that 64 nations were rated as highly favorable to the treaty, 29 as favorable, 2 as noncommittal, 16 as undecided, and 3 against.[54] France was one of the countries opposed to the treaty, and President Kennedy attempted to induce President Charles de Gaulle to sign the treaty. By recognizing France as a nuclear power, it could receive American assistance under the Atomic Energy Act and would not have to rely on atmospheric testing to improve its nuclear capability. However, de Gaulle rejected the offer and refused to sign the treaty, arguing the test ban was so incomplete it was meaningless and that nuclear stocks should be destroyed. On the day the treaty was open to adherence by other countries, August 9, the representatives of 31 countries signed the treaty at the Department of State, and by the time the treaty was approved in the Senate, 102 states formally adhered to the treaty.[55]

A special problem was posed by West Germany. The Federal Republic was concerned lest the East German government receive implicit or explicit recognition when it signed the treaty, thereby gaining enhanced standing in the international community. Chancellor Konrad Adenauer was also concerned about the tone and direction of American-Soviet discussions on Western Europe, particularly as it related to the future of Germany. To

[54] *New York Times,* August 4, 1963, p. 3.

[55] *Ibid.,* August 19, 1963, p. 1. The treaty was open for signature in the capitals of the three original parties. Some countries signed in all three countries but others only in one of them. This was designed to preclude tacit diplomatic recognition to countries not recognized by one of the three major powers. Thus East Germany signed in Moscow but not in Washington or London.

relieve German suspicions, the American Ambassador, George McGhee, called on the Chancellor July 12, three days before the Moscow negotiations to reassure him of the continued United States interest in and commitment to Germany. The United States embassy in Bonn gave daily briefings to German officials throughout the negotiations. On July 24, President Kennedy sent a letter to the Chancellor in which he attempted to allay Germany's fear that its interests had been adversely affected by the treaty, assuring him that the United States and the United Kingdom had not negotiated away any German interests. He also pledged that any discussions which concerned the North Atlantic Treaty Organization or individual members of the alliance would be fully discussed with the parties concerned before any concrete negotiations with the Soviet Union commenced.[56]

Secretaries Robert McNamara and Dean Rusk also spoke to the Chancellor and attempted to assure him that German interests had not been compromised. Rusk promised the Federal Republic that the United States would do everything possible to minimize any advantage the East Germans would gain by acceding to the treaty and that the United States would consult with Bonn on future Soviet-American negotiations. The Secretary of State spent seven hours with the Chancellor on his return from Moscow following the signing of the treaty.[57] A week later the Federal Republic was the 67th country to sign the treaty.[58]

## *Conclusions*

The President attempted to protect and expand his options and controlled information in order to maintain and pursue particular goals. Previous experience had taught him that there was a real danger that his policy could be diluted by agency debate and interagency compromise. Option-management refers not only to expanding the range of choices available to the President, but also to restricting possible dysfunctional moves by his opponents. At the same time, Kennedy was prepared to adjust to some pressures from opponents and skeptics of the treaty to assure as much support as possible without surrendering the basic integrity of the test ban. The President was a strategically located actor because he was in a position to influence outcomes in several political subsystems including the follow-

[56] Sorensen, *op. cit.*, p. 736.
[57] *New York Times*, August 11, 1963, p. 1.
[58] *Ibid.*, August 19, 1963, p. 3.

ing: (1) policy formation and articulation; (2) diplomatic bargaining; (3) public opinion formation; (4) political communication; (5) group articulation; and (6) legislative subsystems. Only some of these roles have been discussed here; others will be analyzed in later chapters where the President and other political participants will be considered in light of their role in that particular subsystem.

The division of labor in the political system increases specialization and tends to restrict the domain of action for a role incumbent, but when an actor occupies roles in several subsystems he may increase his capacity to effect outcomes. Concomitantly, the division of labor also increases interdependency. The resources, information, conflict, support, and options of any role incumbent depend, to a greater or lesser extent, on the behavior of other role incumbents in coupled subsystems. Some political actors are able to move from one subsystem to another with relative ease and attempt to direct or influence other role incumbents or coupled subsystems to behave in desirable ways. However, this is not without its costs; the more attention an actor devotes to a variety of roles, the less control he may have on any single subsystem. However, this does not mean he has necessarily overextended himself. He may increase his range of control through his own judicious use of information, his ability to isolate his opposition, and his formation of a formidable coalition against his opponents. In the case of the test ban, the President attempted to supervise more of the process than was customary in the conduct of foreign affairs, but he considered the issue so important and the threats from internal opposition sufficient enough to warrant his own personal attention.

The President, of course, was also concerned about a variety of issues which restricted the time and energy he could devote to any single issue. He allocated considerable time to the test ban treaty, but he also had to devote attention to other matters. Three other considerations which claimed his time during the summer of 1963 were the impending railroad strike, civil rights, and a personal tragedy – the death of his infant son. Many matters required immediate attention and could not be postponed. The President could not set his own agenda or devote as much time to the test ban treaty as he might have wished.

CHAPTER III

# DECISION-MAKING IN THE EXECUTIVE BRANCH

Several agencies participated in the formulation of American arms control policy, and each was expected to evaluate proposals according to its expertise and judgment of the national interest. Policy was formally constructed in the Committee of Principals where such heterogeneous organizations as the Department of State, the Atomic Energy Commission, the Arms Control and Disarmament Agency, and the Department of Defense were represented.[1] All agreed that national security was their primary goal, that peace was preferable to war, and that unilateral disarmament was unwise. These norms were hardly sufficient to guarantee harmony among the participants who held different interpretations of the elements which defined national security; the institutional ways in which peace might be assured; and the limits, if any, which should be imposed on the testing and use of weapons.

Still the participants at the policy making level had generally internalized "rules of the game" which reduced open hostility between them and enabled them to continue to work with their associates, even after vigorous disagreement. Although the participants had their own goals, they were constrained by other participants, by the environment, by the options which were available and the probable effects of their actions on their future goals. They had a hierarchy of values, and if an actor pursued one goal exclusively, he might endanger some of his other values. In addition, he had to decide on the costs of different strategies.[2] Because he wished to salvage

[1] The Central Intelligence Agency was also an important participant, supplying information and recommendations on the state of Soviet technology and nuclear testing. It recommended the treaty, but the basis and intensity of the recommendation are not known because of security considerations.

[2] No organization is completely open or completely closed. Agencies differed not only because of their specialized goals but also because they were open to outside pressures, support, and constraints. For a discussion of open systems as organizations, see Charles Z. Wilson and Marcus Alexis, "Basic Framework for Decisions," *Journal of the Academy of Management,* 5 (August, 1962), particularly p. 162.

some of the endangered values, he often adjusted his scale of preferences to meet the new situation. Adjusting of values and strategy is neither necessarily wise nor successful. But the actor who is conscious of the conflicts is faced with the options of maintaining his current value preferences, adjusting them, or attempting to alter the environment to a congenial direction. For some, support for the treaty represented little or no problem. It was either positive or neutral, and they were eager or willing to follow the President. For other agencies, however, the test ban was seen as limiting their ability to pursue their goals as effectively as they might wish. Skepticism about the treaty was particularly pronounced in the military services and the Atomic Energy Commission (AEC), where adjustment was more difficult.

In addition to their own agency's goals, the actors had to consider a variety of other factors in the case of the test ban treaty. The President was strongly committed to its ratification.[3] It had been signed, that is, it was no longer a proposal but was a policy on which the prestige of the United States rested.[4] It had considerable popular support, and the chances for ratification appeared good. The effect of these environmental changes can be seen in a comparison of the behavior of some of the participants who opposed the treaty in June, with their behavior in August, after the treaty had been signed and the agencies adjusted to alterations in the environment.

### *The Committee of Principals*

The Committee of Principals was charged with developing the United States' position on disarmament and arms control and reporting its recommendations to the President. It considered the effect of proposals on national security and whenever possible presented a unanimous recommendation to the Chief Executive. Consequently, it had all of the advantages and disadvantages of committee decision-making. Because it was

[3] See McGeorge Bundy, "The Presidency and Peace," *Foreign Affairs,* XLII (April, 1964), pp. 353–365. The President talked with the members of the Joint Chiefs of Staff as a group on July 23, 1963 and discussed the treaty with each Chief individually the week before. He asked them to weigh the military *and political considerations* in their evaluations of the test ban. U.S. Senate, Preparedness Subcommittee of the Committee on Armed Services, *Military Aspects and Implications of Nuclear Test Ban Proposals and Related Matters,* 88th Cong., 1st Sess., 1963, p. 733.

[4] Interview, Washington, D.C., January, 1964. The effect of signing the treaty can be seen in the opposition to the test ban by the members of the Joint Chiefs of Staff when they appeared before the Preparedness Subcommittee in late June, 1963 before the treaty was negotiated and in mid-August when they gave a qualified endorsement after it had been signed. *Ibid.,* pp. 302–305 and 587–591.

cumbersome and proposals were often delayed, the President decided to bypass the Committee when he prepared his American University address.

The criterion by which suggestions were evaluated in the Committee was national security. National security is a word which is difficult to define specifically, but it conveyed a meaning to many of the participants, and appeared to have made compromise more palatable to them. National security still rested on a deterrence strategy. While the Arms Control and Disarmament Agency and many in the military could agree about the concept of deterrence, they differed about what constituted appropriate force levels to achieve deterrence, where one could accept risks stemming from Soviet superiority or uncertainty, and whether deterrence was better served by nuclear payload and delivery superiority or parity. National security tended to constrain participants when they represented their own agency and precluded some of the dissension which might have arisen from a Hobbesian struggle for dominance without some legitimizing norm. National security served as a value which restricted debate, defined acceptable limits, and, by its nature, was assumed to rest on a variety of factors which were unevenly represented in the final equation. Consequently, victory or defeat for an agency might be seen as a matter of degree rather than an absolute, although there were some participants who were more apt than others to accept the results with good humor, and there were some issues which were resolved to the obvious long-range detriment of some participants.

The formal and informal arrangements in the Committee facilitated evaluation from several perspectives. Suggestions from the Office of the President or one of the agencies were circulated to the participants, and each position was then discussed at a Deputies' Meeting. Here an attempt was made to identify the areas of agreement and, if possible, to establish a consensus. After the meeting, the Deputies briefed their superiors on the status of the various proposals and constructed an agency position. In 1962 and early 1963, the Committee generally met from an hour to an hour and a half, leaving little time for a discussion of details. In the words of one adviser, they "must have all of their homework out of the way and dispense with minor issues."[5] When the Committee could not agree on a proposal, it was resolved at the presidential level. After the American position had been constructed, it was sent to the United Kingdom for comment, as the two countries desired to present a united front in their negotiations with the Soviet Union. If the British expressed reservations, the evaluation process

[5] Interview, Department of State, March, 1964.

would normally begin again in Washington with consideration by the agencies, the Deputies, and the Committee of Principals. In the case of the draft test ban treaty, no fundamental changes were proposed by the British, although some modification in its language was suggested.

The test ban treaty of 1963 was based on proposals submitted by the United States and United Kingdom at the Geneva Conference in 1962. Two draft treaties were submitted at Geneva, one prohibiting all nuclear tests and another banning tests in the atmosphere, outer space, and underwater, though permitting underground tests. This latter proposal was introduced as a limited ban, both in its scope and duration. The administration hoped to extend the ban to underground tests after the limited agreement had been accepted. The administration believed that effective inspection of the atmosphere, outerspace, and underwater could be made by the parties without access to the territory of the other nations which adhered to the treaty. However, the United States insisted on having on-site inspection if underground tests were to be part of the treaty.

Both preliminary treaty drafts were circulated in early July, 1962 to the agencies which had been represented in the working committee for study and formal comment. Two weeks later, the Committee of Deputies discussed the proposals. Following their meeting of July 20, two additional drafts of each treaty were circulated for comment in preparation for the meeting of the Committee of Principals, held on July 26. This was followed by three successive meetings of the Principals with the President on July 27 and 30 and August 1. The military services were represented by the Chairman of the Joint Chiefs of Staff, who was not then a formal member of the Committee, and the Secretary of Defense or his representative. The draft treaties were revised slightly during August on the basis of suggestions from the President and were circulated to the interested agencies for comment. Additional inter-agency discussions to work out last minute details were continued at the staff level and the treaties were then submitted by the United States and Great Britain on August 27, 1962.[6]

[6] Senate, Subcommittee of the Committee on Armed Services, *Hearings, Arms Control and Disarmament,* 87th Cong., 2nd Sess., 1962, p. 71. See Appendix 1 for a comparison of the draft treaty of 1962 and the signed treaty of 1963. Also invited to attend the meeting were Ambassador Arthur Dean, chief United States negotiator at Geneva, and two members of the Arms Control and Disarmament Agency's General Advisory Committee, John J. McCloy, its chairman, and Robert A. Lovett a Secretary of Defense in the Truman administration.

*The Arms Control and Disarmament Agency*

The Arms Control and Disarmament Agency (ACDA) is charged with the responsibility of advising the President and Secretary of State on arms control and disarmament matters. Created in September, 1961, it had a staff of 150 in early 1963, and a budget of 6.5 million dollars, two thirds of which was to be devoted to research.[7]

In formulating proposals and recommendations, it obtained current information on both American and Soviet nuclear weapons programs. Its Reference Research Section attempted to collect all significant intelligence reports, publications, special studies, national intelligence estimates, and other relevant intelligence documents at various levels of classification from liaison-officers attached to the Central Intelligence Agency, the Department of Defense, and the Bureau of Intelligence and Research of the Department of State. Informational inputs concerning nuclear weapons development and nuclear effects data also came from the Atomic Energy Commission, the Office of the Director of Research and Engineering in the Department of Defense, and the Defense Atomic Support Agency. In addition to routine receipts and analysis of information, specific requests for data were made to specialists outside of the agency. For example, agency personnel were briefed on May 1, 1963 by John Foster of the Lawrence Radiation Laboratory and by J. Carson Mark, Director of the Theoretical Division of the Los Alamos Scientific Laboratory, on the current state of nuclear weapons technology and prospects for its development with further testing. The agency also awarded contracts to private agencies and individuals to study various questions pertinent to a nuclear test ban, and nongovernmental consultants provided additional information and evaluation.[8]

ACDA is one of the few agencies which included members from other government offices to assure a "balanced" view. To make certain that it considered military, scientific, and diplomatic factors, the State and Defense Departments, the Atomic Energy Commission, and other agencies were assigned to work with ACDA as it constructed and evaluated proposals.[9] Normally, interagency committees develop a policy after each agency presents its own organizational position. Compromise occurs after, and not before, the organization has formulated its recommendations. Agencies often take account of the probable reception by potentially competing or co-

[7] Office of the Federal Registrar, *United States Government Organization Manual, 1964–1965* (Washington: Government Printing Office, 1964), pp. 495–496.

[8] Preparedness Subcommittee, *op. cit.*, pp. 50–51.

[9] *Ibid.*, p. 51.

operating agencies to their proposals and adjust them accordingly. In any event, the compromise is not generally structured by interagency participation within the proposing agency. This was not the case with ACDA. Among its employees were two from the Atomic Energy Commission, twelve from the Department of Defense, and one from the United States Information Agency.[10] There were also twenty-one Foreign Service Officers and Reserve Officers assigned to ACDA. The Agency devoted a considerable proportion of its resources to scientific and technical problems relating to the verification of possible arms control and disarmament proposals. Twelve ACDA officials, five of whom were military officers, spent all or a substantial proportion of their time on these problems. Coordination was also maintained through the Inspection Study Group which was under ACDA auspices. Two of its members were from the Agency, three from the Defense Department, two from the Office of the President, one from the Atomic Energy Commission, and one from private industry.[11]

Although ACDA was not under the control of the military or other possible skeptics of arms control, it obviously had to take their position into account, not only in the Committee of Principals when policy was recommended, but also within the Agency when policy was formulated. Coupling between ACDA and other agencies was more direct than is usually the case in the executive branch.

William C. Foster, Director of ACDA and a Republican, generally found arms control was synonymous with national security. Foster regarded the test ban treaty, in particular, as decelerating the arms race and serving as the first step toward a more comprehensive agreement with the Soviet Union on future arms control agreements.[12] A precondition for national security, according to ACDA, was a stable technological environment. Unanticipated breakthroughs could upset the uneasy balance and encourage reckless behavior. Consequently, the Agency was concerned with a ban on nuclear weapons to countries not possessing them. It was also more concerned about the effects of radioactive fallout than other participants, although it soon became obvious that this argument would not sway many of the other agencies. Nuclear contamination was an acceptable cost for most of the other participants if testing seemed necessary, with the President, his scientific advisers, and ACDA being the major exceptions.

[10] *Ibid.*, p. 57, and U.S. Senate, Disarmament Subcommittee of the Committee on Foreign Relations, *Hearings, Review of Operations of the Arms Control and Disarmament Agency,* 87th Cong., 2nd Sess., 1962, pp. 73–74.

[11] Disarmament Subcommittee, *op. cit.*, pp. 71–72.

[12] Preparedness Subcommittee, *op. cit.*, p. 7.

*The Department of State*

There was some skepticism concerning arms control and disarmament in the Department of State. Secretary Dean Rusk was generally not optimistic about the chances of success for arms control. Like many others, he seriously questioned the Soviets' motivations and was unprepared to accept an agreement unless it was adequately monitored. But the idea of what comprises adequate safeguards or inspections changed with each new scientific and technological discovery. It appears that Rusk's position in this fluid area was more cautious than that of some participants in ACDA, but less intransigent than those of many military officers and Atomic Energy Commission officials. However, many desk officers in the State Department were particularly riled by previous public discussions in the United States about the imminence of an arms control agreement. It was difficult enough for them to work with some of the Western allies who feared the immediate and future effects of a test ban treaty. These officials felt that arms control discussions were causing unnecessary agitation among some allies.

In the late summer of 1962, Secretary Rusk said that he devoted more time to the affairs of ACDA than to any of the units or bureaus in his department, with the exception of the Bureau of European Affairs during the Berlin crisis. The contacts between the Department and the Agency operated at a variety of levels. One of the senior officers of the Agency attended the morning staff meetings of the Secretary. Secretary Rusk also met with members of the Agency about twice a week, spoke with the Director or Deputy Director at least once each day on the phone, and saw all of the Agency's proposals.[13] The Secretary of State rated arms control proposals as one of three of the most important and time-consuming questions discussed with the Secretary of Defense. In addition, he explored arms control problems within his department, including the Bureau of European Affairs, which assigned one of its experts on Eastern European Affairs to the Arms Control and Disarmament Agency.[14] Yet Rusk was not

[13] *Ibid.*, pp. 83–84.

[14] *Ibid.*, p. 84. Arthur Schlesinger, reflecting the attitude of several of President Kennedy's advisers, found that the Department of State was more of a handicap in reaching agreements with the Soviet Union than a help. For example, Schlesinger reported that after Dean Rusk "somewhat tentatively" suggested Harriman as the chief United States negotiator, "State developed second thoughts in the next twenty-four hours." *Op cit.*, p. 903. More directly, Schlesinger charged the Department's leadership with fostering hostility between the two superpowers. "Left to itself, the Department of State would not have persevered with the issue, nor would it have ever proposed an American University speech – that speech which, in its modesty, clarity, and perception,

an advocate for either side. It was relatively easy for him to follow the President's lead in the summer of 1963.

When Rusk appeared before the Committee on Foreign Relations to urge approval of the treaty, he told the Senators that military victory was an unrealistic concept for policy makers when a full scale nuclear exchange was involved. The lessons of the Cuban missile crisis of October, 1962 had demonstrated that a more rational method must be found. At that time, "men confronted decisions that might have moved to a nuclear war. That experience has been sobering for all."[15] The United States was still engaged in a monumental contest with the Soviet Union, and the task before American leaders was to bring it into a less dangerous context.

> No responsible man will deny that we live in a world of vast and incalculable risks. Where decisions may be required in minutes, we must be constantly on guard against accident or miscalculation that can lead where no one wants to go. A local conflict anywhere around the globe in which the interests of the great powers are engaged might suddenly pose the prospect of nuclear war.
>
> Nor can any responsible person say that we can improve our security by an unlimited arms race extending without relief into the future. On the contrary, great as the risks are now, they would rapidly increase. Arsenals will grow larger, weapons more destructive, the frustrations of stalemate and fear more intense. The risks will increase unpredictably as nuclear weapons become available to more and more countries.[16]

Consequently, the Secretary believed that there was a need for "durable international institutions and. . . a respect for law and its procedures." In this setting, the "most important thing about the treaty is, therefore, what it may symbolize and what new paths it may open."[17]

### *The Atomic Energy Commission*

One of the responsibilities of the Atomic Energy Commission (AEC) is to develop nuclear energy for national defense. Among the offices in AEC which evaluated the treaty were the Division of Military Application under the direction of General Austin W. Betts and several research and development facilities including the Los Alamos Scientific Laboratory and E. O. Lawrence Radiation Laboratory. Each operated in different environments,

repudiated the self-righteous cold war rhetoric of a succession of Secretaries of State." *Ibid.*, p. 909.

[15] Committee on Foreign Relations, *op. cit.*, p. 12.

[16] *Ibid.*, pp. 12–13.

[17] *Ibid.*, p. 20.

had distinct organizational purposes, and had diverse backgrounds. At the same time, they shared many similar goals and experiences. AEC provides us with one example of intra-agency debate on arms control. Intraorganizational debates also occurred in the armed services and in the Departments of State and Defense.

AEC had a long history of opposition to arms control proposals during the Eisenhower administration. Many in the Commission thought it would be dysfunctional to their goals.[18] The former Chairman of AEC, Lewis Strauss, vigorously fought any suggestion that his agency be limited in any way by an arms control agreement with the Soviets. The moratoria imposed on testing by Presidents Eisenhower and Kennedy affected the AEC's activities and goals more immediately than those of any other agency. In looking at the impact of the test ban, the directors of the laboratories relied on their experience with the previous moratoria in making their recommendations. John Foster, who succeeded Edward Teller as Director of the Livermore Laboratory, found the 1958 moratorium was a "very serious blow" to his operation, affecting personnel and morale adversely. The technical personnel expected that the order would soon be recalled because "this was a very unrealistic situation, and in general . . . (the) people in the Laboratory felt that the resumption of testing was likely to be six months or twelve months away, and they felt that way month-after-month."[19] However, after more than three years of unfulfilled expectation, a sense of frustration developed. During this period several talented people left, feeling they could be more effective elsewhere. Drawing from these experiences, Foster maintained that the test ban treaty would only exacerbate this problem of maintaining a qualified staff and aggravate attempts to induct new people into the program.[20]

According to Foster, although the laboratory did not atrophy as it waited for permission to test, its research, based on calculations from previously tested data, could not be incorporated into new designs with a high level of confidence unless there was more experimentation. Proof-testing in the past had demonstrated that a system may behave one way in the laboratory but another, unexpected way under more realistic conditions.[21] "Ignorance, ineradicable under the treaty, can thereby increase uncertainty in technical-military judgment."[22] The test ban was unacceptable to Foster because it

[18] For example, see Lewis L. Strauss, *Men and Decisions* (New York: Doubleday, 1962), p. 416, and *passim*.

[19] Preparedness Subcommittee, *op. cit.*, p. 395.

[20] *Ibid.*, p. 396.

[21] Committee on Foreign Relations, *op. cit.*, p. 615.

[22] Preparedness Subcommittee, *op. cit.*, p. 531.

would increase technical uncertainty and reduce the efficiency of the laboratories.

The high value which he assigned to testing was reinforced by his own professional training and experience:

> Among the experts are those whose background is theoretical and those whose background is experimental. My background is experimental. And I have leanings, and those leanings tell me that one should do the experiments to verify the degree to which the capability in fact exists.[23]

Dr. N. E. Bradbury of Lawrence Laboratory at Los Alamos did not agree with Foster's evaluation of the treaty, finding that it held "only mild risks to the national defense posture, but (represented) the possibility of taking the first real, even if small, step in the direction of the prevention of a nuclear war."[24] This latter factor was not mentioned by Foster in his evaluation of the treaty.

Bradbury did not find that the moratoria imposed restrictions on the operations at Los Alamos, and observed that it:

> . . . already had a Division of Basic Research and looked for a number of other peaceful applications of atomic energy, power, nuclear rocketry, fusion power, programs in biology and medicine, and things of that sort.
>
> In contrast, the Livermore Laboratory was established at the insistence of Dr. Teller on a very fundamental assumption, possibly a correct assumption, that its basic objective was to develop nuclear weapons . . .
>
> Therefore, I suppose in a certain sense the Los Alamos Laboratory being older by some twenty years has become somewhat more familiar with these problems and has perhaps less reason for existence because of atomic development.[25]

Bradbury did not believe that additional atmospheric nuclear testing would enhance national security. Additional experimentation was especially important for delivery systems, but this could be tested under the treaty because nuclear detonations were not involved.[26] He insisted that the nuclear scientist must have the basic objective of putting himself "out of business."[27] The fact that the time for this had not yet arrived prompted his recommendation that the federal government initiate an active program of underground testing.

[23] *Ibid.*

[24] Committee on Foreign Relations, *op. cit.*, p. 579.

[25] Preparedness Subcommittee, *Hearings, 1963, op. cit.*, p. 404.

[26] *Ibid.*, p. 406.

[27] *Ibid.*

General Betts was particularly concerned with the ability of the military services to maintain sufficient superior strength to deter or sustain a Soviet first strike. A month before the test ban was negotiated, he told the Preparedness Subcommittee that the only way to achieve this objective was by continued testing in the atmosphere because it enabled the United States to develop new weapons to counter Soviet advances.[28]

There was, then, a debate within AEC over the meaning and effects of the treaty as it impinged on a number of values considered important by some of its participants. As their understanding of national security requirements varied, their evaluations of the effects of the treaty on national security also differed. However, it is the Commissioners who are charged with establishing the policy of the Atomic Energy Commission and who are represented by their Chairman at meetings of the Committee of Principals. In arriving at Commission policy, they rely on information supplied by their laboratories as well as on sources outside AEC. Their recommendations on the treaty were based on "the technical, arms control, and political aspects of the proposal as well as . . . national security" considerations.[29] Prior to his appearance before the Preparedness Subcommittee, Commissioner Leland Hayworth consulted with the Department of Defense and the Joint Chiefs of Staff, as well as the Arms Control and Disarmament Agency and the Department of State. AEC's Division of Military Applications assisted him in drafting his statement.[30]

Hayworth recommended support for the test ban treaty, finding that it would not have adverse effects on American nuclear capabilities.[31] When Dr. Glen T. Seaborg, Chairman of the Atomic Energy Commission, appeared before the Foreign Relations Committee, he insisted that there would be no slowdown on development except for complex multimegaton warheads.[32] Both felt that continued testing would pose problems for the maintenance of American nuclear superiority. Hayworth, for example, did not believe that continued testing by the United States would necessarily assure a superior capability for this country because the Soviet Union would also test and might overtake the United States.[33]

[28] *Ibid.*, pp. 241–242.

[29] Letter from Allan M. Labowitz, Special Assistant for Disarmament, The Atomic Energy Commission, Washington, D.C., July 23, 1964.

[30] Preparedness Subcommittee, *op. cit.*, pp. 223–295.

[31] *Ibid.*, pp. 224–235.

[32] Committee on Foreign Relations, *op. cit.*, pp. 205–212.

[33] Preparedness Subcommittee, *Hearings, 1963, op. cit.*, p. 242.

### *The Department of Defense*

Some observers have noted a unified military opposition to any attempt to limit the application or types of force available to the country and have charged that this negative position held by the military frustrated a more vigorous and favorable arms control policy.[34] This approach ignores the fact that there are several missions within the Department of Defense, and that some branches do not mind seeing other participants under additional control when the services are in competition with one another, particularly if they are not adversely affected.

Secretary of Defense Robert McNamara argued that the United States was not necessarily best protected by a continuation of the arms race but believed that greater protection would be afforded if the military environment could be stabilized. Although he generally insisted that the United States must maintain a superior military position, he often implied that there was a point of diminishing returns in any arms race. In discussing the Cuban missile crisis, he found that concepts of fixed military superiority or traditional notions of victory were no longer applicable. He told a congressional committee:

> As the events of last October have so forcefully demonstrated, the expanding arsenals of nuclear weapons on both sides of the Iron Curtain have created an extremely dangerous situation not only for their possessors but for the entire world. As the arms race continues and weapons multiply and become more swift and deadly, the possibility of global catastrophe, either by miscalculation or design, becomes more real.
>
> More armaments, whether offensive or defensive, cannot solve this dilemma. We are approaching an era when it will become increasingly improbable that either side could destroy a sufficiently large portion of the other's strategic nuclear force, either by surprise or otherwise, to preclude a devastating retaliatory blow. This may result in mutual deterrence, but the prospect is a grim prospect . . . The United States and the Soviet Union, as the two great nuclear powers, are the nations most directly endangered by these weapons, and, therefore, have great mutual interest in seeing that they are never used.[35]

Six months later, he urged support for the treaty, insisting that the United States had a net quantitative nuclear superiority.[36] Finding that "the sheer

[34] For example, see John M. Swomley, Jr., *The Military Establishment* (Boston: Beacon Press, 1964).

[35] U.S. House of Representatives, Subcommittee of the Committee on Appropriations, *Department of Defense Appropriations for 1964* (Part 1), 88th Cong., 1st Sess., 1963, p. 109. The testimony was given February 6, 1963.

[36] Committee on Foreign Relations, *op. cit.*, p. 98.

multiplication of a nation's destructive nuclear capability does not necessarily produce a net increase in its superiority,"[37] McNamara did not agree that the risks, which some professional military men saw in the treaty, were sufficient to reject the test ban.

Although he received information and advice from the members of the Joint Chiefs of Staff, he relied "very heavily on his own staff."[38] His emphasis on civilian advisers caused considerable uneasiness and some antagonism from military officers who felt that their role had been depreciated. After his retirement as Chief of Staff of the Navy, Admiral George Anderson complained there was a tendency in the Department of Defense to "downgrade the role of the men who may have to fight our country's battles" and to "discredit the voices of dissent from the military."[39] The Secretary called on his civilian staff when he wanted technical advice, or when he believed military officers did not possess the necessary flexibility to evaluate all of the facets of a proposal, which was McNamara's prognosis of the Air Force evaluation of the test ban.

One of his principal advisers was John T. McNaughton, General Counsel of the Department. He alone represented the Department at the Moscow negotiations[40] and assisted in coordinating the testimony of military witnesses before Senate committees.[41] Before assuming his post as General Counsel, he was Deputy Assistant Secretary of Defense for Arms Control and had a reputation for being sympathetic to arms limitations. McNaughton found that if arms control proposals were to be meaningful and acceptable to all parties, they must provide "mutual improvement" for all of the participants. Agreements which limited American testing need not adversely affect capabilities if they were offset by parallel or compensating reductions by the Soviet Union. In his view, the task for decision-makers was to concern themselves "with the factors of stability and of the dynamic effect of the arms race." Within this context he believed that there may be a limit on what is necessary for a successful deterrent.[42]

Opponents of the treaty in the Department of Defense believed that the Soviets were generally ahead of the United States in very high megaton weapons and had probably gained valuable data from their high-yield atmos-

[37] *Ibid.*, p. 109.
[38] Preparedness Subcommittee, *op. cit.*, p. 317.
[39] *New York Times*, September 5, 1963, pp. 1–19.
[40] Committee on Foreign Relations, *op. cit.*, p. 203.
[41] Preparedness Subcommittee, *op. cit.*, p. 177.
[42] Address before the International Arms Control Symposium, University of Michigan, Ann Arbor, Michigan, December 19, 1962, as cited in William Kaufmann, *The McNamara Strategy* (New York: Harper and Row, 1964), pp. 142–147.

pheric tests, enabling them to develop an anti-missile system. Dr. Harold Brown, Director of Defense Research and Engineering, rejected these arguments in language which paralleled McNamara's. Brown held that American anti-missile missile development efforts were comparable in magnitude and success to those of the Soviets, and that American missiles could penetrate any existing anti-missile systems without the aid of further atmospheric testing.[43] Both he and the Secretary found little military value in high-yield nuclear weapons.[44]

Each of the military services has its own mission or purpose, tends to approach strategic requirements on the basis of its mission, and seeks to maximize those weapons systems which enable it to perform its perceived function most effectively. Because goals differ between and within the services, the evaluation of any given arms control proposal is not necessarily pre-determined, although the services are certainly skeptical about the inherent desirability of widespread arms control.

The Air Force maintained that the foundation of American defense must be a clear superiority of the country's nuclear striking power. When General Curtis LeMay, Chief of Staff of the Air Force, recalled the lessons of the Cuban crisis, he found that "superior U.S. strategic power, coupled with the obvious will and ability to apply this power, was the major factor that forced the Soviets to back down."[45] The Air Force was particularly concerned about treaty restrictions which precluded further study of missile site vulnerability[46] and which retarded the development of high-yield weapons.[47] General LeMay insisted that high-yield weapons were necessary to destroy certain types of targets such as underground, hardened missile sites which smaller weapons could not effectively demolish. He also felt that there was a "very important psychological factor which is involved with high-yield tests,"[48] and indicated that he "personally would like to go up to 100 megatons or more."[49]

The role of the Navy has expanded with the advent of nuclear power. As one writer identified one of its functions: "The Navy's central missions have become to maximize its ability to project power from the sea over the land

[43] Preparedness Subcommittee, *op. cit.*, pp. 856–58.
[44] *Ibid.*, pp. 855–56.
[45] U.S. Senate, Committee on Armed Services, *Military Procurement Authorization, Fiscal Year, 1964*, 88th Cong., 1st Sess., 1963, p. 333.
[46] Preparedness Subcommittee, *op. cit.*, p. 718.
[47] *Ibid.*, pp. 724–729.
[48] *Ibid.*, p. 739.
[49] *Ibid.*, p. 724.

and to prevent the enemy from doing the same."[50] The Navy found its interests affected principally by the prohibition of the testing of nuclear devices under water. It would be unable to test antisubmarine devices and to study the effects of the Navy's Polaris warhead. The Navy was willing to accept restrictions on further tests on the Polaris warhead but was not altogether satisfied with the prohibition on testing antisubmarine devices. It accepted the limitations imposed by the test ban, expecting that the treaty would also restrict Soviet testing in this area.[51]

Although the Army had incorporated nuclear weapons into its mission, it continued to rely primarily on a large, flexible land force. It read entirely different lessons into the Cuban crisis than the Air Force had done, and the lessons coincided with its evaluation of the requisite requirements for national security. General Earle Wheeler, Chief of Staff of the Army, found that the crisis "demonstrated (the) value of maintaining ready Army forces at a high state of alert in order to equip national security policy with the military power to make a direct confrontation with Soviet power." He found that nuclear forces were in the background and nonnuclear forces were most significant.[52]

The Army felt that there were basic provisions in the treaty which required examination: (1) the use of tactical weapons in training would be prohibited; (2) the use of nuclear weapons in time of war might be compromised; and (3) the development of the anti-missile missile system, which was under Army jurisdiction, might be adversely affected. General Wheeler was satisfied that the treaty did not impose any restrictions on the use of nuclear weapons in war. At that time, the Army Chief of Staff reasoned "this particular treaty would go out of the window as far as there being any limitation on our use of weapons," and he expressed considerable confidence in the statements of the President that the treaty would not inhibit the right of self-defense by the United States.[53] The inability of the Army to conduct manoeuvers without the use of tactical nuclear weapons was not considered to "be too serious a disadvantage" to the overall effectiveness of the service.[54] Moreover, the anti-missile missile presented no serious problem because such a system could be designed "in the absence of atmospheric testing." Underground testing would compensate for some of the problems,

[50] Timothy Shea, "Project Poseidon," *U.S. Naval Institute Proceedings,* August, 1962, p. 31.

[51] Preparedness Subcommittee, *op. cit.,* p. 709.

[52] *Military Procurement Authorization, Fiscal Year 1964, op. cit.,* p. 76.

[53] Preparedness Subcommittee, *op. cit.,* pp. 659–685.

[54] *Ibid.,* p. 657.

although there were some areas where atmospheric testing would be able to supply helpful information.[55]

However, several Army scientists, particularly those connected with the anti-missile missile program, raised objections to the treaty. Like many others, they were concerned about the knowledge the Soviet Union had obtained in its high megaton test series and feared the Russians possessed useful information which the United States did not have. They seriously questioned whether they could accomplish their assigned goals if all atmospheric testing was frozen.

The payoffs for support and opposition were different for the services as well. The Army had occupied an inferior position among the services during the Eisenhower administration, but had grown in size and influence under President Kennedy. Although the Army was concerned about some of the treaty's consequences, it decided to disregard them since they concerned only secondary values to the service. Limited debate on these matters might be interpreted as a form of covert disapproval of the entire treaty. The Army had little to gain and much to lose by attacking the test ban, that is, by unnecessarily antagonizing the President.

The Air Force, which had been in its primacy during the Eisenhower years, found its strategic mission suffering a steady decline during the Kennedy administration. The doctrine of massive retaliation had given way to flexible and selective response; nuclear superiority was being replaced by nuclear parity, and requests by the Air Force to continue manned bombers were rejected by the Secretary of Defense. To many Air Force personnel, the treaty was another step in the process of weakening its mission. They were concerned that the Air Force would not be able to contribute to the national defense most effectively, and that the country would become weaker.[56] Because the costs of the treaty were so much higher and because many in the Air Force believed they had relatively little to lose, that is, the price of opposition was lower for them than for the Army, they were more prepared to find fault with the treaty publically.[57]

Although the services differed in several important respects on their evaluations of the treaty, they finally endorsed it when the Joint Chiefs of Staff appeared before the Senate committees in August. They had periodically been consulted from August 1962, when the draft treaties were introduced at Geneva, to August 1963, when the treaty was before the Senate. During the year, they met with the Service Secretaries and the Secretary of

[55] *Ibid.*, p. 671.
[56] Interview, Washington, D.C., February, 1964.
[57] Interview, Washington, D.C., January, 1964.

Defense six times and with McNamara alone four times, to discuss arms control. In their last three meetings they evaluated Khrushchev's speech in East Berlin (July 8, 1963), reviewed the Moscow negotiations (July 29), and coordinated their testimony before the committees (August 12).[58] In addition to these meetings, the Chairman of the Joint Chiefs of Staff met with the Secretary and Chiefs separately to consider arms control matters coming before the Committee of Principals.

The members of the Joint Chiefs of Staff, as a group, began an intensive review of their position in mid-June, following the President's American University speech. The address by the Soviet leader on July 2, 1963, intensified their efforts. General LeMay reported that it had not been until he saw the instructions to Governor Harriman on July 14 that he had realized "we were really serious about trying to negotiate a treaty."[59]

The Joint Chiefs consulted with a number of agencies and individuals during this time, including Teller,[60] Bradbury,[61] Foster, Seaborg, and Harriman.[62] The Central Intelligence Agency, the Office of the Secretary of Defense, the Department of State, and others were also contacted. The Chiefs were concerned with the present state and growth capacities of Soviet technology and military organization, as well as with an evaluation of American power and its probable increase with and without testing. The prospects for continued investigation into weapons effects, the development of an effective anti-missile missile system, testing weapons under realistic conditions, and measuring the blackout effects[63] of high yield atmospheric explosions were among the more important questions examined.

When they appeared before the Preparedness Subcommittee in June 1963, the Joint Chiefs of Staff reported that the two proposed treaties, a comprehensive one including underground tests, and a partial treaty, were "not consistent with the national security" of the country without inclusion of a number of recommended safeguards.[64] By August, with a negotiated treaty before them, the safeguards were somewhat altered, and the language was phrased positively for the limited test ban rather than negatively. They found that, subject to recommended modification, "the risks inherent in this treaty can be accepted in order to seek the important gains which

[58] Preparedness Subcommittee, *op. cit.*, p. 607.

[59] *Ibid.*

[60] *Ibid.*, p. 594.

[61] *Ibid.*, p. 672.

[62] *Ibid.*, p. 658.

[63] The blackout effect refers to the phenomenon of radar becoming inoperative during and immediately after the blasts of high megaton nuclear explosions.

[64] Preparedness Subcommittee, *op. cit.*, p. 305.

may be achieved through a stabilization of international relations and a move towards a peaceful environment in which to seek resolution of our differences."[65] The safeguards they recommended were (1) continued underground testing, (2) continued availability of men and facilities for nuclear research, (3) the maintenance of laboratories in a state of readiness, to retest in the event of Soviet abrogation or American withdrawal from the treaty, and (4) the improvement of United States detection techniques in order to discover any treaty violations.[66]

## *Conclusions*

The treaty was the result of several previous decisions to work for some type of arms control measure with the Soviet Union within the framework of American security interests. The successful negotiation of the treaty brought the need for new decisions – whether underground testing should occur; what proposals might be presented for future arms control agreements; and what steps might be taken to even further reduce tensions with the Soviet Union.

The decisions leading to the American University speech and instructions to Ambassador Harriman were made by only a few individuals. In each instance the final decision rested with the President not only in an institutional setting, but also in a personal way. Kennedy had participated in the discussions in August, 1962, which formulated the American position on testing, and therefore had the relevant information. In 1963, he bypassed this cumbersome decision-making process and controlled the number of participants and the flow of information. By isolating several agencies from the immediate decisions relative to the July negotiations, particularly the military services and some of the laboratories, he increased his personal control over the policy-making process.

Although little had been accomplished at the negotiating table before July 1963, the agencies devoted a substantial portion of their time to arms control. For some, such as the Arms Control and Disarmament Agency, the test ban represented a positive value. The attention given by several other agencies can be explained by their fear of any adverse effects of an agreement and hence their attempt to secure safeguards before a draft was submitted to the Soviets. The military services did not allocate limited time, resources, and personnel to arms control because they wished to see

65 *Ibid.*, p. 591.
66 *Ibid.*, pp. 589–591, *passim.*

sweeping disarmament. They were primarily concerned about the possible adverse consequences of proposals on their specific missions.

In the debates over arms control, agencies mustered impressive collections of data to substantiate their position, either that arms control had a beneficial or a detrimental effect on national security. Arms control was not judged on an abstract scale, but rather as an input whose eventual outcome would be to increase or diminish the agency's ability to maintain national security, as it defined the requirements. The data which the agencies collected often originated in their own offices, but they borrowed heavily from other participants. Sharing information has two effects: it increases the amount of data available to all participants, and it enables agencies to scrutinize the material in a variety of ways. Consequently, information is not necessarily given a single interpretation reflecting the experience and goals of the agency which originally collected the information. Although it can be subjected to analysis from many different perspectives, there is the danger that even after analysis there might be serious flaws which go undetected. The data may not be complete, data may be withheld, collateral data might not be available, and the information may be grouped by the agency in such a way as to obliterate distinctions which another agency wishes to emphasize. The latter is particularly a problem because it is time consuming to subject all of the raw data to new tests. It may be helpful to have greater consultation among the agencies when they collect data from weapons tests, particularly if the lead time between the tests and policy recommendations is short.

It is simplistic to assume that arms control is universally opposed by the military services or that it is always supported by ACDA. There are differences of opinion within these large and complex organizations, and one easy and automatic response is unlikely. Reactions to proposals depend not only upon the substance of a policy, but also on the costs associated with opposition and the benefits which might accrue from support. If we are to predict agency behavior, it is necessary to identify the agencies' experiences, goals, resources, and options, as well as the situation which exists at the time. The varied history of the AEC laboratories indicates that there are a variety of experiences among smaller operating units and that the past consequences of a policy on an agency are used to judge current proposals. The personnel in agencies learn not only from their own earlier personal behavior but also from the experiences of their associates in the agencies.

Personnel are more often socialized in the norms of smaller, specialized branches of which they are members, rather than in the larger organization to which they also belong. Some Army scientists, State Department desk officers, and scientists at the Livermore Laboratory opposed the treaty, although the organizations of which they were a part had publicly endorsed the agreement. These specialists had specific tasks to perform and had accumulated a variety of experiences which indicated that arms control would cause stress in their individual systems or for the constituents with whom they worked. However, they accepted the agency's decision and subordinated their private misgivings to the policy of the parent organization.

National security was an ambiguous term, and most of the participants had their own individual notions of its meaning. For the State Department, the alliance structure of the West and a stable international system were the major ingredients. The Secretary of Defense emphasized a rough parity of overall strength, and held that American security would not be endangered if the Soviet Union did not gain an appreciably superior military position. The services, particularly the Air Force, rejected this proposition, insisted on military superiority for the United States, and argued that the American lead must be clearly substantial. ACDA looked at military and technological stability as a foundation of national security and maintained that radical increases in the arms race could just as easily benefit the other side. The AEC contended that the country was best protected under the present arrangements, whereby the United States held a superiority of power. There were, of course, differences within each of the agencies, and many of the official positions of the organizations overlapped with the positions of other organizations. The State Department's emphasis on alliances, for example, was not its exclusive concern; the services, ACDA, and others were also interested in the strength and stability of the American alliance structure. Nor did the State Department's concern about treaties preclude its interests in military or scientific questions. Because of these overlapping interests, members of the Committee of Principals shared several common values although they often defined them according to their own perspective. The fact that they emphasized one particular value did not mean that they were opposed to all of the values of the other side. The debate in the Committee of Principals centered on the priority which should be given to different objectives.

CHAPTER IV

# THE MEDIA AND THE TREATY

The mass media act as the major channel of information to the general public and to decision-makers as well. Although society and government have changed in many important respects since Jefferson's time, his observation that a free press is the foundation of a democratic system is still appropriate. To the extent that government officials rely only on private or restricted-use channels to communicate selectively among one another, the general public becomes an irrelevant participant in the policy-making process, left only with the alternatives to approve or disapprove the actions of officials *in toto* at election time. When the mass media reports an event, they do not bestow on every citizen who follows the news the same power or information as the President or Senators. They give the individual information which may stimulate his interests and activity for or against a policy. In concert with other citizens, he may effectively set the appropriate boundary for a decision-maker.

With specialists and several interest groups, the media not only perform a communication role but also comprise part of the articulate public in the United States. They are articulate not simply because they discuss issues more regularly than the average citizen but because they have access to decision-makers not customarily available to the man in the street. An important segment of the articulate public is the prestige press which includes those newspapers which "command the attention of a highly politicized and very influential audience."[1] The *New York Times*, *New York Herald Tribune*, *Washington Post*, *Washington Star*, and *Baltimore Sun* have been identified by most students of the press as the prestige papers because they were generally read more consistently by official Washington than other papers.[2] Although many decision-makers who read the prestige

[1] V. O. Key, *Public Opinion and American Democracy* (New York: Alfred A. Knopf, 1961), p. 405.

[2] *Ibid.*, and Bernard Cohen, *The Press and Foreign Policy* (Princeton: Princeton

papers disagree with their editorial policy and rely on papers in their constituencies for domestic issues, they consider them to be a reliable source of news about foreign policy issues.

The press and other components in the mass media perform three basic political roles: a communication role when they report an event which has political significance, a barometer role which acts as an index of interest and support for an issue by a segment of the articulate public, and a decoding role when the media offer their rationale for supporting or opposing an issue. In the last role the media can provide simplistic interpretations to the public or stimulate the interest of both decision-makers and the public when issues are analyzed in depth and with sophistication. Most of the following analysis is based on the reaction of the press to the treaty because newspapers lend themselves more thoroughly to analysis than the electronic media which shall be briefly discussed in a later section.

## *The Communication Role of the Press*

The press, radio, television, and magazines devote uneven attention to political events, giving considerable time or space to some issues but ignoring others completely. When the national media decline to report an event fully, the information available to the public diminishes, but it does not necessarily disappear for everyone because interest groups have their own specialized media and send reports about various issues to their members as well as others. Magazines, newspapers, and special bulletins from organizations such as the American Legion or the AFL-CIO often alert their members to issues not routinely covered in the press, or they supplement stories carried in the media. Moreover, local press, radio, and

University Press, 1963), pp. 139–140.

A study made for the *Washington Post* reported that the number of editorials by newspapers inserted in the *Congressional Record* from 1947 through 1961 for the five most represented papers were:

| Paper | No. of Editorials |
|---|---|
| *Washington Post* | 3,118 |
| *New York Times* | 2,755 |
| *Washington Star* | 1,538 |
| *New York Herald Tribune* | 861 |
| *Washington News* | 783 |

"Other higher ranking papers in this respect are the *Christian Science Monitor, Wall Street Journal, Baltimore Sun* and *St. Louis Post Dispatch.*" Letter to author, from Frank McArdle, Associate Promotion Manager, *Washington Post,* Washington, D.C., August 28, 1964.

television coverage supplement the national magazines, network newscasts and the group media.

Not every message transmitted by the mass media is accepted by each individual who receives it. The evaluations of the sender of the news and its content are basic determinants of the ways a person treats the message and the media. Most people tend to listen to programs and read materials which they have grown to trust and to depend on.[3] Generally, Americans put confidence in the mass media and consider them to be reasonably fair, although some people prefer television over newspapers, and a smaller group primarily relies on magazines because they consider them to be most objective. Individuals higher on the socio-economic scale are more apt to select the press as their first choice of the most truthful and accurate segment of the media (42.2) while those lowest on the scale rely on television more (43.9 per cent). This pattern follows for college and grade school groups, and those in cities over 25,000 and those in towns less than 10,000 and in rural areas.[4]

In his study of public opinion, V. O. Key found that the impact of the mass media on American society has been grossly exaggerated and that individuals often reject messages directed to them. At the same time, "despite the stratagems by which people screen themselves from the flow of communications, it must not be deduced that the media lack influence."[5]

Messages attributed to sources which are judged positively are more likely to be influential than sources an individual does not know or trust,[6] provided he has not already made a judgment about the issue. If recipients of messages do not have strong preconceptions, they tend to accept the recommendations of experts over non-experts (individuals who are not considered competent in the field).[7] When the mass media in the United States report news, they often emphasize experts – scientists, military men,

[3] John W. Riley and Matilda W. Riley, "Mass Communication and the Social System," in Robert Merton, *et. al.*, eds. *Sociology Today: Problems and Prospects* (New York: Basic Books, 1959), p. 544.

4. Bruce Westley and Werner Severin, "Some Correlates of Media Credibility," *Journalism Quarterly,* 41 (Summer, 1964), pp. 328–29.

[5] Key, *op. cit.*, p. 370.

[6] Carl I. Hovland, "Reconciling Conflicting Results Derived from Experimental and Survey Studies of Attitude Change," *American Psychologist* XIV (January, 1959), pp. 12–13.

[7] Joseph T. Klapper, *The Effects of Mass Communications* (New York: The Free Press, 1960), p. 61 and Carl I. Hovland and W. Weiss "The Influence of Source Credibility on Communication Effectiveness," *Public Opinion Quarterly,* XV (Winter, 1951), pp. 635–650.

diplomats, or politicians who have credibility because of their work in a particular area.

Key's observation is particularly pertinent to foreign policy issues such as the test ban because the issue was highly complex, opinion was very unstable, and several conflicting cues were presented to the public. The complexity of the issue not only involved the issue of fallout, the intricacies of monitoring devices, and the logic of a self-propelling arms race; it was also complicated by the military considerations of the cold war including possible clandestine testing, the blackout effect of high-megaton explosions, and the impact of nuclear explosions in outer space. The experts were not in agreement, and, as the following analysis will indicate, the mass media presented conflicting interpretations about these questions. Public opinion fluctuated throughout the Eisenhower and Kennedy administrations, but so did reactions of public officials, interest groups, and the media. Intense feelings are less apt to develop when opinions are not fixed. In addition, the public had to balance several conflicting goals, most notably the desire for peace and the feeling that only a strong military establishment could insure national security. In such a fluid situation, replete with ambiguous attitudes and changing recommendations, the mass media have a more potent role to play in fashioning public opinion than when citizens have intense, stable opinions about issues.[8]

The efforts of papers to change voters' preferences in presidential campaigns have been notably unsuccessful as have been attempts to build support for foreign aid or reciprocal trade. But all of these issues not only had an economic cast to them which made them more relevant to citizens, they were also matters about which individuals often had longstanding ideas, frequently reinforced by their neighbors, co-workers, or occupational groups who seemed to be more accurate and appropriate interpreters on such issues. On the test ban issue, no such large-scale, interested, stable constituency existed. It is a central premise of this and the following chapters that opinion-leaders in the United States, including the mass media, were highly influential in bringing public acceptance of the test ban treaty because the conditions were appropriate.[9] Because the issue was supported by sources the public trusted, it was likely that individuals would

[8] Bernard Berelson, "Communications and Public Opinion," in Wilbur Schram (ed.), *Mass Communications* (Urbana: University of Illinois Press, 1949), p. 500.

[9] For the effectiveness of the different types of media, see Sidney Kraus, *et al.*, "Mass Media and the Fallout Controversy, *Public Opinion Quarterly*, Vol. XXVII (Summer, 1963), p. 197.

accept the message as credible, even when they had not totally supported nuclear suspensions only a year earlier.[10]

Editors of papers are confronted with a variety of competing news inputs. They have limited space and limited manpower and deadlines to meet as well as more stories than can be printed. A foreign policy story must compete with domestic items as well as with other stories about international relations. Judgments about what should be printed, how much space should be allotted to it, and where it should be placed are conditioned by the sense of importance an editor attaches to the story, by his evaluation of what his readers expect, and his competition with other papers and other media elements.[11]

The treaty received considerable attention in the mass media as the following analysis will indicate. The editors of the major news agencies and networks rated the treaty as the fifth "top news story" of 1963, following in importance the assassination of President Kennedy, continued tensions over civil rights, the death of Pope John XXIII, and the mounting conflict in Vietnam.[12]

Even when an event is widely reported in a medium the public normally follows, not everyone may be receptive to the message. Some readers skip from the front page to devour the sports or fashion pages. Others may read the headlines or the lead stories but ignore other news items. Therefore, placement of a story on the first page and the space allotted to stories are relevant for the communication function of the press. It is instructive to compare coverage of the treaty with another "foreign" news story which was developing in a London courtroom when the test ban was signed in Moscow. The Stephen Ward trial, with its sex and scandal, provided entirely different copy from the test ban. The trial appealed to a different type of audience. In addition there was a host of other stories, generally the purely local story, which might have impinged on the coverage of either of these stories. Neither the August nor September samples had a clearly competitive story, but a variety of articles from local to international attention generally took precedence over the treaty. Papers involved in some degree of competition gave higher coverage to either the Ward trial or the test ban treaty in the July sample while monopoly papers in smaller cities generally gave the treaty and the trial routine coverage and concentrated

[10] Carl I. Hovland, "Assimilation and Contrast Effects in Reactions to Communication and Attitude Change," *Journal of Abnormal Social Psychology*, XIV (January, 1959), pp. 12–13.

[11] Cohen, *op. cit.*

[12] Combined news judgments of editors responding to a survey as reported in the *Columbia Journalism Review* (Winter, 1964), p. 41.

on a local story. One Eastern paper, for example, highlighted plans for a new Main Street office building while a Southern paper in its lead headline told its morning readers of a rooftop shooting.[13]

In the July sample of the treaty, each paper gave the treaty some type of front page coverage, but the Ward trial received front page attention in only 45 per cent of the papers.[14] The announcement of the treaty's initialing on the front page in all of the papers compares to 58 per cent front page coverage in August for testimony before the Committee on Foreign Relations and 35 per cent front page coverage for the closing days of the Senate debate.

Another indication of interest by the press is the space or column inches it devotes to a topic. The non-prestige press and the prestige press devoted approximately the same space to the Ward trial (43 and 35 column inches respectively), but the prestige press outranked other papers in treaty coverage for all three sample days, devoting at least two and a half times as many column inches to the treaty. The most notable difference occurred in the July sample when the texts of the treaty and speeches were included in their copy, but in only a few of the non-prestige papers. The *New York Times* ran 590 column inches for the treaty on the twenty-sixth of July while it devoted only about five per cent of that figure to the Ward trial. The treaty was an important event for official Washington, and it was treated as such by the prestige papers which devoted an average of 300 column inches to the subject. Coverage on the treaty in July fell from these lofty heights for the prestige papers to an average of 84 inches for all other papers in the July sample. Some of these papers devoted as little as seven or fifteen inches to the announcement that the treaty had been signed. As the Senate approached its vote, attention proportionately diminished for all papers, including the prestige press. Having informed their readers about

[13] *Buffalo Evening News,* July 25 and the *Houston Post,* July 26, 1963 respectively.

[14] The material for this analysis of space and placement is partially based on a sample drawn by the *Columbia Journalism Review* (Fall, 1963), p. 15. The two additional days of coverage sampled imposed some restrictions since the papers in the Library of Congress did not duplicate many of those in the Columbia study. About half of the papers surveyed in the original study were dropped, and additional ones were added, selection being based on geographic area. A complete list of the Columbia sample was suppled by James Boyland, Managing Editor of the *Columbia Journalism Review*. The other two days surveyed were August 13 and September 20. Secretary Rusk's appearance before the Committee on Foreign Relations on August 12 provided most of the material printed in the morning papers of August 13. The afternoon papers generally featured Secretary McNamara's testimony to the Committee given earlier that day. The Senate debate provided most of the copy of September 20 for both morning and afternoon papers. The sample does not purport to be representative, but suggestive of newspaper reaction.

the treaty when it was signed, the press generally lost interest in the issue in the following months. In August, the prestige press printed 135 column inches and in September, 55 column inches on the treaty while the non-prestige press published 48 and 21 column inches respectively. Most of the later coverage was perfunctory and did not include full reporting on the subtleties or qualification various Senators, generals, or scientists offered when they commented on the test ban.

### *The Barometer Role of the Press*

The barometer role informs observers of the position of the press just as opinion surveys report on the percentage of the public supporting or opposing a policy. Because government officials see the press as an important indicator of articulate and effective opinion on foreign policy issues, the barometer role is a gauge of one of the factors decision-makers take into account before they act. Indeed, Bernard Cohen reported that one State Department official stated that the press was the department's "major source of knowledge of public opinion."[15] Although many Senators paid attention to the recommending features of the prestige papers, they also followed editorials in their home state because of wide-spread interest in the test ban compared to other foreign policy issues. Even though Senators had access to public opinion surveys published in newspapers, editorials continued to be an important indicator of articulate opinion particularly since most of the public opinion surveys were national and did not indicate the level of support in any specific state. The value placed on editorials can be seen in the numerous insertions of press endorsements for the treaty in the *Congressional Record*. Senator Hubert Humphrey was interested in building a case of popular support for the treaty and offered numerous editorials published throughout the country. To offset Humphrey's campaign a few opposition Senators also inserted editorials from papers which evaluated the treaty negatively. Another indicator of governmental interest in the reaction of the press was found in the Public Opinion Studies Staff in the Department of State which clipped editorials from newspapers throughout the country and summarized the press mood for the White House and other government agencies, including the United States Information Agency.

The sample used to identify the barometer role is based on the editorial positions of 155 daily newspapers throughout the country. A conscious

[15] Cohen, *op. cit.*, p. 237.

attempt was made to include all of the larger newspapers. After the forty papers with a circulation over 250,000 were selected, all others available in the Library of Congress and the Public Opinion Studies Staff of the Department of State were divided into regions, and a random selection was made from this universe. Because of the restricted universe, larger papers are overrepresented.[16]

Seventy-three per cent of the papers sampled supported the treaty, and twenty-six per cent opposed it. But 40 per cent of the Southern and Western papers rejected the test ban, compared to 18 per cent in the Midwest and East. However, Table 4–1 shows that when circulation figures are considered, regional differences narrow. The largest papers in the South tended to favor the treaty, while the two papers with the greatest circulation in the East and Midwest both rejected the treaty, inflating the circulation figures of the opponents in these two areas. Nevertheless, there was a clear tendency for editorial support for the treaty to grow as the size of the paper increased. Papers with a circulation between a 100,000 and 250,000 supported the treaty 70 per cent of the time, and 90 per cent of the papers with a circulation over 250,000 endorsed the test ban, but only 66 per cent of the papers with less than a 100,000 circulation supported the treaty. The smaller and medium sized papers shared more with one another than either of them did with the largest papers. Much of the South's inflated editorial opposition to the treaty is accounted for by the overrepresentation of smaller circulation papers in that region.

TABLE 4-1. *Newspaper Reaction to the Treaty by Region and Circulation*

| Region | Position on the Treaty | No. of Papers | Per Cent in Region | Circulation | Per Cent in Circulation |
|---|---|---|---|---|---|
| East | for | 43 | 86.0 | 9,765,000 | 78.5 |
| | against | 7 | 14.0 | 2,746,000 | 21.5 |
| Midwest | for | 36 | 80.0 | 8,246,000 | 72.7 |
| | against | 9 | 20.0 | 2,082,000 | 27.3 |
| South | for | 23 | 57.5 | 3,372,000 | 66.3 |
| | against | 17 | 42.5 | 1,715,000 | 33.7 |
| West | for | 12 | 60.0 | 1,602,000 | 66.7 |
| | against | 8 | 40.0 | 800,000 | 33.3 |
| Total | for | 114 | 73.5 | 22,985,000 | 73.4 |
| | against | 41 | 26.5 | 7,343,000 | 26.6 |

[16] At least one paper is represented for all but two states. Of forty-two papers published in the United States in 1963 with a daily circulation of over 250,000, forty are included in the sample. One of the excluded papers did not take a position although

### *The Decoding Role of the Press*

Papers used several different criteria for evaluating the treaty. For some, military factors were particularly important, but others emphasized diplomatic and health considerations. A content analysis enables us to determine the rationale of support or opposition and to compare the evaluations of different categories of papers. The analysis which follows is based on a survey of themes in 50 of the 155 papers previously sampled. After the five prestige papers were selected, 45 others were drawn randomly: 32 were pro-treaty and 13 were anti-treaty papers. Each was examined for three five-day periods: in July when the treaty was initialed, in August during the Senate hearings, and in September during the Senate debate. The prestige press had 27 editorials with 96 themes, other pro-treaty papers ran 100 editorials with 359 themes, and the anti-treaty press editorially commented on the treaty 36 times with 127 themes.

The decoding behavior of the press will be contrasted with the attitudes of Senators in a later chapter. Because 74 per cent of the papers supported the treaty, and 80 Senators voted for it, and 81 per cent of the public approved it in September, it is tempting to construct linkages among these three participants. However, the content analysis of the press will indicate that its rationale for supporting the treaty does not easily accord with the evaluation of the public or Senate.

The pro-treaty press disagreed among themselves about the nature and importance of the test ban, while opponents of the treaty tended to share the same perspective. Many of the pro-treaty editorials defended the treaty against the charges that the Soviets would break it and would then test, thereby benefiting militarily. This defensive theme received more attention in the pro-treaty press than any other single topic, representing 25 per cent of all editorial themes, excluding editorial discussion about foreign countries and domestic participants. The pro-treaty press insisted the United States could develop an antimissile system in the future and that present defenses would not be endangered by the treaty. Several papers supported the contention of Secretary of Defense Robert McNamara that the United States would maintain superiority in some areas and parity in others, but in no event would America's capacity to defend itself be impaired. The treaty's proponents also contended that the treaty was mutually beneficial to

it did call for careful examination of the treaty while the other clearly did not discuss the treaty. Eight other papers chosen from the Library of Congress sample did not discuss the treaty, and none of these papers are included in the following analysis.

the two superpowers and would reduce tensions between them. This, they believed, made abrogation unlikely. Table 4-2 reveals that when they pressed positive themes, the pro-treaty press emphasized the reduction of tensions, the elimination of fallout, and the control of the arms race. For example, the *New York Herald Tribune* found that the importance of the agreement rested in its provision for "the framework of a world relatively free of nuclear fallout and hopefully free of nuclear war."[17] The *Washington Post* thought the treaty might "lead to further progress in the disarmament field" as well as help to "reduce some of the points of contention and differences that have caused the arms race."[18] Humanitarian and moral justification provided little rationale for the proponents of the treaty; when they did, they were always coupled with other themes.

Opponents of the treaty saw two beneficiaries of the treaty, the Soviet Union and the President. They believed the Soviets would increase their lead in high nuclear weapon technology leaving the United States hopelessly behind. The *Chicago Tribune* proclaimed that the treaty was a "fateful decision in a game that is being played for keeps with national survival. If the step is taken, there could be no second chance."[19] Opponents believed the administration was offering the country a house of straw which would collapse in the gales of the cold war. In capital letters, the *Manchester* (New Hampshire) *Union Leader* warned its readers, "In the end it will be the average American citizen, all of us, who will pay for the present administration walking into the death trap of a test ban with Russia."[20] Earlier the *Chicago Tribune* wondered "whether the Kennedy administration is committed to national suicide or whether it is conducting a planned drive into surrender to communism."[21] The opposition press also charged the President's support of the treaty was politically motivated. President Kennedy needed a "victory of some sort, for his record and prestige are at a low ebb."[22] The suggestion that the Chief Executive was more concerned with his image than with the security of the nation was a recurring theme in the opposition papers.

The major theme in the opposition press was that the Soviet Union would not honor the treaty. The anticipated abrogation of the treaty by the Soviets was regarded as *prima facie* evidence that it should not be accepted by the

[17] August 6, 1963, p. 20.
[18] August 6, 1963, p. 12A.
[19] August 21, 1963, p. 16.
[20] August 21, 1963, p. 8. This was one of the few editorials which urged its readers to write their Senators on the treaty.
[21] August 18, 1963, p. 14.
[22] *Chicago Tribune*, July 16, 1963, p. 16.

United States. One paper calculated a 95 per cent probability that the "current agreement will be broken by the Reds."[23] Another paper reasoned that if the Soviet Union really expected to abide by the terms of the treaty, it would withdraw its "army of spies which infest our land" or "begin to

TABLE 4-2. *Thematic Analysis of Editorials in 50 Selected Newspapers*

| Theme | Pro-Treaty | Anti-Treaty |
|---|---|---|
| Treaty Benefits | 130 | 2 |
| Reduce Tensions | 45 | 1 |
| Reduce Fallout | 31 | 1 |
| Reduce Arms Race | 28 | 0 |
| Hopeful Sign | 20 | 0 |
| Humanitarian | 6 | 0 |
| Treaty Disadvantages | 18 | 60 |
| Cannot Trust Soviets | 6 | 26 |
| Soviets Benefit Militarily | 2 | 18 |
| Euphoria | 8 | 4 |
| Destroys Balance of Power | 0 | 3 |
| Others | 2 | 9 |
| Discuss Delays and Reservations | 17 | 3 |
| Defensive Themes | 72 | 8 |
| No Military Danger | 64 | 1 |
| Use Caution in Examining the Treaty | 8 | 7 |
| Domestic Participants | 149 | 37 |
| The President | 28 | 7 |
| Secretary of Defense | 20 | 2 |
| Secretary of State | 17 | 4 |
| Senator Goldwater | 11 | 3 |
| Foreign Relations Committee | 7 | 1 |
| Military Officers | 17 | 5 |
| Dr. Teller | 8 | 3 |
| Other Scientists | 6 | 3 |
| Senator Fulbright | 5 | 2 |
| Other Senators | 16 | 3 |
| Others | 14 | 4 |
| Foreign Countries | 69 | 17 |
| Germany | 16 | 3 |
| China | 15 | 4 |
| France | 14 | 3 |
| NATO | 7 | 1 |
| Others | 17 | 6 |
| Total Number of Themes | 455 | 127 |

[23] *Dallas News,* August 9, 1963, p. 18.

honor their promises of Yalta and Potsdam."[24] These arguments did not go unanswered in the editorials of papers favoring the treaty. The *Louisville Courier-Journal* insisted that it was not a question of trusting the Russians because the treaty was based on mutual interest, and each side would avoid taking those steps which would lead to a nuclear war.[25] The *Washington Post* echoed this theme when it insisted that the question of trust was extraneous. "Enforcement of no part of it now depends on America's acceptance of the Soviets' word."[26]

The hearings before the Committee on Foreign Relations elicited comments from many editorial writers. The positions advanced by Secretary of Defense McNamara, Secretary of State Rusk, and Dr. Teller received the greatest attention in August, although their arguments drew little comment in September. Washington was reading that the Defense Secretary's testimony was a "powerful argument for ratification,"[27] that the United States would "maintain and prolong" its nuclear superiority,[28] and that McNamara presented a military rationale "even more persuasive than the political rationale" conveyed by Rusk.[29] But the *Chicago Tribune* examined the same testimony and concluded that there were more dangers inherent to American security with the treaty than without it. It reasoned that the testimony of the two cabinet members demonstrated no need for the treaty.[30]

Dr. Teller's appearance stimulated considerable comment from both sides. Opponents of the treaty found that he was a capable, politically disinterested expert who directed serious challenges against the treaty.[31] Reacting to suggestions that Dr. Teller seemed obsessed with the big bomb and that such thinking would lead us closer to nuclear war, the *Cincinnati Enquirer* vehemently charged that "we are close to imperiling the reputation of an authentic American for the incredible reason that he has been right too often."[32] However, the *Washington Post* found that Teller's contribution was simply that a powerful nuclear arsenal was the only source of security, an assumption which the paper rejected.[33] The *Christian Science Monitor*

[24] *Chicago Tribune*, August 6, 1963, p. 18.
[25] September 3, 1963, p. 8.
[26] August 27, 1963, p. 14A.
[27] *Washington Star*, August 14, 1963, p. 24A.
[28] *Washington Post*, August 14, 1963, p. 18A.
[29] *Ibid.*
[30] August 14, 1963, p. 16.
[31] *Chicago Tribune*, August 26, 1963, p. 18.
[32] *Cincinnati Enquirer*, September 4, 1963, p. 6.
[33] August 16, 1963, p. 16A.

summarized the feelings of many other papers when it observed that "the parade of responsible scientists and weapons experts who support Mr. McNamara is more impressive than the list of critics."[34]

Unlike the pro-treaty press, opposition editorials did not feel compelled to comment on the arguments of the other side. The opposition papers almost exclusively emphasized the military aspects of the treaty and previous Soviet behavior, ignoring the Sino-Soviet dispute and the possibility of any areas of mutual interest between Washington and Moscow, areas in which they thought the test ban was especially vulnerable. Because most generals and admirals who publicly spoke on the treaty supported it with varying degrees of enthusiasm, these papers relied on Dr. Teller and retired military officers. Indeed the *Chicago Tribune* interpreted for its readers that the heart of the military was not really for the treaty. The Joint Chiefs were "like the condemned man led to the gallows" who "dutifully testified" for the administration.[35] But the *Washington Star* rejected the suggestion that the Joint Chiefs of Staff were under duress and insisted they were not the kind of men who would bow to pressure when the issue involved American security,[36] a theme echoed in many pro-treaty papers. The opponents largely ignored diplomatic, health and humanitarian consequences of the test ban.

The proposed reservations to the treaty was another recurring topic, becoming more pronounced in September.[37] One editorial caption expressed the response of many pro-treaty papers to reservations offered by opponents relating to Cuba and the United Nations debt with the injunction, "No Box Tops with the Test Ban."[38] The *Washington Star* predicted that Senator Goldwater who offered his own reservations would regret that he had dealt "so shallowly and even frivolously with the test ban."[39] The *Kansas City Times* argued that Cuba, the subject of one reservation, was "an irrelevancy." Like many other papers, it feared that adoption of any of the reservations would force the entire treaty into a renegotiation which might be unsuccessful.[40] While one paper simply found Goldwater "sounding querulous,"[41] another saw him taking his place alongside General De Gaulle, the Chinese Communists, and the militant faction of the Kremlin.[42]

[34] August 15, 1963, p. 18.
[35] August 21, 1963, p. 16.
[36] September 11, 1963, p. 14A.
[37] See Chapter VIII.
[38] *New York Herald Tribune*, September 8, 1963, Sec. 2, p. 5.
[39] September 7, 1963, p. 4A.
[40] September 9, 1963, p. 32.
[41] *Chicago News*, August 21, 1963, p. 16.
[42] *St. Louis Post Dispatch*, September 4, 1963, p. 14A.

The large mass circulation papers called the treaty one of the most important postwar issues to come before the Congress. Editorial writers generally believed that the outcome of the Senate vote would have important ramifications for future American foreign and defense policy. Proponents were not only concerned about the reduction of tension, the arms race, and the control of fallout, but also about the role of America in the world. "If the Senate," wrote the *New York Post*, "were to repudiate President Kennedy on this issue, the long range consequences could be as grave as Woodrow Wilson's tragic debacle in his fight for the League of Nations."[43] Finding that rejection of the treaty would bring "an abysmal setback to the cause of peace and irreparable damage to American leadership," the *Washington Post* argued that there was no reasonable alternative to ratification,[44] while the *New York Times* insisted that the treaty's implications for international relations were particularly important because the communist world was in disharmony due to Sino-Soviet discord which had given the Soviet Union an interest in reaching some agreement with Washington.[45]

The press shifted its editorial priorities on the treaty each month. The pro-treaty press enthusiastically catalogued the benefits of the agreement more often in July (68 per cent) than in both August and September combined. The opposition papers had not mounted their attack until August at which time they concentrated on its possible military disadvantages. Several opposition editorials in July attacked the President, suggesting he engineered the treaty to bolster his political standing or charged in general terms that he was weakening American defenses. But the major anti-treaty theme appeared as soon as the agreement was announced and persisted in the following months, namely that the Soviets would break the treaty. The Yalta agreements and Soviet missiles in Cuba were recurring topics all three months. Table 4-3 shows that the debate moved from the political ramifications of the test ban discussed by the President in July to its military implications, reflecting the tone of the skepticism in the Senate.

Three events occurred during the sample periods: the announcement of the signing of the test ban, the Senate hearings, and the debate on the floor. Most of the papers which were initially skeptical about the treaty and asked for its careful consideration but later endorsed it generally emphasized the defensive themes in August and ignored the topics of delays and reservations to the agreement in September. However, those which quickly

[43] July 22, 1963, p. 24.
[44] August 13, 1963, p. 14A.
[45] August 6, 1963, p. 30.

approved the test ban in July gave greater attention to the positive aspects of the treaty in August and attacked delays in the Senate in September.

The papers generally commented about individuals when they made news and did not use these persons later as sources to lend support to a position the editorial was propounding. The President was a more popular topic in July when he announced the treaty than in August, when Secretary of State Rusk and Secretary of Defense McNamara testified before the Committee on Foreign Relations. Although their arguments were germane in September, these men were seldom mentioned. What was true for domestic participants also held for press treatment of foreign countries. Specific mention of France, Germany and the North Atlantic Treaty Organization declined in August and virtually was non-existent in September after the French had made clear they would not sign the treaty and the Germans had announced they would associate themselves with it. While news stories react to events and relay information about day-to-day affairs, editorials might be expected to be more reflective and not bound by deadlines. Nevertheless, editorials usually ignored previous relevant material about the treaty and as the news stories focused on day-to-day problems, editorials summarized and interpreted the events of the week.

In many themes, the editors followed, rather than led, influential decision-makers. The monthly distribution indicates that as new attention moved from the White House to the Senate and as public support appeared to be confirmed by published opinion surveys, editorial writers shifted their priorities from positive to defensive themes. This movement to defensive themes tended to allay fears rather than educate the public to the opportunities the treaty opened for future agreements with the Soviet Union.

*Regional Decoding*

Just as public support for the treaty was unevenly distributed in the four major regions of the country, editorial opinion also showed diversity not only in its recommendations about the treaty but also in the rationale the press offered when it discussed the test ban. The denial that the treaty carried military dangers for the United States was the most discussed topic in every region except the Midwest where it ranked third with 15 per cent of that region's contributions. In that area, the most often repeated theme (18 per cent) dealt with efforts to delay the treaty and the second most popular theme (17 per cent) centered on the reduction of cold war tensions.

Readers in the East and Midwest were presented with the positive bene-

TABLE 4-3. *Frequencies of Editorial Themes on the Test Ban*

| Theme | *Pro-Treaty* July | *Pro-Treaty* Aug. | *Pro-Treaty* Sept. | *Anti-Treaty* July | *Anti-Treaty* Aug. | *Anti-Treaty* Sept. |
|---|---|---|---|---|---|---|
| Treaty Benefits | 87 | 33 | 10 | 2 | 0 | 0 |
| Reduce Tensions | 32 | 9 | 4 | 1 | 0 | 0 |
| Reduce Fallout | 19 | 9 | 3 | 1 | 0 | 0 |
| Reduce Arms Race | 17 | 8 | 3 | 0 | 0 | 0 |
| Hopeful Sign | 15 | 5 | 0 | 0 | 0 | 0 |
| Humanitarian | 4 | 2 | 0 | 0 | 0 | 0 |
| Treaty Disadvantages | 12 | 5 | 1 | 18 | 35 | 7 |
| Cannot Trust Soviets | 6 | 0 | 0 | 8 | 15 | 3 |
| Soviets Benefit Militarily | 2 | 0 | 0 | 5 | 11 | 2 |
| Euphoria, Apathy | 3 | 4 | 1 | 1 | 2 | 1 |
| Destroys Balance of Power | 0 | 0 | 0 | 0 | 2 | 1 |
| Others | 1 | 1 | 0 | 4 | 5 | 0 |
| Discuss Delays of Reservations | 0 | 0 | 17 | 0 | 0 | 3 |
| Defensive Theme | 21 | 38 | 13 | 4 | 3 | 1 |
| No Military Danger | 14 | 37 | 13 | 0 | 1 | 0 |
| Use Caution in Examining Treaty | 7 | 1 | 0 | 4 | 2 | 1 |
| Domestic Participants | 39 | 84 | 26 | 10 | 20 | 7 |
| The President | 14 | 8 | 6 | 4 | 2 | 1 |
| Secretary of Defense | 2 | 18 | 0 | 0 | 2 | 0 |
| Secretary of State | 2 | 15 | 0 | 1 | 3 | 0 |
| Senator Goldwater | 6 | 2 | 3 | 1 | 0 | 2 |
| Foreign Relations Committee | 1 | 5 | 1 | 0 | 1 | 0 |
| Military Officers | 2 | 12 | 3 | 1 | 3 | 1 |
| Dr. Teller | 1 | 6 | 1 | 0 | 3 | 0 |
| Other Scientists | 1 | 3 | 2 | 1 | 2 | 0 |
| Senator Fulbright | 0 | 4 | 1 | 1 | 1 | 0 |
| Other Senators | 3 | 8 | 5 | 0 | 1 | 2 |
| All Others | 7 | 3 | 4 | 1 | 2 | 1 |
| Foreign Countries | 38 | 20 | 11 | 11 | 4 | 2 |
| Germany | 2 | 8 | 6 | 3 | 0 | 0 |
| China | 10 | 2 | 3 | 2 | 1 | 1 |
| France | 11 | 3 | 0 | 2 | 1 | 0 |
| NATO | 5 | 2 | 0 | 1 | 0 | 0 |
| Others | 10 | 5 | 2 | 3 | 2 | 1 |
| Total Number of Themes | 197 | 180 | 78 | 45 | 62 | 20 |

fits of the treaty more often than those in the South or Far West where editorial opposition was not only more numerous but where the pro-treaty press either presented more defensive arguments for the treaty or were less enthusiastic about the treaty. More than two-thirds of the Eastern and Midwestern editorial themes were positive compared to half that percentage in the South or West.

With 64 per cent of their editorials defensive, skeptical, or negative, readers of Western newspapers were seldom presented with the positive benefits of the treaty. The South followed the pattern of the West, publishing these themes 54 per cent of the time compared to 37 cent in the East and 38 per cent in the Midwest. The Midwestern and Eastern papers were not only closer to one another on their assessments of the treaty, they were closer to the Southern editorial reaction than to those in the Far West.

Although more Southern papers attacked the treaty than those in any other region in the country and many papers in the old Confederacy strongly opposed President Kennedy's civil rights proposals, treaty opposition was not directly related to the papers' civil rights stand.[46] Several of the larger papers in the South urged compliance to the civil rights act although they usually had opposed Congressional approval of the bill earlier. Papers in Birmingham, Atlanta, Little Rock or Miami did not picture the President's dispatch of troops to Mississippi as a step to be countered with violence or state interposition, although some of the smaller Southern papers attacked the patriotism and ambitions of John Kennedy's support for equal rights for the Negro and these negative perceptions carried over into some of their editorials against the test ban. Those Southern papers which were part of a national chain generally responded to the treaty as other large papers elsewhere in the nation did. Positions on civil rights and treaty reactions were not closely related in the South except that smaller papers which were violently opposed to the President's support for equal rights usually opposed the treaty.

The behavior of Western papers does not fit into any expected patterns of reaction. One factor to account for the regional differences is that Western papers are more conservative than those in the East and Midwest. While some of the Western papers have reflected populist ideals, many others have emphasized the virtue of individualism, were skeptical of federally administered programs and carried their conservatism over to foreign policy. This observation is reinforced when editorial endorsements for presidential candidates in 1960 and 1964 are examined: 35 per cent of the Western sample supported both Richard Nixon and Barry Goldwater,

46 See Alfred Hero for the relationship between opinions about civil rights and foreign affairs in the South in *The Southerner and World Affairs* (Baton Rouge, La.: Louisiana State University Press, 1965), pp. 409–10; 418.

the more conservative candidates in 1960 and 1964 respectively, but only 23 per cent of the Southern sample did while the other two areas showed even less support. In addition, more Southern papers switched from a pro-Nixon or independent position in 1960 to support Lyndon Johnson in 1964 than Western papers, indicating more editorial flexibility in the old Confederacy, although the effect of the religious issue in the South may have also been a factor in 1960.

Even though there was not a national editorial reaction to the treaty, neither was there a clear-cut regional cleavage. Rather there were differences of emphasis on the test ban. While all papers editorially reacted to the signing of the treaty and the hearings conducted in the Senate, few papers outside of the Midwest reacted to delays on the Senate floor or to the reservations which might be attached to the treaty but echoed chords sounded earlier.

### *Decoding by Circulation Size*

The papers with a circulation of less than 100,000 not only tended to oppose the treaty more often and give it less coverage in its news columns than larger papers, they also showed a generally negative disposition when they interpreted the treaty, whether they favored or opposed it. While the dominant theme in all sizes of pro-treaty papers denied there was any military danger to the nation, defensive, skeptical and negative themes were almost twice as prevalent in papers under 100,000 circulation than those over 250,000. Readers of smaller papers were presented with military arguments more often than those relying on larger circulation papers. The three most popular topics among papers with less than 100,000 circulation were defensive or negative, accounting for 45 per cent of their total editorial output compared with 37 per cent for medium-sized papers and 33 per cent for those with a circulation over 250,000. When the smaller papers discussed the positive effects of the treaty, the most popular topic was the general one that the treaty was a hopeful sign for future American foreign policy; but they seldom analyzed this theme, presenting it in the most simple terms.

The smaller papers lacked diversity and sophistication, while the largest papers saw more subtleties in the effects of the treaty, and gave four times more consideration to the reduction of tensions, fallout, and the arms race than did the smallest papers. Although some of the mass-circulation papers did not analyze these topics with much care, simply printing glowing reports that the arms race, for example, would be diminished, several of the largest newspapers did take the trouble to analyze the immediate and potential effects of the test ban.

When papers under 100,000 circulation turned their attention to domestic participants, they gave twice as much attention to home-state Senators than the larger papers did which gave more attention to the President and the Secretaries of State and Defense. The positions of military men also played a disproportionate role in papers with less than a quarter of a million circulation (14 per cent to 5 per cent of the themes on domestic participants). Interestingly, there was relatively little variation among the papers in the effects of the treaty on other countries.

The smallest papers shared the same editorial themes with the medium-sized papers 63 per cent of the time and with the largest papers 59 per cent of the time. However, the papers with the circulation between 100,000 and 250,000 and over 250,000 had overlapping themes 75 per cent of the time, indicating a greater similarity between the largest and medium sized papers than either one of them shared with the smallest papers.

Papers under a 100,000 circulation customarily do not concern themselves with foreign policy either in their news features or on the editorial page as much as the largest papers.[47] Generally the editorial writers on the smaller papers painted the treaty in broad strokes and in vivid colors rather than using subtle shadings to examine the agreement. In part, this reflected their own conception of what their readers desired, but lack of attention and sophistication could be due to the absence of foreign-policy specialists on the editorial desks of most small papers which simply could not afford to have a large staff. Moreover, many of them did not have their own correspondents in Washington and were forced to rely on the wire services for information or editorials. Direct contact with their own man on the scene would probably have facilitated the flow of information and intensified interest in editorial writers on the issue. Duplicate editorials tended to be negative or defensive about the treaty, and none of them clearly informed readers about the possible benefits or dangers in the treaty. The canned editorial was usually inoffensive, calling for caution, asking for consultation with the Joint Chiefs of Staff, requesting a continued state of readiness, and emphasizing the role of the Senate in the treaty-making process. Such generalized and innocuous comments are to be expected when a syndicate does not want to lose possible customers with extremely intense editorials which might disagree with the publisher. A few canned editorials,

[47] Cohen, *op. cit.*, p. 238.

however, came from right-wing groups which violently attacked the treaty. Editors opposed to the treaty occasionally used this material to attack the President, the Foreign Relations Committee, and the Soviet Union.

*Political Decoding*

Newspapers, like individuals, develop relatively stable perceptions of the world around them; and these standards show considerable consistency over time. Of the 145 papers examined in the sample on the barometer role of the press, only two of the papers which favored Lyndon Johnson for President in 1964 opposed the treaty, regardless of whether they supported John Kennedy or Richard Nixon in 1960. Only two of the papers which supported Barry Goldwater in 1964 supported the treaty, with most of the opponents of the test ban coming from the 17 papers in the sample which endorsed both Nixon and Goldwater and the second highest contribution coming from the 13 papers which supported Nixon but were independent in 1964.

Returning to the smaller sample used in analyzing the decoding role of the press, none of the papers which endorsed John Kennedy opposed the treaty while 35 per cent of those which supported Richard Nixon did. Among the 15 papers the Public Opinion Studies Staff of the Department of State classifies as "nationalist" because they have usually vigorously opposed the bipartisanship which has characterized post World War Two American foreign policy, only one supported the treaty while another did not take a clear position.[48]

If the reaction of the "nationalist" press was predictable, so was the response of most of the papers which endorsed John Kennedy in 1960. Papers like the *New York Post* and the *St. Louis Post-Dispatch* not only were traditionally Democratic, they also were staunch proponents of arms control, and many of these papers roundly praised the President's proposal to create an Arms Control and Disarmament Agency early in his administration. Twelve of the fifty sample papers endorsed the new agency in 1961, and most of them had endorsed Kennedy for President the year before. However, 27 papers were noncommittal about the proposal and they represented the type of papers the White House most needed to create the kind

[48] H. S. Foster, "POS List of 'Representative' Newspapers vs. 'More Comprehensive Coverage,'" Public Opinion Studies Staff, Department of State, January 28, 1964 (Mimeographed), p. 3.

of popular mood and to provide the articulate support when the Senate considered the treaty. These papers, which had generally supported Nixon over Kennedy in 1960, were the flexible papers which might either support or oppose the test ban. The President did not lobby with specific publishers or editorial writers, but by quickly establishing the relationship between the need for ratification and America's prestige in the world and bringing several endorsements for the treaty before the public as well as isolating his opposition, he helped to create a favorable mood for press reaction which in turn helped him fashion majorities in the Senate and with the general public.

Two characteristics typify the Nixon papers which supported the treaty: they endorsed it later than the Kennedy papers did and they published more negative themes than the Democratic papers of 1960 did. The Democratic papers emphasized the positive features of the treaty more than the Republican papers (54 to 43 per cent). For example, both types of papers agreed that the reduction of fallout was important and ran this feature 12 per cent of the time, but the Nixon papers gave only 13 per cent of its themes to the reduction of tensions compared to 20 per cent of the Kennedy papers. There was also an eight percentage point difference between these papers on their discussion of the arms race. While both types of papers defended the treaty against military security arguments in about a quarter of their themes, the Nixon papers urged caution lest the Soviets break the test ban more often than the Democratic papers. Interestingly, the Republican papers of 1960 featured the President more than the Democratic editorials which gave cabinet members equal footing with him. Another difference between these papers was the attention they devoted to other countries, with pro-Kennedy papers concerned about this topic 23.3 per cent of the time compared to 15.6 per cent for the pro-Nixon papers, reflecting the appreciation of the Democratic papers that the treaty had important diplomatic consequences, and the prestige of the President and nation rested on Senate approval. The pro-Nixon papers devoted more time to the possible disadvantages of the treaty and were more cautious in approving the agreement.

None of the papers in the sample which opposed the test ban in 1963 supported Lyndon Johnson for the Presidency in 1964, although several anti-treaty papers preferred to remain neutral than to endorse his opponent Senator Goldwater, a leading critic of the treaty. Only one out of twelve of the pro-treaty papers in the sample supported the Senator's candidacy in 1964, but these were papers which only reluctantly endorsed the test ban, emphasizing its possible military dangers and accordingly calling for adequate safeguards to protect American national security. Like the treaty of 1963, Lyndon Johnson's presidential campaign in 1964 was presented as a contest between marginal improvements with the Soviet Union while maintaining American national security on the one hand and the continued hostility with the USSR and the primacy of military solution to protect American national interests on the other hand. Both Kennedy with the treaty and Johnson in his campaign successfully preempted the middle ground, establishing a temporary consensus, and isolated their opposition in extreme positions. The papers which opposed the treaty were generally already estranged from the bipartisan foreign policy norms of the post war period, and they continued to decode international relations in 1963 and 1964 as they had done earlier. This continuity of interpretation is seen in the reactions of papers in the sample to two other issues related to arms control. None of the anti-treaty papers supported the creation of the Arms Control and Disarmament Agency in 1961 while there was a six to one ratio among the pro-treaty papers supporting the Agency. In June 1963, 15 pro-treaty papers applauded the President's American University Speech which signaled the initiation of a new arms control move by the United States, three of them opposed it and 18 did not comment. However, none of the anti-treaty press welcomed the President's move to press for arms control, with half opposing the speech and the other half not commenting.

### *Magazines*

The mass magazines shifted their position on nuclear testing from one of opposition in 1958 to support in 1963. In the earlier period, *Life, The Reader's Digest, The Saturday Evening Post, Time* and *U.S. News and World Report* had favored nuclear testing while only *Look* opposed it and *Newsweek* took a neutral position.[49] In a survey of college students, Snell Putney and Russell Middleton found that information concerning nuclear war came from all media sources, but these mass magazines supplied most of the information for these people.[50] They reported that these publications tended to present thermonuclear war as "possible and plausible."[51] For

[49] Eugene J. Rosi, "How 50 Periodicals and the Times Interpreted the Test Ban Controversy," *Journalism Quarterly*, XLI (Autumn, 1964), p. 547.

[50] Snell Putney and Russell Middleton, "Some Factors Associated with Student Acceptance or Rejection of War," *American Sociological Review*, XXVII (October, 1962), p. 666.

[51] *Ibid.*

example, the front cover of *Life* proclaimed that "97 out of 100 can be saved" if shelters were used in a nuclear attack,[52] and the *Saturday Evening Post* subtitled an article by Edward Teller with the comforting assertion that "radiation for test fallout might be slightly harmful to humans . . . or slightly beneficial."[53] However, on the specific issue of the test ban in the summer of 1963, three of these magazines clearly favored the treaty, *Life, Saturday Evening Post,* and *Newsweek.* Neither *The Reader's Digest* nor *Look* commented directly on the treaty, although the former had recently cautioned against agreements with the Soviets and called for a high state of military preparedness while the latter ran several articles outlining the dangers of fallout. Only *U.S. News and World Report* was clearly opposed to the treaty, while *Time* tended to support the treaty but found more fault with it than the other supporters did. While these mass magazines enter homes of all socio-economic and educational levels, higher income groups and college-educated individuals were more apt to receive them than those lower on the income and educational scale.[54]

Magazines with smaller circulation but read by many politically influential and concerned citizens generally supported the treaty both in 1958 and 1963.[55] In both periods, *Atlantic Monthly, New Republic, Saturday Review, Nation,* and *The Reporter* endorsed the treaty although some of them often did so by the tone of their articles rather than with a direct recommendation of the treaty. The *Bulletin of Atomic Scientists,* read by both scientists and laymen alike, vigorously campaigned for the limitation of testing in 1958 and 1963. New to the list of magazines with a select audience which supported an end of testing in 1963 were *Scientific American, Business Week,* which shifted from an anti-ban position, and *Harpers.* In both periods, most of the religious magazines which commented on the issue supported a ban. Of the select-audience magazines, the conservative *National Review* which ran several articles against the ban was alone in 1963 in opposing the treaty.

Both the mass and limited circulation magazines followed the same pattern found in the daily newspapers in the country; they endorsed the treaty by a considerable margin. The magazines should not simply be

[52] *Life,* 51 (September 15, 1961).

[53] "We Must Face the Danger," *Saturday Evening Post,* 235 (February 10, 1962), p. 36.

[54] Cf. Key, *op. cit.,* pp. 364–366; and *The Audiences of 5 Magazines,* a survey sponsored by Newsweek and conducted by Audits and Surveys Company, 1962, p. 23.

[55] For 1958 figures, see Rosi, *op. cit.,* pp. 549–550.

considered as a reinforcement of the tone of the newspapers supporting the treaty, but also as an important source of information and recommendation for those people Professor V. O. Key has classified as the political activists.[56]

### *Radio and Television*

The network news programs prominently featured the treaty when it was initialed in Moscow. In July and early August as the test ban received favorable treatment, the treaty news was being made by the administration and supporters of the treaty while little opposition had formed. For example, adherence of other countries to the test ban received considerable attention. The Mutual Broadcasting System's 25 minute "World News Roundup" devoted its entire program to the 31 nations signing the treaty in Washington on August 9. It had the impact of emphasizing the leadership of the United States in the free world and the strong expectations of many foreign countries that the treaty would be ratified.

There were some programs which gave the opposition more coverage than most network newscasts, such as "Three Star Extra" on the National Broadcasting System; but most of the unfavorable treatment came from interpretative programs which normally rejected administration foreign policy. Fulton Lewis, Jr. argued over the 445 stations of the Mutual Broadcasting Company that Mr. Harriman had been "the architect for the sell-out of Laos to the Communists," and had duplicated his record in Moscow with the test ban treaty. Lewis found the disarmament agency was left-wing and suggested it desired to appease communist tyranny.[57] Another program which consistently departed from network news interpretation was the "Manion Forum of the Air." During the Senate debate, Clarence E. Manion told his radio audience that:

> . . . the Kennedy administration is committed to suicide and surrender. It has made its covenant with death and its agreement with hell for the promise of a world without war in which Mr. U. Thant will keep universal peace, using American soldiers who will wear United Nations uniforms.[58]

In order to counteract these messages, the Committee for the Nuclear

[56] Key, *op. cit.*, pp. 357–358.

[57] Quoted in Americans for National Security and the Liberty Lobby, *The Moscow Treaty* (Washington: Liberty Lobby, 1963), pp. 21–24.

[58] Inserted by Senator Thurmond in the *Congressional Record*, September 10, 1963, pp. 15777–15778.

Test Ban Treaty asked organizations supporting the treaty to request their members to call any opposition editorials on radio or television to the attention of the Committee. On August 16, 1963, under the signature of James Wadsworth, the chairman of the Committee, a request was submitted to each of the stations broadcasting Life Line programs 66, 73, and 96 for time to answer the program. He based his request on the "Fairness Doctrine" of the Federal Communications Commission of July 26, 1963. In a clarification of its position, the Commission held that the other side must be presented, but the manner and content of presentation was the proper concern of the broadcaster. It held that with the exception of personal attacks, no single group or person could claim the right to present a reply to positions advocated by any given station on the issue.[59] Anti-treaty stations generally did not give equal time to the supporters.

The Senate did not overlook coverage of the treaty by the electronic media. When more than half of a news special on the test ban was devoted to Dr. Teller, Senator Fulbright complained that the program was a "gross distortion" of the hearings conducted by his committee.[60] However, Senator Hickenlooper, who had not announced his position on the treaty at the time, found that the networks had generally emphasized the administration's position and that the mass media, radio and television included, had presented the treaty as "the greatest thing that has ever been presented before the American people."[61]

Most of the news reported on radio and television was similar to that reported in the daily press, that is, considerable attention was given to treaty supporters or to accounts which did not detract from the treaty, such as the acceptance of the test ban by the Federal Republic of Germany. Although Dr. Teller commanded considerable publicity when he testified before the Senate Hearings, most of the newsmakers in and out of the country who reacted to the treaty supported it. The fact that the Communist Chinese and the French opposed the agreement, at a time when relations between these two countries and the United States was relatively low, did not add to the case for opposing the treaty. Five and ten minute news reports particularly tended to report stories to their audiences in only an outline form, with the qualifications or subtleties left unreported. This further gave support to the administration position because several

[59] Federal Communications Commission. Report No. 4800, Public Notice B, September 19, 1963.

[60] Committee on Foreign Relations, *Hearings, The Nuclear Test Ban Treaty,* 87th Cong., 1st Sess., 1963, p. 772.

[61] *Ibid.,* p. 773.

of those supporting the treaty expressed reservations which were not always reported in the short newscasts. This is not a peculiarity of the electronic media, however, because many of the very short newspaper stories often had the same format of reporting only the bare essentials. Nevertheless, there was some shrill domestic opposition, and decision-makers and citizens who distrusted the move to accomodation had easy access to reinforcement through selected media sources.

### *Uses of the Press by Decision-Makers*

Members of Congress and their staffs rely on stories and editorials in the prestige press and the major columnists as an important source of "ideas, insights, and interpretation in the field of foreign affairs."[62] A decision-maker also finds it helpful to know what others are thinking about issues and uses the press "as a convenient basis for locating and formulating his thoughts."[63] Bernard Cohen observed that members of Congress and officials in the executive branch tend to accept the priorities of the prestige press as appropriate because of their confidence in the mass media.[64] He also found that legislators, even when they came from remote constituencies, usually gave more attention to the prestige papers, particularly the *New York Times* and the *Washington Post* than to their local papers on foreign policy. They followed both the news stories and editorials in the prestige papers more often than they relied on the papers in their constituencies which often did not devote much attention to foreign policy. Apart from their content, the prestige papers were more accessible to Washington decision-makers than most other papers.[65]

[62] Cohen, *op. cit.*, p. 222.

[63] *Ibid.*, p. 223.

[64] *Ibid.*, p. 224.

[65] *Ibid.*, p. 238. A Survey of members of Congress indicated that most of them read the *Washington Post* and *Star* on a regular basis. Reproduced below are the responses to the following question, "Which of the following Washington, D.C. newspapers do you read regularly?"

| | Senate (Base: 98) | | House of Representatives (Base: 410) | | Congress (Base: 508) | |
|---|---|---|---|---|---|---|
| Newspapers | # | % | # | % | # | % |
| *Post* | 94 | 95.9 | 390 | 95.1 | 484 | 95.3 |
| *Star* | 91 | 92.9 | 367 | 89.5 | 458 | 90.2 |
| *News* | 37 | 37.7 | 136 | 33.2 | 173 | 34.0 |

Prepared for the *Washington Star* by Walter Gerson and Associates, "Readership Study Among Members of the United States Congress," December, 1963. (Mimeographed.)

On the basis of interviews with Senators and senatorial assistants concerning the treaty, the conclusions of Cohen tend to be confirmed with only minor modification. The press served as a source of information not only to the general public but also to decision-makers. Senators, members of the executive branch, and lobbyists used the press as one of their chief sources of information about the treaty and the positions and activities of other participants. Because the test ban was an issue which stimulated considerable public concern, many Senators followed their homestate press more closely on this issue than they customarily did on foreign policy issues both in order to determine what information was available to their constituents and how articulate opinion in their states was reacting to the treaty. The degree of dependency of the Senator on the prestige press was related to his committee assignments and interest in the treaty. If he were concerned about the issue but did not sit on a committee handling it, he relied on the prestige press more for information about the proposal than if he were an active committee participant. One member of the Committee on Armed Services reported there was nothing in the papers which had not been available to him in the committee's files for some time.[66] However, committee members did read the prestige press both for its interpretative features and its barometer features as well as to identify the positions and behavior of other decision-makers.

On the other hand, many of those members of the Senate who opposed the treaty had deep suspicions of the prestige press and refused to accept its claims of objectivity or reliability. When the prestige papers recommended a position a Senator consistently and intensely opposed, he often turned to other newspapers to fill the function the *New York Times* and a few other select papers played for most other Senators, and the *Chicago Tribune* served as the most prevalent substitute. One respondent summed up his position by saying that the "so-called prestige press" was too hurried in its analysis and tended to accept the administration's position uncritically. The legislative assistant of another Senator who had a continuing record of opposition to administration foreign policy and who voted against the treaty found that there was nothing new in the prestige press. "They are generally internationalist, anyway." He believed the administration had preempted the news on this issue and had a considerable public relations advantage over the opposition. Senate opponents also argued that

[66] Material for this section is based on interviews conducted in Washington, D.C. March and April, 1964.

because all of the facts were not available to the press and the public, it was impossible for most of the newspapers to react other than they did unless they refused to take the word of the President, his cabinet members, and others they normally trusted. They believed the press would have reacted differently if it had all of the information several of them felt was available to them. Many Senators were able to explain away press reaction when they found it disagreeable on the grounds that it was ill-informed or prejudiced. An administrative assistant admitted that the Senator he served "respected those papers that are closer to his own political philosophy." When local papers found fault with the test ban, they occupied a more important interpretative role for many Senate opponents than the prestige papers.

The White House relied on the mass media for information about the activities of other decision-makers, groups and foreign governments to supplement reports from the Department of State. The office of the President also used the mass media to reach both decision-makers in Washington and foreign capitals as well as the American public. The President used his press conferences not only to satisfy the news curiosity of reporters but also to speak to Senators and foreign leaders. The treaty occupied a disproportionate attention in the Kennedy news conferences in August and September. Twenty-five of the 60 questions in his August news conferences, and in the following month 6 of the 36 questions were devoted to the treaty. To communicate with selected audiences the President used both open and restricted-use channels. In open channels there is relatively easy access to the message sent by a transmitter, and several outlets facilitate the dispersal of information to different types of audiences. His most notable use of the open channels was his television and radio announcement of the agreement in Moscow concerning the treaty. A restricted-use channel was used when Marquis Childs was invited to inspect the Kennedy–Khrushchev correspondence. The White House expected that this influencial columnist would ally fears, particularly in the Senate, that the letters contained some devious material prejudicial to the American interest. Childs' article may not have satisfied every Senator, but the President was able to transmit his message through a columnist who was generally respected by both Republicans and Democrats in Congress for his objectivity.

The White House provided reporters with material favorable to the treaty, including speeches by cabinet members and leading scientists, often solicited by White House aids. The *ad hoc* Committee for the Nuclear Test Ban Treaty acted as an important funnel of information coming from the White

House to the press and directed at the Senate and the public. The President relied on such groups to reinforce his contention that the treaty had popular support as well as to demonstrate that leading scientists and influential interest groups favored the treaty. As the President talked to some groups, he often had other audiences in mind, and his office often used groups to communicate the interest of the President to the public at large or to their members. Moreover, the President facilitated the work of the groups, particularly the *ad hoc* committee, in gaining publicity for their pro-treaty positions because whatever assisted them assisted him as well.

## *Summary*

The mood of the press clearly was favorable to the treaty, not primarily because most newspapers and magazines openly endorsed the treaty, but more especially because stories reported in all of the media generally gave coverage to material favorable to the treaty. The media do not offer 'equal time' to both sides but afford attention to newsmakers and events which can claim public attention, and most of them pictured the test ban as beneficial, wise, and popular. An endorsement of the treaty by General Eisenhower was more important in the national media than an attack on it by Senator Strom Thurmond of South Carolina and received more attention. Moreover, reporting did not necessarily have to be centered on endorsements to have a favorable impact for the treaty on the public. By giving only passing attention to a statement by the German Chancellor or the announcement that several more countries had acceded to the treaty reinforced earlier favorable news. In addition, when the press reported that Communist China had opposed the treaty, many Americans could not help but think that the agreement could not be completely detrimental to American interests. Even though there was more attention given in most papers and on most radio and television programs to treaty news than is customary for foreign policy issues, the doubts and qualifications of many who endorsed the treaty were nevertheless ignored. Interestingly, the subtleties of the endorsement of the military officers received more attention in the prestige papers than in the anti-treaty press which tended to treat skeptical supporters simply as supporters, without offering any fine distinctions. Germs that might have been planted in the mass public were not sown because of the structure of attention given by the press to foreign policy stories.

CHAPTER V

# GROUP ARTICULATION AND ACTIVITY

The group basis of American politics can be used more profitably to explain domestic politics than the conduct of foreign policy. Organizations are more active concerning the distribution of tangible values for their members than for foreign policy goals which appear less immediate to them. When David Farnsworth studied the Senate Committee on Foreign Relations in the early 1950's, he found the major political interest organizations were relatively inactive in the foreign policy process. While there has been a notable increase in group participation since then, it is more of an alteration than a transformation of the earlier pattern. Activity by organizations continues to be selective, and groups do not devote their limited resources equally to all international issues such as foreign aid, military assistance agreements, arms controls proposals, and the appointment of ambassadors. Having developed a hierarchy of preferences, the groups have accordingly allocated their time, money, energy, prestige, and talent to those issues which are most important to their leaders and members. Since foreign policy is a peripheral issue for most groups in the United States, their contributions are often limited to statements of support or opposition. Endorsements, while an activity, are a low-level activity and not comparable to intensive lobbying and mass public relations campaigns.

Lobbying is not a simple one way channel from organizational centers to decision-makers. Group leaders not only interact with decision-makers but also communicate with their own members, other groups, the mass media, the general public, and other decision-makers. Not every member of a group may be informed or interested in an issue, and the leadership therefore marshalls the organization's media to build membership support for a proposal. Several national and local groups were sampled and asked if they participated in the test ban debate in any way. Of the 42 who did participate, all of them informed their members, and seventy per cent of them urged their members to take an active part in the ratification process.[1] All but one of these organizations requested their members to write their Senators and about two-thirds of the groups suggested to their members that they arouse their friends to support the group's position. One-half of the active groups also suggested that Senators ought to be personally visited, and several organizations urged their members to write letters to newspapers for the purpose of stimulating support.

Groups concerned with enlarging their coalition, will attempt to induce potential supporters to cross the boundary of political disinterest and inactivity to political concern and activity. Additional interest groups not only add more resources but may also increase the range of effective contacts available for the coalition thereby enlarging the number, and possibly the kind, of decision-makers with whom they have access. In addition, narrow special interests appear to be more effective when they are endorsed by other organizations which do not receive any direct benefits from the proposal. Active groups use the mass media to inform the public about their position, and they presumably work with decision-makers to influence other decision-makers. An organization seldom lobbies in Congress without any contacts in the legislative branch. It relies on its supporters there to facilitate contacts, to help swing votes, and to add stature to its position.

All but two of the 42 organizations communicated their position to at least one Senator. Table 5–1 indicates local groups contacted fewer Senators, generally concentrating on their homestate Senators. When national organizations contacted less than half of the Senate, they generally devoted their attention to the members of the Committee on Foreign Relations, Senators whom they had previously contacted on other matters, or Senators whose position on the treaty was thought to be flexible. One of the opposition groups identified 22 Senators whose vote it thought was doubtful, and an *ad hoc* organization of groups supporting the treaty listed 24

[1] The data for this analysis were collected from the returns of a questionnaire sent to 110 organizations which were identified as or suspected of being participants in the ratification process. Replies were received from 67, or 60.9 per cent, of the sample. Sixteen stated they did not take a position on the treaty, and nine reported their official position but did not complete the questionnaire. Of the 26 groups appearing before or submitting statements to the Committee on Foreign Relations, 18 returned completed returns.

Replies were received from 12 local Councils on Foreign Relations, and none of them took a position on the treaty. They were constitutionally prohibited by their charters from making endorsements on public policy questions such as the test ban treaty. However, a few of them did sponsor speeches or discussions about arms control or the test ban during the summer of 1963.

Senators who were considered to be undecided. Both the opposition group and the *ad hoc* organization devoted most of their attention to the Senators whom they thought were not strongly committed at that time.

TABLE 5-1. *Number of Senators Contacted by Groups*

| Number of Senators Contacted | Groups | | |
|---|---|---|---|
| | Total | National * | Pro-Treaty ** |
| All of the Senate plus the House | 5 | 5 | 4 |
| All of the Senate | 11 | 11 | 10 |
| More than 50 Senators | 9 | 9 | 8 |
| More than 25 Senators | 5 | 4 | 3 |
| More than 2 Senators | 6 | 3 | 6 |
| Two Senators | 4 | 0 | 3 |
| Did not communicate | 2 | 2 | 1 |
| No. of groups | 42 | 34 | 35 |

* The number of local groups is the difference between the total and the national groups.

** The number of anti-treaty groups is the difference between the total and the pro-treaty groups.

Most groups wrote to Senators, but 55 per cent of the organizations reported they had personal conversations with at least one Senator.[2] When groups used the telephone, they always supplemented it with personal conversations and letters. Communications with a Senator were not simply designed to inform him of the organization's position. More than half of the groups worked with Senators who were committed to their position: sixteen groups supplied information for speeches; nineteen gave moral support to the Senator; and ten helped him generate popular support for his position in his home state. National groups were much more active in assisting Senators in all these categories than were the local organizations.

There was considerably less contact between the groups and the executive branch. While 94 per cent of the groups communicated with the legislative branch, only 75 per cent contacted the executive branch. But even this figure inflates the attention the groups paid to the executive branch. The most popular recipient of attention was the White House, which generally received messages approving its efforts in support of the treaty.

[2] Interviews with Senate staff members indicate that a letter was considered as effective as telegrams.

The opposition groups, as might be expected, tended to ignore the executive branch. While somewhat more than one half of the groups personally saw Senators, only 33 per cent saw officials in the executive branch. Because their work was basically centered on the treaty vote in the Senate, few organizations believed that they assisted the executive branch. The thirteen organizations which reported that they assisted the executive branch believed their greatest contribution was stimulating public support for the treaty.

The mass media was another object of attention by the groups. Thirty-five of them sought to publicize their position to the public and used a general news release to the press more than any other technique to gain attention. However, thirteen placed special emphasis on selected newspapers, columnists, reporters, or magazines. They had established a working relationship with them and believed that selected emphasis would more likely produce publicity than would a general news release.[3] A few groups used paid advertising to publicize their position. Proponents of the treaty placed more advertisements in the prestige papers while the opponents concentrated on smaller papers. Twenty-two groups also asked their members to present the viewpoint of the organization to their friends and other members of the community.[4]

### *Primary and Secondary Goals*

For some of the groups, a strong and active position on the test ban treaty was highly predictable because it coincided with one of their central purposes and, moreover, was highly salient for the leadership and probably for the membership. For others, the treaty had a profound impact on the leadership, although the membership did not share the same intensity of interest. This situation was most apparent for mass organizations whose primary interest was related to economic benefits for their members. A primary goal is a value which corresponds to the organization's purposes, while secondary goals are important only in an auxiliary way. Organizations generally do not react to secondary goals with the same intensity they exhibit when primary goals are at stake.

[3] In an examination of newspapers, it was found that little attention was paid to group positions. The *New York Times* covered the positions of more groups than other newspapers, but even the *Times* restricted coverage to 12 of the groups. No other paper had more coverage, although the *Chicago Tribune* tended to give more attention to anti-treaty groups than did the *Times*. Despite their efforts, the groups did not effectively reach the public through the mass media.

[4] See TABLE 5–4.

Inasmuch as organizations possess only limited resources, they generally appropriate the major proportion of their resources to those goals which are considered most important. Although labor unions may be interested in civil rights and civil rights groups may be interested in economic questions, the former concentrate their resources on economic questions which materially affect their members, while civil rights groups devote most of their resources to their own primary interest. This is particularly true when the immediate issue is directly related to a high priority organizational goal where action cannot be postponed, and resources are perceived to be in short supply. Goals may compete within organizations where several issues demand or provide opportunity for action, but where resources are limited. The Civil Rights Bill was the test ban treaty's major competition for organizational attention in the summer of 1963.

Many groups that lobbied for the test ban treaty were also supporters of the administration's Civil Rights Bill and allocated time, money, and effort to the March on Washington for Jobs and Freedom in August of 1963. Of the eighteen groups which testified on behalf of the treaty before the Committee on Foreign Relations, eleven participated in the March on Washington or supported the Civil Rights Bill at the time. That competition of issues and the need for selection affects allocation of resources was indicated by the observation of one organization official who admitted that its activity "was a modest effort since our resources are limited and this organization was concentrating last summer on the Civil Rights Bill and the March on Washington . . ."[5] Liberty Lobby, which opposed the treaty, devoted three regular issues of its monthly publication *Liberty Letter* to the Civil Rights bill, sent out two special mailings, and distributed a half million pieces of literature opposing the proposal.[6]. With this high level of activity allocated to civil rights, resources which might have been available to oppose the treaty were substantially diminished for this organization.

### *The Activity and Position of the Peace Groups and Their Allies*

The peace groups reacted energetically to the President's American University speech, and the successful negotiation of the treaty intensified their activity. Having a core of determined members whose time and energy

[5] Reply to author, Unitarian Universalist Fellowship for Social Justice, March 18, 1964.

[6] "1963 Progress Report," *Liberty Letter*, January 25, 1964, p. 2.

had been devoted to the goals of peace and disarmament, they responded almost automatically to the events of the summer of 1963. They had previously lobbied before executive agencies and Congress and attempted to educate the public to the need for arms control. Especially energetic in lobbying for the act which created the Arms Control and Disarmament Agency in September, 1961, they worked for subsequent appropriations for the Agency and amendments to the act in 1963.[7] In early May, 1963, the Women Strike for Peace and the Women's International League for Peace and Freedom lobbied on behalf of a test ban treaty, contacted half of the members of the House and the offices of seventy-nine Senators, and saw a number of advisors to the President.[8] The Senators seen, the petitions signed,[9] the publications distributed, the letters sent, the meetings held, and the speeches delivered were considered to be necessary stimuli for congressional and public support of arms control. Their basic objectives were to keep the issue before decision-makers and the general public, to reinforce the positions of proponents of arms control in Washington, to urge others to keep an open mind to a test ban treaty, and to alert the public to the dangers of future testing, fallout, nuclear proliferation, and the arms race. Although a number of peace activists were disappointed that the treaty was a "limited ban," none opposed it for that reason. One activist summarized the approach of the majority of the peace groups in her comment that the treaty was "the reason for our being."[10]

The local peace groups and many of the patriotic organizations shared one lobbying technique: both showered the Senate with letters, phone calls, and petitions, not distinguishing between politically relevant and irrelevant activity. In part, this reflected a hope that they could demonstrate to the Senate that the public was concerned about the treaty and was willing to support its position. It also reflected the notion of these groups that activity was a moral or civic responsibility and that it had an accumulative educational impact in the community. Even if they were not successful on that issue, they hoped that more people would be alerted to the issues and

[7] U.S. Senate, Committee on Foreign Relations, *To Amend the Arms Control and Disarmament Act,* 88th Cong., 1st Sess., 1963, pp. 39–72.

[8] Women Strike for Peace, "Report – May 7 *et seq.,* Test Ban Lobby," (Washington, 1963), pp. 1–6.

[9] On July 8, 1963, a number of peace and religious groups presented a test ban treaty petition with 20,000 signatures to Averell Harriman's assistant.

[10] Aileen Hutchinson, Women Strike for Peace, before the U.S. Senate, Committee on Foreign Relations, *Hearings, Nuclear Test Ban Treaty,* 88th Cong., 1st Sess., 1963, p. 744.

would support them in the future. Activity, particularly by smaller groups, also had a reinforcing function. This was especially true in those areas of the country where the activists were clearly in a minority and where group interaction reassured them that their program was necessary because the community was not enlightened.

While most of the opposition to the treaty came from organizations which were generally conservative on both domestic and international issues, many of the peace groups did not announce positions on domestic questions, and this opened membership and leadership in many of these groups to individuals who might be conservative on economic matters but not on international issues. Paul Walters of Cleveland, President of the United World Federalists, had formerly worked for the late Senator Robert Taft's nomination for President and for Robert Taft, Jr. in his campaigns for the House and Senate. Through such men as Walters, the peace groups had contacts with conservatives, and doors were opened which otherwise might have been closed.

A number of organizations favoring arms control met at the Dodge House in Washington on April 23, 1963, at a luncheon meeting chaired by Edward Snyder of the Friends Committee. The meeting was addressed by Senator Joseph Clark and attracted representatives from fifty national organizations. At the close of the session, a request was made that any group which could work on a test ban treaty or on appropriations for the Arms Control and Disarmament Agency remain to discuss formation of an *ad hoc* committee. The fifteen organizations which volunteered were coordinated by Sandy Pearsons of the United World Federalists, and they began immediately to plan an integrated program. Contacts were reactivated at once in Congress and in the executive branches. John Stewart, Senator Humphrey's legislative assistant, met with the *ad hoc* committee and discussed the prospects for an agreement and the difficulties bound to be encountered during the Senate ratification process. Communication flowed in each direction, with the groups and supporters in the Senate assisting one another in their common goal, a nuclear test ban treaty.[11]

The successful negotiation of the treaty three months later brought an increase in both the number of participants and the intensity of their activity. With White House encouragement, James J. Wadsworth, a Republican, Norman Cousins, and others formed the Citizens Committee for a Nuclear Test Ban Treaty. Prominent members of the committee included

[11] Interviews, Washington, D.C., April and August, 1964.

two of Dwight Eisenhower's former Secretaries of Health, Education, and Welfare, Marion Folsom and Arthur Fleming.[12]

The Citizens Committee worked closely with the White House throughout this period. Presenting the treaty as a non-partisan goal of Republican and Democratic administrations, the committee sought to stimulate the broadest possible support for it. With a number of leading Republicans on the committee as well as businessmen, labor leaders, churchmen, scientists, and civic leaders, it was hoped that treaty support would be bipartisan and broadly based. Through the use of advertisements in the *New York Times, New York Herald Tribune, Washington Post, Washington Star,* and the *Wall Street Journal,* the Committee not only attempted to stimulate public opinion, but also to communicate directly with the Senators who generally read these papers.[13]

The day the formation of the Citizens Committee was announced, several of its members met at the White House to discuss plans with the President and expressed their determination to utilize all recognized avenues of communication to build support for the treaty. Later in the day the peace groups met at the Statler Hotel in Washington to map strategy and coordinate activities between the Citizens Committee and the *ad hoc* committee, now expanded to twenty groups. In addition to those already mentioned as participants were the United Automobile Workers, the National Farmers Union, the Americans for Democratic Action, the Division of Peace and World Order of the Methodist Church, the American Veterans Committee, the American Association for the United Nations, and the Committee for a Sane Nuclear Policy. From the time of its formation until Senate approval of the treaty, the *ad hoc* committee met every ten to fourteen days. Together with sympathetic Senators, particular-

[12] *New York Times,* August 8, 1963, p. 1.

[13] Two basic advertisements were used, a full page statement by scientists supporting the test ban and a two page endorsement signed by business leaders who also welcomed the treaty. The former contained the names of 52 prominent scientists, including nineteen Nobel Prize recipients, and appeared in the *New York Herald Tribune* and *Washington Star* on September 13, 1963. The statement by leading business figures included the names of presidents, chairmen of the board and partners of leading American corporations, investment houses, and brokerage firms and appeared in the *New York Times* and *Washington Post* on August 15, 1963. The committee also enlisted the support of the presidents of ten state universities and 24 other academic heads in a communication directed to the Senate and made available to the press; in another release, the Committee included the names of one hundred and three "leaders in science, art, medicine, music," and these names can be found in the *Congressional Record,* September 16, 1963, pp. 16186–16187. The Committee, which also engaged in an extensive literature campaign, reported spending $61,240.00. *Washington Post,* November 26, 1964, p. 44A.

ly Hubert Humphrey and Joseph Clark, it worked to influence those Senators who were not strongly committed to support the treaty. Supporting organizations clipped editorials and sent them to Senators for future insertion in the *Congressional Record.* Allan Howe, President of the Young Democrats, who worked out of the office of Senator Frank Moss of Utah, received material supplied by the groups for West Coast speeches and, in turn, suggested contacts for them in some of the critical states.[14] Paul Walters of the United World Federalists, James Wadsworth, and Norman Cousins maintained contact for the groups with the White House through McGeorge Bundy, the President's national security advisor.

A nucleus of eight organizations worked to mobilize support for the treaty in those states represented by undecided Senators. They agreed on the following points:

1. It is important for each organization to work through his own channels, in every state where it has contacts, to encourage letters and visits to Senators. Even Senators who are announced for or are expected to support a Treaty should be encouraged. Those who are presently on the fence should not be taken for granted.
2. The action suggestions include: (a) letters to Washington; (b) personal visits, especially of weighty delegations, to Washington or in the Senator's home state; (c) newspaper editorials, letters to the editor, joint statements, etc. . . .
3. Special efforts should be made to concentrate in key areas. Key states were divided into three classes: critical areas (5 states); second priority (4 states); and third priority (10 states). A person in Washington was tentatively selected to be primarily responsible for encouraging field activity in each of the states. The resources of each state were canvassed in the light of information available to this group. A state coordinator on the scene, familiar with the situation, was then suggested.[15]

The Senators from these states were not confirmed opponents of the treaty, but were marginal. No attempt was made to convert the irreconcilables, such as Senators Thurmond and Goldwater.[16] The groups wished

[14] Pro-treaty Senators worked more closely with groups favoring the treaty than anti-treaty Senators with organizations opposed to the test ban. According to the administrative assistant of one of the Senate's leading opponents, the right-wing groups were poorly organized, ill-informed about the technical implications of the treaty, mobilized too late to mount any effective opposition. Accordingly, in response to requests for help by these organizations, his office made the Senator's speeches available to the group but did little more.

[15] "Field Work in Crucial Areas on the Nuclear Test Ban Treaty," August 9, 1963, p. 1. (mimeographed).

[16] A right-wing organization, the Communications Network of America also identified several Senators who might vote against the treaty if they received enough mail to

to optimize their resources and tactically selected their objects for attention. In the letter-writing campaign the groups pursued two objectives: to encourage as large a volume of mail as possible in order to indicate strong public support for the treaty, and to attract new names and faces in order to demonstrate the depth of support. The organizations were interested in mail especially from businessmen and labor leaders.[17]

The peace groups and their allies were especially active at the local level. Having an existing grass roots organization, they called on chapters and churches to arouse interest. The Washington offices promoted and coordinated those activities most likely to have a positive effect on an individual Senator. One midwestern Senator, who was thought to be more responsive to businessmen than "do-good pastors", was bombarded with letters and calls from small businessmen. Methodist ministers and members of their congregation were active in another state where they were thought to be more effective; while the Baltimore chapter of the United World Federalists called on Maryland Senator J. Glenn Beall with Baltimore Mayor Theodore McKelden, a group of businessmen, and prominent women of the community. The Friends Committee arranged to have Arthur Watson, the president of a college in Iowa and a Republican, testify on its behalf at the hearings of the Committee on Foreign Relations. After his appearance, Dr. Watson met with the two Republican Iowa Senators whose votes were in doubt. The groups did not expect any of these activities to be decisive, but saw them as a part of a pattern of reinforcement.

Three peace groups testified before the Committee on Foreign Relations during the test ban hearings, and one submitted a written statement. Each emphasized the need to end future radioactive pollution of the atmosphere, to arrest the arms race, and to increase the prospects for peace. The representative of the Women Strike for Peace assumed the role of translator for concerned citizens when she asked the committee to:

show them that the test ban placed the United States "in the role of protector of the Soviet Union in all of its future schemes for expansion by means of subversion and conquest." August 23, 1963. Several of the same Senators were targets for other groups but few Senators who could be considered as strongly committed to either side were identified as appropriate objects for attention. The peace and religious groups used a more moderate approach while the rightwing groups tended to take positions which not only seemed to make their arguments untenable – that is, there was a mammoth conspiracy – but also their letters were more easily identifiable as stimulated mail because of the unique content and language. In order to encourage their members to write, the right-wing groups made the treaty seem more important to national security than it appeared to many Senators, and accordingly made the appeal less realistic.

[17] United World Federalists, *Newsletter,* August 5, 1963.

. . . pause amid the clamor of intricate political concerns and harken to the one voice which has pledged its power to you. We ask that you remember the human concern, the fresh hopeful voices of your children and grandchildren, the patient wisdom of your wives. In the vastness of history, this is the testimony which holds the key to man's survival.[18]

Stanford Gottlieb, representing SANE, rejected the objections of the treaty opponents who complained that the Soviets could not be trusted and that the treaty would endanger American security.[19] The representative of the United World Federalists was Brigadier General J. H. Rothschild (U.S.A. Ret.) who introduced himself to the committee as a man who had "spent 32 years in the Army" and discussed his research in chemical, biological, and radiological warfare material. His background, he felt, qualified him "to speak on the subject of the test ban treaty." He insisted that military security was no longer a credible goal in a world in which weapons systems continually underwent revolutionary changes.[20] Group spokesmen often assumed roles which did not seem to coincide with their primary goals because many learned that they were more effective when they addressed themselves to questions which troubled committee members than when they simply reported the group's position.

### *The Religious Groups*

Most of the religious institutions supported the treaty, and many were active on behalf of its ratification. For some, the treaty was not simply a matter of international relations but represented a moral question; and consequently, they concentrated on peace and the danger of fallout as the central features. There were, however, many churchmen who went out of their way to examine the treaty's security ramifications.

The Protestant churches in the United States officially affirmed their support of disarmament and the cessation of nuclear testing on a number of occasions.[21] Without arms control there was the distinct possibility that nuclear destruction would be visited upon mankind. The abstention of testing nuclear devices was generally considered by many churches as a necessary first step to be taken if man were to withdraw from the abyss.

[18] Committee on Foreign Relations, *op. cit.*, p. 745.

[19] *Ibid.*, pp. 751–756.

[20] *Ibid.*, p. 741.

[21] For a compilation of positions by the Churches see Committee for World Development and World Disarmament, *Disarmament and Nuclear Weapons Tests* (New York: 1960), pp. 15–37, for the period to 1960. For subsequent statements, see Committee on Foreign Relations, *Hearings, op. cit.*, pp. 939–945.

Although not discussed in many of the churches, fallout concerned several churchmen. A resolution of the American Baptist Convention expressed concern over "the damaging effects of Strontium 90 as conveyed to the populace through milk and other foods."[22]

Although the churches shared several goals with the peace groups, the religious groups placed more emphasis on national security and argued that the strength of the free world must be sufficient to deter potential Soviet aggression.[23] Former Assistant Secretary of State Francis O. Wilcox, representing the National Council of the Churches of Christ before the Committee on Foreign Relations, rejected the notion that churchmen were indifferent to Soviet power. They realized that world peace directly depended on the strength of the free world to deter Soviet expansion.[24] The selection of Wilcox provided the National Council with a representative who had greater credibility as a witness to the committee because of his previous experience in foreign affairs than a church official might have had. The use of specialists or nationally respected figures fortified the position of the group.

Finding the treaty consistent with the teachings of Pope John's *Pacem in Terris,* the Catholic association for International Peace supported the test ban. Although it welcomed the treaty as an opportunity for peaceful progress for mankind, it warned that the Soviet Union had not rejected its ideology or its objectives of conquering the West.[25]

A number of Jewish groups had taken a strong position favoring a test ban treaty before the summer of 1963. The Central Conference of American Rabbis emphasized the reduction of fallout, the alleviation of tensions, and the prospects of new disarmament proposals.[26] This group believed that it may have been effective in the debate in the sense that it had "reconfirmed congressional assessment of the liberal(ism) . . . of American Jewry." Noting that those states which had a heavy concentration of Jews were represented by Senators who generally favored policies such as the test ban, this group believed that it had "told them that it was politically expedient for them to maintain their policies."[27]

[22] Resolution and Cessation of Nuclear Tests, June 7, 1960.

[23] See H. F. Reissig, United Church of Christ, Committee on Foreign Relations, *op. cit.*, p. 946.

[24] *Ibid.*, p. 934.

[25] *CAIP News,* July–August, 1963, pp. 2–6.

[26] Rabbi Leon Feuer for the Agencies of National Reform Judaism in Committee on Foreign Relations, *Hearings, op. cit.*, p. 987.

[27] Note to the author from Rabbi Norman Misrsky, Central Conference of American Rabbis, New York, March 1964.

In a joint statement released in the second week of September, a number of the prominent church leaders in the country urged treaty ratification. Included among the sponsors were two Catholic cardinals, an Episcopal bishop, the Archbishop of the Greek Orthodox Diocese of North and South America, and the heads or presidents of the following religious institutions: United Presbyterian Church in the USA, the Lutheran Church in America, the United Church of Christ, the Rabbinical Assembly of America, the Synagogue Council of America, and the World Methodist Union.[28]

There was a notable exception to the generally favorable response to the treaty by the religious institutions. The American Council of Christian Churches, a dissident group generally opposed to the policies of the National Council of Churches, took a position similar to many of the self-proclaimed patriotic groups. Appearing before the Senate Committee on Foreign Relations, it vigorously opposed the treaty because it was "morally wrong to covenant with a godless power which has no standard of morality and which has announced its purpose to destroy us." Because the Soviet Union was evil incarnate and would obliterate religious freedom, the United States should not blind itself with a deceptive peace. Its leader also insisted that the "universe belongs to God" and under no circumstances should we "tie our hands in searching for its mysteries, like the atom."[29]

### *The Economic Groups*

For the economic groups, the treaty represented a secondary issue. The industrial trade unions, which announced a position, and the Farmers Union supported the treaty with enthusiasm, while the AFL–CIO Executive Council expressed skepticism of Soviet motivations. The United States Chamber of Commerce suggested recommendations to clarify treaty language and to insure American security. The Economic Council, a conservative-oriented organization, urged outright rejection of the treaty. Most of the economic groups, however, did not take a position.

The AFL–CIO Executive Committee viewed the treaty as a first step to arms control, which they had generally favored, but emphasized the need for underground testing and continued vigilance.[30] In his testimony before the Foreign Relations Committee, George Meany, President of the Federation, supported the treaty but devoted considerable time to detailing

[28] *New York Times*, September 9, 1963, p. 8.
[29] Committee on Foreign Relations, *op. cit.*, pp. 734–740.
[30] *Ibid.*, pp. 881–882.

the record of Soviet perfidy. The treaty might lessen world tensions and might improve the prospects for world peace only if "we have no illusions about the enemy threatening us and are united and strong enough to deter and defeat any aggression which he might consider."[31] Meany argued the less we expected from the treaty the more realistic we were. The greatest danger was that Americans might relax their guard. Other unions were more enthusiastic in their reactions. The United Automobile Workers, the United Electrical Workers, and the Longshoreman's and Warehouseman's Unions emphasized the positive aspects of the treaty rather than the shortcomings which Meany found so crucial.[32] When the UAW asserted that "a vote for the nuclear test ban could save our children,"[33] it saw benefits which were not germane to the president of the AFL–CIO. Although there was no organized opposition from labor, trade unions were hardly in agreement about the meaning or salience of the treaty.

The Chamber of Commerce paralleled the skeptical approach of the executive council of the AFL–CIO. The president of the Chamber welcomed the purpose of the treaty but recommended clarifications in its language to permit the United States to employ nuclear weapons in time of war and to use nuclear energy for peaceful purposes.

Two of the three major farm groups in the country supported the treaty, although the largest, the American Farm Bureau, did not take a position. The National Farmers Union, the smallest and most liberal of the big three, vigorously endorsed it and worked with the Citizens Committee for favorable Senate action, while the National Grange favored the test ban but did not actively participate in the ratification campaign. The Cooperative League, a federation of consumer, service, and supply cooperatives with a combined membership of fifteen million persons, also endorsed the treaty.

The test ban treaty was a secondary goal for the economic groups, and many did not participate in the debate, or simply made a recommendation and did not engage in further activity. When they did take an active role, it was generally less intense than that of the peace groups. The activists from the trade union were traditionally liberal and had supported President Kennedy on other occasions.

[31] *Ibid.*, pp. 879–880.

[32] Cf. *Ibid.*, pp. 952, 954–955 and *ILWU Dispatch,* August 9, 1963, p. 2.

[33] *UAW Solidarity,* August, 1963, p. 1. For a discussion of the differences between George Meany and his supporters in the craft unions on the one hand and Walter Ruther and several industrial unions on the other hand over foreign policy issues, see John P. Windmuller, "The Foreign Policy Conflict in Organized Labor," *Political Science Quarterly,* LXXXVII (June, 1967), pp. 205–234.

### *Veterans' Organizations*

Veterans' organizations have often lobbied on a variety of foreign and military policy issues. The American Legion and the Veterans of Foreign Wars have consistently supported a high level of military preparedness and were generally skeptical of peaceful co-existence with the Soviet Union. Although these two groups shared a common perception of the risks entailed in accepting the treaty, they adopted different positions on it. While the two giants of the veterans organizations insisted that security could come only from superior strength, many of the smaller veteran groups did not share this evaluation.

Late in the test ban debate, the American Legion held its annual convention and, after a stormy session, approved a resolution conditionally supporting the treaty. Most of the leaders of the Legion did not wish to reject the goals of the test ban but were not prepared to endorse its implications of future arms control agreements. The resolution demanded that the test ban should not be considered a step toward disarmament by the United States nor a surrender of national sovereignty. The policy statement expressed the deep concern of the Legion with the motives of the Soviet Union because it believed the Communists could use the treaty to improve their position economically, politically, and militarily.[34] The Legion took the view that what benefited the Soviet Union was necessarily disadvantageous to the United States.

The Veterans of Foreign Wars (VFW) saw the same dangers inherent in the treaty as did the Legion but drew a different conclusion – specifically, that the test ban would seriously weaken American military superiority. The VFW feared the treaty would impose intolerable technological restraints on the United States where it was weakest and would inevitably lead to Soviet nuclear superiority. Consequently they opposed the test ban.[35]

The smaller American Veterans Committee regarded the arms race and nuclear testing as a "mortal danger to mankind" and found that national security could best be realized through the rule of law rather than by the threat of force. At the same time it insisted that agreements with the Soviet Union should insure that communism would not be imposed on unwilling

[34] American Legion, *Summary of Proceedings, 45th Annual National Convention*, September, 1963, p. 89.

[35] *New York Times*, August 30, 1963, p. 16.

peoples.[36] When the representative of the American Veterans Committee appeared before the Foreign Relations Committee, he spoke for his fellow members who had served in the armed forces, members who did not claim unusual military expertise, but who did know the horrors of war and desired to withdraw from the abyss.[37] The American Council of the World Veterans Federation, composed of six smaller veterans organizations, urged ratification, reaffirming its conviction that "none can speak more eloquently for peace than those who have fought in war" and expressed the hope that future steps would bring the country closer to disarmament.[38]

While the administration courted several different groups, it paid special attention to the veterans. The peace and church groups were already allies, many economic groups were largely indifferent and were considered potentially more helpful for assistance in the Civil Rights Act, and the patriots were irreconcilably opposed. The veterans were interested in the outcome; and if they opposed the treaty, they could add respectability and numbers to an otherwise isolated opposition. Secretary Dean Rusk addressed the American Legion,[39] and the Administrator of the Veterans Administration told the Veterans of Foreign Wars' convention that the treaty was our last hope for peace.[40] Assistant Secretary of State G. Mennen Williams discussed the treaty with the American Veterans of World War II and Korea.[41] During this period some of the opponents also brought their message to the veterans. For example, Senator Richard Russell told the Veterans of Foreign Wars that he feared the treaty might pave the way for other treaties which would seriously weaken American defenses.[42]

### *Opposition and Patriotic Groups*

Discussion of the position and activities of the groups has generally focused on those organizations supporting the treaty.[43] The opposition

[36] *AVC Bulletin*, June, 1963, p. 1.

[37] Committee on Foreign Relations, *op. cit.*, pp. 722–723.

[38] Resolution reprinted in *Congressional Record*, September 10, 1963, pp. 16560–16561.

[39] Press release 464. September 10, 1963, *Bulletin of the Department of State*, XLIX, No. 1266, September 30, 1963.

[40] *Washington Star*, August 29, 1963, p. 8A.

[41] Press release 436, August 2, 1963, *Bulletin of the Department of State*, XLIX, No. 1264, September 16, 1963, pp. 432–436.

[42] *New York Times*, August 25, 1963, p. 47.

[43] The Veterans of Foreign Wars, the Economic Council, and the American Council

groups would include such groups as the John Birch Society on the right of the political spectrum, would . . . include such groups. They were primarily concerned with protecting America from perceived dangers of the left at home and abroad. For them the treaty was a step, but not the small one President Kennedy envisaged, nor in the direction the President felt it pointed. Rather, it was a giant step toward national disaster. Nor was it the first step. It was only one of a series of blunders into which the administration's foreign policy was leading an unsuspecting public. The patriotic groups often identified those who supported arms control as being, directly or indirectly, in league with the enemy. The Americans for National Security insisted that the forces which sought "to trick Americans into accepting a false peace . . . come from such as the Communist Party and the Council on Foreign Relations." The National Council of Churches was "a leftist church group" which delighted in "joining with atheists and communists on every opportunity."[44] Like many opposition groups, it attributed superior intelligence and sinister motives to the enemy[45] and judged current Soviet behavior by previous Soviet conduct. It said the changes between Stalin's and Khruschev's policies were tactical, and there was no reason to assume the Soviets were in the least bit concerned about reaching an agreement with the United States which would reduce chances of nuclear war. Mutual interest between the two super-powers was an alien concept for the patriots. International relations was a zero-sum game and anything which profited the Soviets must result in a corresponding loss for the United States.

Part of the difficulty with the patriotic position was that its language was discordant to most political participants and the general public; its targets were highly respected men or organizations; the motivations it attributed to its opponents were monstrous; and the evidence it marshalled was incomplete and shaky. Not surprisingly, the very behavior and language of these groups served to isolate them. The shrillness of the Communications Network of America is a case in point. It held that the "administration's paid civilian propagandists, muzzled military leaders, and controlled outlets in the press chorused a monotonous tune of slavish acceptance of the master plan for appeasement embodied in this death pact."[46] Because the test ban would not allow the United States to use

of Christian Churches opposed the treaty and were discussed earlier under other appropriate headings.

[44] *Newsletter*, October 15, 1963.

[45] Senate Committee on Foreign Relations, *op. cit.*, pp. 745–751.

[46] Communications Network of America, "News Alert for Immediate Action," New York, August 23, 1963.

nuclear weapons against the Soviet Union in wars of liberation, the treaty placed the United States "in the role of *protector* of the Soviet Union in all of its future schemes for expansion by means of subversion and conquest."[47] This attack, not dissimilar to many others by the patriots, made no sense unless there was a mammoth conspiracy, a proposition most Americans found untenable.

In August, The Committee Against the Treaty of Moscow had been formed at a breakfast meeting at *National Review* editor William Buckley's New York apartment. The *National Review* had opposed moves relaxing tensions with the Soviet Union because such actions were perceived as enhancing the diplomatic, economic, and political position of the enemy while diminishing American strength, and the magazine carried editorials opposing the treaty.[48] Three other editors of the magazine, and Buckley's brother-in-law L. Brent Bozell, along with Marvin Liebman, a public relations man, long active in conservative causes, were present.[49] Liebman's public relations office handled the promotion for the American Committee for Aid to Katanga Freedom Fighters, the Committee for the Monroe Doctrine, and other anti-communist *ad hoc* groups.

Within a week after their meeting, the committee released its aim to the press, and 1,500 "influential persons" were sent statements of the organization's purpose.[50] The immediate goal was to attract prominent individuals to the campaign against the treaty. Because the anticipated response did not materialize, the committee sent out a fund-raising letter to 3,500 persons who had previously contributed to one or more similar campaigns. In its solicitation letter, the committee reported that it had "established liaison with various senators and will work closely with them to mobilize support against the treaty."

On August 30, two additional mailings were sent, the first to members of Congress and others in public life, and the second to 20,000 political activists whom the committee "knew would react automatically" to the appeal. On September 5, 1963, the committee ran its ad in the *Washington*

[47] *Ibid.* Italics in the original.

[48] For example see James Burnham, "Who is Conning Whom," *National Review*, August 13, 1963, p. 101.

[49] The material for a description of the Committee Against the Treaty of Moscow was collected from the *New York Herald Tribune*, August 20, 1963, p. 1; an interview with Marvin Liebman by Richard Reston for the *San Francisco Chronicle*, September 8, 1963, pp. 1, 19; and material distributed by the Committee.

[50] The committee hoped to generate a sufficiently large enough response to enable *National Review* to fade into the background, and a citizen group with a potentially wider appeal would publically lead the opposition.

*Post*. The names of college professors, doctors, and retired military officers were included to give the message a broader appeal than might be the case if it carried a *National Review* image. One additional mailing occurred during the Senate debate and called for a flood of letters, telegrams, and phone calls to the Senate asking for the defeat of the treaty.

In detailing its skepticism of the treaty, the American Security Council speculated that "it was in the Soviet interest that there be no change in Administrations."[51] Consequently the Soviet leaders wished to shift attention from Cuba to the test ban. The Council feared that the treaty had "set in motion and (is) continuing to fuel a ground-swell of popular optimism and hope that the Cold War is ending,"[52] thus weakening our will to fight communism. The Council distributed its bimonthly *ASC Washington Report* to over 3,400 member institutions. However, it is difficult to estimate the extent to which the affiliates agreed with the position of the Council.

The John Birch Society probably had the most effective grass-roots organization of any of the patriotic groups. Extending into many communities and spread throughout the country, it appeared to have greater membership support than most of the other organizations, although its potency in Congress has been overstated at times.[53] Some observers from other patriotic groups believed that the Society was the most effective group opposing the test ban, particularly as indicated by the volume of mail sent to the Senate. One of the active opponents of the treaty felt that much of the treaty opposition had been coordinated by the Society.[54]

Two features of the response of patriotic groups to the treaty differentiate them from the peace groups and most of their allies. Although each side had intense feelings based on its own perception of reality, most of the patriotic groups had a more conspiratorial view of their opponents than the supporters of the treaty did of theirs. Opposition groups identified more organizations, individuals, and institutions in their assessment of the conspiracy. Not only were the administration and pacifists included, but much of the press also occupied a special place in the conspiracy since it was considered to be pro-Communist or manipulated by the Communists.

[51] American Security Council, *Washington Report*, August 3, 1963, p. 2.

[52] For a partial list of individuals and groups associated with the American Security Council, see *Peace and Freedom*, American Security Council Press, 1964, pp. 9–12.

[53] For a discussion of their effectiveness in activating membership support, see Harry and Bonaro Overstreet, *The Strange Tactics of Extremism* (New York: W. W. Norton, 1964), pp. 114–118.

[54] Letter to the author, Chicago, Illinois, May 29, 1964.

Although the patriotic groups were intense in their feelings and viewed the opposition as united against them, there was remarkably little coordination of their activities. Some groups which might have been expected to participate did not, and a few participants fired one volley against the treaty and became preoccupied with other problems. Even when there was coordination, it generally centered on an exchange of views, newspaper mats, petitions, and exhortations on the need for letters. These observations must be tentative because most of the patriotic groups did not discuss their activities in depth and tended to be suspicious of questions addressed to them by individuals who were not clearly identified with them.

### *The Experts*

The groups which have been discussed could not effectively claim knowledge in specialized areas which interested many Senators, namely, scientific and technological factors as they impinged on the military ramifications of the treaty. The scientific community could make such claims and, as groups and individuals, actively presented its positions and analyses of the treaty to the Senate.[55] A specialist is defined here as one who has expertise and experience in a given field, is in possession of current data relevant to the field, and is considered to be free from extraneous pressures which would compromise his ability to evaluate the data on its merits. That is, he is expected to be disinterested in the political outcome. In fact, however, the scientists were highly involved in the outcome.

Most of the undecided Senators were concerned with four technological questions: (1) What would be the effect of prolonged inactivity on manpower and facilities if the United States found the need to retest in the atmosphere because of Soviet abrogation or violation of the treaty? (2) What was the comparative position of the United States in nuclear technology and capacity *vis-à-vis* the Soviet Union, and how would testing in any specific environment affect this standing? (3) Was it possible to develop an anti-ballistic missile system without testing in the atmosphere? and (4) What was the reliability of the country's capacity to detect and identify clandestine testing? Some of these questions required judgments which were speculative and not scientific. The scientists were asked to interpret facts in terms of their effect on American national security; but national security is a set of interrelated assumptions and facts and does

[55] The role of the scientist in executive decision-making has been discussed in Chapter II.

not lend itself to scientific analysis exclusively. Does national security rest on a superiority of American nuclear power, and if it does, how much additional power is needed over the maximum Soviet capacity? Does national security rest on a stabilized military environment in which there is a relative parity of power or does it rest with a radical reduction of military power? In his study of scientists and their impact on the policy-making process, Robert Gilpin noted that:

> . . . advice of experts to the policy-maker, including that of scientists, is seldom if ever solely technical. While advise generally appears technical, careful analysis of its substance will reveal it to be political in nature . . . (E)xplicit or implicit in the reported technical data are numerous nontechnical assumptions including political assumptions concerning what ought to be done.[56]

Incomplete information about the Soviet Union was an additional problem which the American scientist faced. Even with all available intelligence information, it was difficult to make a concrete comparison of the relative state of American and Soviet nuclear technology. An evaluation, even when based on complete information about the American position, would necessarily have to introduce hypotheses about the Soviet Union which could not be fully tested.[57] Considering these limitations, the best the scientist could offer were the probable effects of the test ban.[58] It was not surprising to find disagreement within the scientific community about the consequences of the nuclear test ban treaty.

The Citizens Committee for a Nuclear Test Ban collected the signatures of fifty-two prominent scientists, including nineteen Nobel Prize recipients.[59] The Berkley Chapter of the Federation of American Scientists distributed a questionnaire to chemistry, physics, and biology professors and staff scientists, and, of those returned, 97 per cent favored the treaty.[60] The *New York Times* reported that 150 scientists at the Massachusetts Institute of Technology supported the treaty.[61] The thirty-five members of

[56] Robert Gilpin, *American Scientists and Nuclear Weapons Policy* (Princeton: Princeton University Press, 1962), p. 15. Also see Bentley Glass, "Scientists in Politics," *Bulletin of Atomic Scientists,* IXVIII, (May 5, 1962), pp. 2–7.

[57] For problems relating to intelligence estimates as they relate to policy formation, see Arnold L. Horelick, "The Cuban Missile Crisis: An Analysis of Soviet Calculations and Behavior," *World Politics,* XVI, No. 3 (April, 1964), pp. 363–389.

[58] For a discussion of probabilities and approaches of what is an acceptable probability for detection of illegal tests, see Gilpin *op. cit.,* pp. 265–269.

[59] *Congressional Record,* September 16, 1963, p. 16186.

[60] *Ibid.,* August 20, 1963, p. A5411.

[61] *New York Times,* September 15, 1963, p. 23.

the Los Alamos chapter of the Federation of American Scientists also vigorously supported the treaty.[62]

The Federation of American Scientists noted its "members who have participated in the development of nuclear weapons welcome this first step in the control of the arms race."[63] In their testimony before the Committee on Foreign Relations, Donald Brennan and Freeman J. Dyson, representing the Federation, directly opposed Dr. Edward Teller, who argued that the Soviets had collected much valuable information from their last set of high-yield tests. Dyson found that any information gained would soon be out of date. The value of any such information would rapidly diminish "as the strength and penetration of offensive forces increase over the next few years."[64]

Dyson expanded his expertise when he told the committee that "scientists have always felt that we have two distinct claims on your attention." Their technical knowledge represented one claim, and the other stemmed from their "long experience of operating a genuinely international enterprise, namely science." Their contacts with Soviet colleagues and administrators had given them "some political insights which may be of more general validity."[65] Soviet society was seen as a complex of diverse groups which did not completely agree on military policy or strategy. While some Communists supported an unlimited arms race, others preferred various degrees of restraint. The latter appeared to be in ascendancy at that time, but the rejection of the treaty by the Senate would probably shift the balance of power in the Soviet Union to the more militant group. Drawing on his experience in scientific collaboration with the Soviets, Dyson expected the results of the treaty to be beneficial, "pushing Soviet society into more reasonable and liberal directions."[66]

When he closed his statement to the committee, he shifted from these political considerations and offered to answer questions raised by the anti-missile missile issue or others on which there was scientific disagreement. What he had to offer was scientific expertise, and this was most apparent in the final sentence of his statement.

> We hope that our responses, based on our combined experience in the field of nuclear weapons system design, missile technology, missile communications, and arms control, will be helpful to you.[67]

[62] Senate Committee on Foreign Relations, *op. cit.*, p. 993.
[63] Released July 31, 1963, reprinted in *ibid.*, pp. 894–896.
[64] *Ibid.*, p. 899.
[65] *Ibid.*
[66] *Ibid.*, p. 900.
[67] *Ibid.*, p. 901.

The group entitled Physicians for Social Responsibility did not strictly fall into the category of experts for many Senators, although it assumed the role of "scientist and . . . clinician," in examining the treaty. As physicians the members of this group felt they had the responsibility of studying the medical consequences of nuclear testing, and its representative told the Committee that radioactive fallout was a problem which was "significant enough . . . to enter into your final assessment" of the treaty.[68] Its scientific interest was so distant from many Senators' definition of the problem they dismissed the Physicians for Social Responsibility as irrelevant. Not only was the scientist involved in making political recommendations, but the politician was also defining what was properly scientific.[69]

Most of the individual scientists who participated in the treaty debate emphasized their own expertise, and some rejected the competence of scientists with whom they disagreed. Dr. George Kistiakowsky introduced himself to the Committee as one who had worked "on chemical explosives, rocket fuels and the A-bomb; [and had served] as the Special Assistant for Science and Technology to President Eisenhower." Having presented his own credentials, he suggested that the Senators give special weight to the testimony of Harold Brown, Director of Research and Engineering in the Department of Defense, for he was the "only witness so far heard who can speak with real authority regarding the total ABM problem, and the related developments in offensive systems." Thus, he rejected Edward Teller's credentials to speak effectively for the treaty.[70] Stanislaw Ulam who had worked with Teller on the hydrogen bomb wrote to the *Washington Post,* dismissing the need for atmospheric explosions of very high yield nuclear devices;[71] and Hans Bethe wrote to Senator Fulbright questioning the ability of Teller to speak as an expert on intercontinental ballistic missiles.[72]

Dr. Edward Teller was the most prominent scientist opposed to the treaty and was characterized by Senator Fulbright as the "leading opponent of the treaty."[73] The testimony, speeches, conversations, and

[68] *Ibid.,* pp. 926–930. The American Medical Association did not examine the treaty nor address itself to the question of fallout at this time.

[69] For example Senator Thurmond dismissed fallout as a serious issue. "(T)he fallout mentioned by some of those who favor this treaty, [was] propaganda that is being disseminated, [and] the fallout is imperceptible." Foreign Relations Committee, *op. cit.,* p. 633.

[70] *Ibid.,* pp. 852–858.

[71] August 17, 1963, as cited in *ibid.,* p. 505.

[72] *Ibid.,* pp. 1007–1008.

[73] *Ibid.,* p. 860.

writings of Dr. Teller during the summer of 1963 were directed to the defeat of the treaty. He considered it as a step to an inevitable war which would result from American military weakness. If the United States did not have the capacity to resist aggression, then the danger of war increased proportionately to the enemy's belief that he could destroy the United States without substantial damage to himself. Teller maintained that adequate protection could be achieved through an anti-missile missile system which could destroy the enemy's missiles after they were fired out before they could strike their targets, but such a system could only be perfected by testing high megaton nuclear devices in the atmosphere. The Soviet Union had done this in 1961 and 1962. Following those "magnificent test series . . . [Khruschev] now knows how to defend himself. He now knows, probably, where the weaknesses lie in our defense." Teller believed the treaty froze American knowledge while the Soviets had progressed to the development stage of an antiballistic missile system.[74]

For some time Dr. Teller fought a test ban, arguing that it was not a realistic solution to the possibility of avoiding a nuclear third world war, because proliferation of knowledge was "unavoidable,"[75] detection methods were incomplete, and methods of concealment of clandestine tests were relatively easy.[76] He also found that the dangers of war have been exaggerated out of all proportions. Through the effective use of fallout shelters, "reasonable defense" could be obtained.[77] If the country kept a "sensible organization under attack," it could "after a number of austere but not necessarily terrible years, rebuild our country to its old strength, and to a better strength."[78] Teller also dismissed concern about radioactive fallout as "a minor worry." Radioactive contamination of the air "would be blown away from the continental United States" in three days.[79]

In late June, 1963, Teller expressed his opposition before a breakfast meeting of one hundred members of Congress.[80] After the treaty had been negotiated, he carried his case to the public, appearing on "Meet the

[74] *Ibid.*, p. 423, *passim.*

[75] Edward Teller, "The Feasibility of Arms Control and the Principle of Openness," in Donald G. Brennan (ed.) *Arms Control, Disarmament and National Security* (New York: Braziller, 1961), p. 125.

[76] *Ibid.*, pp. 128–129.

[77] Edward Teller, "Peace through Civil Defense," *Vital Speeches*, XXVIII (February 1, 1962), p. 245.

[78] *Ibid.*, p. 246.

[79] Edward Teller, "We Must Face the Danger," *Saturday Evening Post*, 235 (February 17, 1962), p. 35.

[80] *Washington Post*, June 26, 1963, p. A16.

Press,"[81] and speaking to the National Press Club.[82] An attempt was made by Republican Governor Henry Bellmen of Oklahoma to invite Teller to the Southern Governors' Conference to discuss the effect of the treaty on the South, but Democratic governors loyal to the President learned of this and protested to Conference Chairman Orval Faubus who rescinded his earlier invitation.[83] During the Senate Committee hearings and debate, Teller discussed his objections to the treaty with a number of Senators as well as several members in the administration.[84] Six days before the treaty was initialed, he sent a letter to Congressmen suggesting it could prove "fatal" to the security of the United States.[85]

Supporters of arms control in the scientific community were also active before the Moscow negotiations. An eleven-week "Defense and Disarmament Seminar" was conducted by the Peace Research Institute for congressional assistants and included lectures by distinguished scientists from several disciplines, administration officials, and experts in peace research.[86] Scientists participated in several informal sessions, and breakfast meetings were also held during the Senate debate to acquaint Senators and their assistants with the position of scientists supporting the treaty. Many scientists actively presented their position to individual Senators. As they visited Senators in their offices, most of the scientists emphasized the need for the treaty and the absence of any serious problems inherent in the treaty as it affected national security.[87] The scientific community may have divided on its assessment of the treaty, but the preponderance of articulate scientific opinion was clearly on the side of the treaty.

Only one group of specialists who were experts in the use and delivery of nuclear power, the Air Force Association, opposed the treaty, a course not followed by the other service associations. One-third of its 75,000 members were active Air Force personnel, although they were not permitted to have a vote on policy questions in the Association. It insisted the options available to the military strategists and national policy-makers were rapidly declining. "In trying to avoid a choice between holocaust and humiliation,

[81] "Meet the Press," September 1, 1963, as reprinted in the *Congressional Record*, September 16, 1963, pp. 16161–16163.

[82] *New York Times*, August 22, 1963, p. 24.

[83] *Ibid.*, pp. 1, 24.

[84] Interviews, 1964 also see U.S. Senate, Preparedness Subcommittee, *Military Aspects and Implications of Nuclear Test Ban Proposals*, 88th Cong., 1st Sess., p. 764.

[85] *Washington Post*, August 11, 1963, p. A4.

[86] "Congressional Assistants and Science Seminar," *The Nation*, 196 (March 2, 1963), p. 170.

[87] Interviews, Washington, 1964.

the nation is in danger of passing to a strategic posture in which any choice at all may well be eliminated."[88] The Association charged that the administration had moved from a position of nuclear superiority to one of nuclear stalemate, and the treaty "would entail unacceptable risks to the security of this Nation and the Free World."[89] There was an attempt to amend the policy statement within the board of directors so that the association would merely warn that the test ban involved "grave" rather than "unacceptable" risks, but this was defeated by a three to one vote.[90]

When the opposition of the Air Force Association was announced, Eugene Zuckert, Secretary of the Air Force, denounced it, refused to attend the Association's reception in his honor, and canceled his appearance as the keynote speaker. In a letter to its president, the Secretary said the statement was "immoderate and based on such information as to disregard completely the best interests" of the country and the service. He also deplored the "alarmist tone" of the resolution which was a resort to "irrationalism which can lead only to passionate rather than reasonable discussion."[91]

## *The Active Groups*

A group can be identified not only on the basis of its major goals but also by its activity. The peace and patriotic groups were smaller than labor unions, veterans' organizations, or some of the other participants on the test ban issue; but they were more energetic throughout the process and concluded their work with greater satisfaction than those groups which might be expected to identify the treaty as a secondary goal. Of 42 groups in the sample, the thirteen peace and patriotic groups can be characterized as primary goal groups and the remaining 29 groups are identified as secondary-goal groups.

The primary goal groups exhibited a higher level of satisfaction than did the other groups. For purposes of analysis, groups were highly satisfied when they reported they helped to change an undecided or negative position in the Senate to a positive one or felt their activity helped to maintain a friendly Senator from deviating to the other side. All other responses were considered to be an indication of lower satisfaction.

[88] *New York Times*, September 12, 1963, p. 16.
[89] *Ibid.*
[90] *Ibid.*
[91] "Zuckert Attacks AFA on Test Ban Stand," *Air Force and Space Technology*, September 16, 1963, p. 31.

Table 5–1 shows that most of the peace groups believed they had influenced a vote in the Senate from a neutral or negative position to one favorable to their position.

TABLE 5-2. *Goal Priority and Perception of Effectiveness on the Senate Vote*

| Effectiveness | Primary Goal Groups | Secondary Goal Groups |
|---|---|---|
| * Yes, helped swing Senate vote | 8 | 1 |
| * Yes, reinforced a Senate vote | 7 | 7 |
| Yes, alerted the membership | 2 | 21 |
| Yes, alerted the general public | 9 | 10 |
| Yes, but not sure | 2 | 4 |
| Yes, other | 3 | 0 |
| No. of groups | 13 | 29 |

* High satisfaction categories.

Primary goal groups used an average of four communication channels to inform their members of the treaty and the organization's position, while the secondary goal groups used less than two, generally concentrating on official publications. The primary goal groups also employed a greater variety of techniques in their communications with the press and accounted for almost all of the organizations which directed special attention to selected columnists, reporters, or magazines. The major economic groups, such as the Chamber of Commerce and AFL–CIO, had access to several media outlets but did not pursue them on the treaty, preferring to use these contacts for issues of central and immediate concern to the group.

The primary goal groups communicated with more Senators than the secondary goal groups and relied on twice as many different communication channels than the latter which customarily sent only a letter. Three-quarters of the primary goal groups personally contacted Senators, while less than two-fifths of the secondary goal groups used this channel, not wanting to exhaust their credit with senators on issues peripheral to their major interests.

Another distinction is the manner in which the two categories of groups worked with Senators. The primary goal groups assisted more Senators more often and offered more assistance per organization than the secondary goal groups rendered. As seen in Table 5-3, half of the primary goal groups helped write speeches or supplied information for speeches, while less than

TABLE 5-3. *Goal Priority and Types of Assistance Rendered to Senators* Types of Assistance

| | No. of Groups | |
|---|---|---|
| | Primary Goal Groups | Secondary Goal Groups |
| Supplied information for speeches, etc. | 6 | 10 |
| Gave moral support | 9 | 9 |
| Helped in Senator's home state | 7 | 2 |
| Other | 2 | 1 |
| | — | — |
| Total types of assistance | 24 | 22 |
| No. of groups | 13 | 29 |

30 per cent of the other groups did. The former also believed that they offered more moral support and helped stimulate public opinion in the Senator's home state more than did the other groups. Actually, some of the secondary-goal groups with a membership of several hundred thousand probably stimulated more public support for their position than did a local peace or patriotic group, although the latter was more apt to be optimistic about its accomplishments.

The primary goal organizations recommended more types of activity to their members, individuals who found the treaty more salient to them than the average member of secondary goal organizations. The former voluntarily affiliated with the group because of its position on peace or national security. Only 22 per cent of the secondary goal group urged their members to write to newspapers and 35 per cent suggested that their members should urge their friends to support the organization's position, Table 5-4 indicates that the primary interest groups made each of these recommendations 92 per cent of the time.

Not only did the primary goal groups have a greater stake in the outcome of the treaty, they also behaved differently. They saw more Senators and rendered them more assistance; they contacted more offices in the executive branch, and they urged their members to engage in more activities than did the secondary goal groups. The members of an informal interest group coalition differ not only on their intensity of interest but also on their intensity of activity. When an issue is not of primary concern to an organization, it does not commit its full resources to the contest. Furthermore, many of the representatives of large economic interest groups knew that many Senators believed the treaty required technical and scientific scrutiny, and persistent lobbying by them would not only be considered

TABLE 5-4. *Goal Priority and Recommended Activity to Members*

| Recommended Activity | Primary Goal Groups | Secondary Goal Groups |
|---|---|---|
| Write Congressmen | 12 | 17 |
| See Congressmen | 10 | 9 |
| Write newspaper | 11 | 6 |
| Urge friends to support position | 12 | 10 |
| Sign a petition | 7 | 1 |
| Other | 2 | 3 |
| Total | 54 | 46 |
| No. of groups | 13 | 29 |
| Average number of recommendations | 4.1 | 1.6 |

irrelevant but unwelcome. Consequently, they endorsed the treaty, often at the request of the White House or other groups, and slipped into a state of relative inactivity. Falling between the highly active and passive groups were a few large economic interest organizations whose leaders had supported President Kennedy on several other issues and had strongly endorsed arms control earlier. Activity for these groups was more a function of the interests of their leaders' preferences than the members' articulated goals.

CHAPTER VI

# PUBLIC OPINION AND THE TEST BAN TREATY

It has become a truism that the general public is not as concerned with foreign relations as much as it is with domestic issues.[1] The cost of living, civil rights, law and order, taxes, labor relations, and education affect most citizens more directly and immediately than international relations. The public consequently exhibits greater fluctuation, less intensity, and less saliency in foreign policy issues which often seem remote from everyday life.[2] While officials court citizens on both national and international issues, leaders tend to be more sensitive to constituency opinions on domestic questions than on foreign policy matters because voters judge the performance of officials on their domestic record except in times of an acute national crisis. James Rosenau suggests that the mass public usually becomes interested in foreign policy only in periods of acute peace-or-war crises, and not always then.[3] Issues relating to war and peace do not fall into this analysis and are analogous to the issue of a dynamic economy or a recession.

In the model of opinion formation of James Rosenau, those who hold opinions and are knowledgeable about foreign policy on a continuing basis are identified as members of the attentive public. Most Americans generally are unconcerned with foreign policy and are identified as the mass public.[4] Preoccupied with immediate, palpable concerns of family, job, and a variety of economic, social and personal problems, they often view foreign policy as something they cannot hope to influence.[5] Not having formed stable or

[1] In particular, see James N. Rosenau, *Public Opinion and Foreign Policy* (New York: Random House, 1961), and Gabriel Almond, *The American People and Foreign Policy* (New York: Frederick Prager, 1960).

[2] V. O. Key, *Public Opinion and American Democracy* (New York, Knopf, 1961), pp. 158–59.

[3] Rosenau, *op. cit.*, p. 36.

[4] *Ibid.*, pp. 35–36 and Almond, *op. cit.*, p. 69.

intense opinions about international relations, the mass public is more apt to follow the recommendations of opinion leaders on these issues than on domestic issues where they already have a general idea about the consequences of the proposal. The mass public does not sort out the complicated facts in foreign policy issues but tends to follow the tone set by the mass media as well as opinion leaders.

Since the end of World War II, Americans have fluctuated in their support for arms control in general and a test ban in particular, and survey results appear to sustain the Rosenau model. The history of opinion is not a progressive development from little support in the early days of the cold war to substantial acceptance of a test ban in 1963. The man in the street shifted his preferences about a cessation of nuclear testing as tensions fluctuated between the United States and the Soviet Union and as American leaders reinterpreted their understanding of the requirements of national security. Because most American foreign policy has been bipartisan, the public was usually offered non-conflicting cues about the appropriate course of action to support; and an opinion consensus often developed. When there were sharp differences in the public at large, bipartisanship had usually collapsed at the opinion-maker level. For example, the greatest cleavage in American opinion on a nuclear test suspension came in 1956 when it was a partisan issue between the Republican and Democratic presidential candidates; after the elections, public opinion tended to be homogeneous as the matter was no longer hotly debated between the parties.[6]

There is often a contradiction between supporting abstractions and favoring the concrete policies which may endanger those abstract values. Samuel Stouffer has shown that most people accept the abstract concepts of the Bill of Rights; but when confronted with choosing between the First Amendment and keeping atheists from teaching in public schools, the Bill of Rights loses its significance for many citizens who would prohibit the atheist from teaching.[7] This pattern is also manifested in foreign relations. Most Americans have desired to avoid a nuclear confrontation with the Soviet Union, but

[5] This holds for many domestic issues as well. Herbert McClosky found that 61.5 per cent of his sample believed the comment, "Nothing I ever do seems to have any effect upon what happens in politics." "Consensus and Ideology in American Politics," *American Political Science Review*, LVIII (June, 1964), pp. 370–371. Combined with low saliency, political futility only accentuates the unconcern of many individuals to foreign policy issues.

[6] Eugene J. Rosi, "Mass and Attentive Opinion on Nuclear Weapons Tests and Fallout, 1954–1963," *Public Opinion Quarterly*, XXIX, (Summer, 1965), p. 238.

[7] Samuel Stouffer, *Communism, Conformity and Civil Liberties* (Garden City, N.Y.: Doubleday, 1955), pp. 26–57.

when faced with the possibility that the Soviets might gain an advantage unless the United States vigorously counteracted, the public has loosened its support for peace and supported a more militant policy.

Nevertheless, most Americans do not recognize the contradictions. While opposing a preventive war they often support policies that might lead to a nuclear war. Even when a considerable body of Americans expressed alarm over fallout, many of the same respondents were prepared to support atmospheric tests. Most of these complex contradictory values are latent, and one or more of them will be activated only when stimulated.[8] If the administration tries to strike some chords, but ignores others to muster support for a controversial issue, opposition leaders will try to strike a missing chord.

Public opinion is not formed in the abstract for either of Rosenau's two categories. Leaders have greater influence over citizens when the public does not have preconceived opinions about the issue, when the opinion-makers are respected, when their recommendations do not seem antithetical to the past experiences of the public, and when the audience considers the issue is important. This last factor is the distinguishing characteristic between the attentive and mass publics. Rosenau holds that while the attentive public seeks information, the mass public will respond to foreign policy issues when they are heavily publicized in both the mass and specialized media. The attentive public seeks out issues while the mass public responds to issues when it is affected by them.

Four inputs interact in the public opinion system before the public arrives at its position: "objective events", leadership response, media attention, and interest group response, although the latter may be relatively inactive and is not always an essential input. At the most elementary level, leaders respond to events, the media report and analyse the event and groups provide supporting or alternative interpretations. By attempting to activate the support of their members in making it salient to them, organizations often supply their members with information not readily available to the general public.

The public generally responds to the tone of the leaders and the media rather than the specific contents of proposals and counterproposals. In the test ban case, it was interested in whether the policy under consideration would promote peace without endangering national security, rather than

[8] Carl Hovland observed that when a message comes from a positively regarded source, individuals often find more agreement than actually exists. "Assimilation and Contrast Effects in Reactions to Communication and Attitude Change," *Journal of Abnormal Social Psychology*, LV (September, 1957), p. 251.

the specific elements of a policy such as the concrete capabilities and limitations of remote monitoring systems to detect nuclear explosions.

The response of leaders to "objective events", the attention given to leadership reaction by the mass media, and the activity stimulated by the groups set the tone of the message which reaches the public. The sequence for the public opinion system is an *event* which is interpreted by officials and opinion-makers who provide a *tone* which in turn influences opinion, and that is translated as a *mood*. When interpretations are conflicting, or when the tone marks a sharp shift in opinion-maker behavior, then opinion cleavage increases as the public decides on what it considers reliable recommendations.[9] Bipartisan recommendations will consequently be relatively effective in influencing opinion.[10]

The President is the customary cue in foreign relations for most of the public, although citizens generally have other alternatives when they do not accept the reliability of the Chief Executive. With the test ban, the presidency provided an effective cue for most Americans. Although John Kennedy had been elected by a slim margin, his popularity as President was relatively high throughout his administration. The mid-July, 1963, survey of the American Institute of Public Opinion (AIPO) indicated 61 per cent of the public approved of his handling of the presidency, while 27 per cent disapproved. His popularity was much greater outside the South and naturally higher among Democrats than Republicans.[11] For those who disapproved of his conduct, other sources of information and recommendations were readily available.

"Objective events" are simply those events which occur in the international environment and are perceived as having an effect on American interests, however defined. The Cuban missile crisis of 1962 or the con-

[9] Carl J. Hovland, "Reconciling Conflicting Results Derived from Experimental and Survey Studies of Attitude Change," *American Psychologist*, XIV (January, 1959), pp. 8–17. Hovland finds that when the respondent is not highly committed to a position, he is more likely to react positively to the communications than when he is either committed to the position or sees the communicator negatively or ambiguously, pp. 12–13.

[10] Elmo Roper and others have found that when the public does not have confidence in one of the mass media channels, such as the press or television, other media sources are considered trustworthy. Cf. *The Public's Attitudes toward Television and Other Media* (New York: Elmo Roper and Associates, 1962).

[11] AIPO, July, 1963. For a discussion of the opportunities of presidents to influence public opinion see Doris A. Graber, *Public Opinion, the President, and Foreign Policy*, (New York: Holt, Rinehardt, and Winston, 1968).

struction of the Berlin Wall in the previous year fall into this category. It is not important whether the United States is a participant or simply a witness to an event, so long as opinion-makers believe it is important to American interests and respond to it. The "objective events," generally external to the system, having received attention by opinion-makers, are communicated to the public for assessment and possible choice. One of the powers of opinion-makers stems from their role as gatekeepers to the public opinion system. They may not report some events to the public which then do not enter the system, or they may attempt to minimize the reliability of alternate channels to the public when authorities wish to ignore the event. However, they do not automatically excite the public when they desire to activate opinion because the problem is not intense enough to make it salient to a large segment of the public.

The energy with which the administration pursued arms control proposals and the acceptance of these policies by the public are inversely related to the current level of tension between the United States and the Soviet Union.[12] Tension is related to distance; a high state of tension separates the parties while a low state of tension tends to bring them closer together.[13] In periods of low tension, arms control proposals have been more acceptable to the public, especially when the administration had publicly supported greater cooperation with the Soviet Union. But the early stages of a period of low tension have not necessarily produced support for an accomodation with the U.S.S.R. Events which earlier resulted in a state of high tension are likely to be recalled when leaders or citizens interpret the current policy of another state. The residual effects of previous events lead to suspicion or trust between the participants. Consequently, conciliatory-intended moves do not necessarily reduce tension, and leaderships' responses are crucial in educating the public to changes in the behavior of other states.[14] Therefore, when they attempted to influence opinion on arms control, the leaders customarily took into account that the earlier actions of the Soviet Union were stored in the memory of the general public; and

[12] For a discussion of tension levels in foreign policy and public opinion, see Jessie Bernard, "Parties and Issues in Conflict," *Journal of Conflict Resolution,* I (1957), pp. 111–121.

[13] David Krech and Richard Crutchfield, "Theory and Problems of Social Psychology," in Wilbur Schram, *The Process and Effects of Mass Communications* (Urbana: University of Illinois Press, 1961), p. 133.

[14] See Bernard Berelson and Gary Steiner, *Human Behavior* (New York: Harcourt, Brace, and World, 1964), pp. 574–84 and Carolyn Sherif, M. Sherif, and Roger Nebergal, *Attitude and Attitude Change* (Philadelphia: W. B. Saunders, 1965), *passim.*

opinion makers presented policy shifts as marginal rather than as radical ones.

When a country which has been considered a serious threat suddenly becomes friendly, it is more likely that the country's former enemies will question his motivations than celebrate the conclusion of the contest. The conciliatory actions of former enemies are likely to be seen as exercises in duplicity by some observers,[15] that is, as alterations in technique, not substance. When President Kennedy presented the test ban treaty to the American public, he offered it as a step in reducing conflict and not as a solution to the cold war, that is, not as a sharp break with previous policy. Furthermore, he insisted it would not weaken American defenses, implying that the United States was not willing to put complete trust in the goodwill of the Soviet leaders. Because the agreement was presented as a marginal improvement, it had a better chance of public acceptance than if it had been publicized as the beginning of a new area of peace and mutual harmony with the communist block.[16]

In examining public response in the United States to the Soviet Union, it is necessary to treat Soviet behavior on a continuum, as part of a pattern of enmity or friendship, and not as a series of isolated acts. To plot moves without consideration of previous conduct would allow certain events to be perceived in themselves as relatively innocuous or less important than they were.[17] By itself, the Soviet resumption of nuclear testing in 1961 may not have been as important a tension-provoking move as the construction of the Berlin wall; but, following the construction of the wall, Soviet nuclear testing in the atmosphere increased distance with the Soviet Union for both decision-makers and the public.

Tension-producing moves may come in rapid succession, resulting in a hostile attitude in the threatened state. However, if there are no tension-producing moves over a period of time, one of three reactions will occur. Distance will continue at the level of the last act, residual suspicion operating to maintain homeostasis; distance will increase in the absence of any conciliatory moves, feeding on suspicion that the other actor is preparing to engage in new hostile moves; or distance might narrow over a period of time as the hostility-provoking moves are forgotten and other issues become

[15] For a discussion of the role of enemies in opinion formation, see David J. Finlay, Ole R. Holsti, and Richard R. Fagen in *Enemies in Politics* (Chicago: Rand McNally and Company, 1967), pp. 1–24.

[16] Much of the following analysis is based on William A. Gamson and Andria Modigliani, "Tensions and Concessions: The Empirical Confirmation of Belief Systems about Soviet Behavior," *Social Problems*, XI (Summer, 1963), pp. 34–48.

[17] Krech and Drutchfield, *op. cit.*, p. 133.

more salient. The third alternative characterized American attitudes prior to the test ban because the Kennedy administration worked to reduce fear of the Soviet Union as an immediate threat to the United States after the Cuban missile crisis. As the succeeding discussion will indicate, the Soviet Union was considered as a hostile country between 1961 and 1962: but as tension-producing moves declined in 1963, distance and, concomitantly, suspicion also diminished. When there were no perceived Soviet threats, the public was more susceptible to accepting an accomodation sponsored by major opinion-makers than during a crisis.

The fluctuations of American public opinion on foreign policy are considerably greater than a surface examination indicates because 65 to 80 per cent of the public is not committed to a particular perspective on international relations and alters its opinions. The remaining 20 to 35 per cent at the poles of the opinion continuum hold intense and stable opinions about arms control. Therefore, the American public can be divided into three groups, the first and third categories showing less flexibility: (1) the "hardliners" who espouse a more aggressive policy toward the Soviet Union as a permanent fixture in American foreign policy, (2) a middle group who accepts the general lines of current policy and tends to change positions as policy changes, and (3) the "softliners" who prefer a more energetic policy toward disarmament.[18] Individuals in each category have their own perceptual framework for judging events and often arrive at conflicting interpretations of the same event. There is a tendency for the softliners to see Soviet tension-producing moves as reactions to Western provocations and for hardliners to insist that mutual interests between the United States and a communist state are impossible and any conciliatory-appearing move is a Soviet attempt to lull the American people to sleep in order that the communists may overcome the United States.

The hardliners hold victory as a priority and see the West and communist systems on a collision course with the Soviets planning the destruction of the West. Accomodation is impossible for the hardliners. Peace is the primary policy goal of the softliners who believe the Soviet Union is interested in avoiding nuclear destruction and will accomodate with the West to reach a mutually beneficial solution.[19] The middle group, which includes the vast majority of the American people, desires both peace and

[18] Gamson and Modigliani, *op. cit.*, pp. 35–36.

[19] See Chapter IV below on groups, particularly the peace and right-wing groups. Also see Daniel Bell, (ed.), *The Radical Right* (Garden City, N.Y.: Doubleday and Company, 1963) for a discussion of some of the psychological properties of dogmatic anti-communists.

military security. Since they combine two goals, which tend to be conflicting in a nuclear environment aggravated by the cold war, the general public has not held stable or intense opinions on arms controls.

The size of the soft- and hard-liners can be approximated from those survey items which produced overwhelming majority responses to foreign policy questions but also included a small group which deviated from the consensus. These deviations generally run to about eight to fifteen per cent at each extreme, leaving about 65 to 80 per cent of the public in the middle group. For example, a 1963 survey indicated that only 3 per cent of the American public supported a preventive war, probably a rockbottom indicator of the hardliners, while in the 1961 crisis period, eight per cent reported they thought Khrushchev was sincere in wanting complete disarmament. In a study of one community, Peter Rose found that a little over two-thirds of his sample believed the United States should seek peace through firmness, while fifteen per cent felt the United States would eventually have to fight with the Soviet Union and should not accommodate with the Soviets, and twelve per cent believed a peaceful settlement was possible and desirable even if a few concessions were made. Only two per cent insisted that the United States should avoid war at all costs, even if it meant concession on a broad range of issues.[20]

The analysis of how tension levels and opinion-makers' reaction act as cues applies particularly to the middle group, and not to the public at large. As the tone of policy fluctuates, the middle group responds most quickly, provided it is concerned enough with the issue to formulate opinions at all. The confidence levels of the middle group in opinion-makers, particularly the President, are important in gauging its reaction; for if it trusts the president (or a national leader), there will be a tendency to opinion consensus; but when the middle group divides into two or more partisan, regional or other subpublics, placing more of their confidence in opinion-makers other than the President, opinion will be divided. To the extent he can maintain his credibility with the public and fashion a coalition of diverse opinion-makers to present a bipartisan policy, the President can mold a consensus for his program.

## *Inputs and Responses*

Public opinion on the test ban treaty must be considered in relation to previous administration policy with the Soviet Union. Table I lists tension

[20] Peter I. Rose, "The Public and the Threat of War," *Social Problems*, XI (Summer, 1963), pp. 72–73.

levels, twelve events and official responses to them, and several surveys on nuclear testing during the Kennedy administration. The events, with the exception of the hot-line negotiations culminating in an agreement in June, 1963, were widely reported in the mass media. Events chosen were of national interest; were unconnected with domestic economic issues; elicited government, group and other opinion-maker response; and many were described by editors and reporters as among the top ten news stories of their respective years. Some of these events are best understood as extending over a protracted period such as the crisis in the Congo in 1961 and the military conflict in Laos and Viet-Nam.

The public generally favored a test ban treaty or a moratorium on testing during the second Eisenhower administration, but this trend was reserved during President Kennedy's first months in office, only to swing upward after his American University speech. When the United States submitted its arms control proposal at Geneva in 1958, two out of three Americans supported a mutual American-Soviet moratorium on nuclear tests.[21] The high point of support for arms control was reached in November, 1959, when nearly four out of five persons supported the extension of the moratorium for another year.[22] This survey was conducted after Khrushchev's tour of the United States, when there were noticeably warmer relations between the two countries and when major American public figures supported an agreement.

While tensions increased with the U-2 crisis; the frustrated Paris summit conference; the growing influence of pro-Communist elements in Cuba, the Congo, and South East Asia; and anti-American rioting in Japan, which forced President Eisenhower to cancel his visit to that country, support for an agreement decreased. In the final month of the Eisenhower administration, only 50 per cent of the public believed that it was possible to reach a peaceful settlement with the Soviet Union.[23] The abortive invasion of Cuba, the "sobering" Kennedy-Khrushchev summit meeting, the construction of the Berlin wall, and the resumption of testing by the Soviet Union were events which lessened the confidence of many Americans in any agreement with the Soviet Union and increased the distance between the two countries. In June, 1961, only 27 per cent of the American public believed the country should not resume testing.[24] At the end of the year,

21 AIPO, May, 1957.
22 AIPO, January, 1961.
23 AIPO, December, 1960.
24 AIPO, June, 1961.

less than ten percent believed Khrushchev was sincere when he said he wanted total disarmament.[25]

In September, 1961, the Soviet Union conducted an atmospheric nuclear test and continued testing high megaton weapons producing very high radioactive fallout yields. The administration responded to this unilateral termination of the moratorium by exclusively testing underground and in the laboratory. The President argued that the United States would continue its current nuclear lead over the Soviet Union without atmospheric testing; and fallout, however small, would be avoided.[26] Reflecting not only the tension between the United States and Soviet Union but also conflicting cues from several national leaders,[27] 45 per cent supported the President and 41 per cent opposed his position. Along with other public figures, both former Vice-President Nixon and Governor Nelson Rockefeller opposed a test ban at that time.[28] As tension increased and the Soviet's testing continued, the administration reassessed its position. In early March, 1962, President Kennedy emphasized the need to maintain America's deterrent nuclear capacity when he announced a new test series in the atmosphere.[29] At that time, other national opinion-makers and the press supported his position and 67 per cent approved of atmospheric testing, a shift of 22 per cent in two months in favor of testing.[30]

Most Americans were not concerned about fallout during this period. Despite a number of published reports in the press and intensive campaigns by a number of peace groups, only 21 per cent of the population estimated there was enough fallout in the atmosphere to constitute a danger.[31] Nevertheless, many Americans were not ignorant about the nature of the effects of fallout. While only 17 per cent could correctly define fallout in 1955, 57 per cent could in 1961.[32]

The apparent contradiction between support for tests and knowledge about fallout can partially be explained by the treatment given fallout in several of the mass circulation magazines which pictured fallout as a potential future danger but not critically important at that time.[33] Since indi-

[25] AIPO, November, 1961.

[26] *New York Times,* September 2, 1961, p. 1 and other September issues detailing the administration's position.

[27] AIPO, November, 1961.

[28] *New York Times,* November 15, 1961, p. 3.

[29] *Ibid.,* March 3, 1962, p. 2.

[30] AIPO, March, 1962.

[31] AIPO, December, 1961.

[32] AIPO, April, 1955 and December, 1961.

[33] Cf. Chapter IV on the mass media, particularly pp. 10–12.

viduals often tend to minimize unpleasantries which are inevitable side effects of a program they believe is necessary for national defense, it is not surprising they rejected any resulting dangers as unimportant and distant.[34] However, rationalizations do not necessarily satisfy all anxieties, and a person will often support alternate policies which reduce his frustration. Because survey questions did not indicate whether people were completely satisfied that fallout was irrelevant, it is difficult to determine whether they were rationalizing. Nevertheless, there was a sharp increase in concern over

TABLE 6-1. *Public Opinion, Tension Levels, and Leadership Reaction to Events*

| Tension Level | State of Opinion * | Event | Leadership Reaction * |
|---|---|---|---|
| 1961 High | Consider it possible to reach peaceful settlement with the Soviet Union. Yes. 50%. January, 1961. | U.S. breaks diplomatic relations with Cuba. January, 1961. | Reaction to increased "anti-American" policies of Castro. |
| | | Unsuccessful invasion attempt of Cuba. Soviets pledge aid. March, 1961. | Kennedy warns Soviets U.S. will not tolerate outside military interference. Nixon backs Kennedy. |
| | Continue moratorium Yes. 27%. June, 1961. | Kennedy-Khrushchev conference. June 1961. | "Ends in hard controversy." *New York Times,* June 1961, p. 1. |
| Rising | | Berlin wall constructed August, 1961. | Kennedy sends 2500 troops to Berlin. Says this is a "most dangerous time." Bipartisan support. |
| Rising | | Soviets unilaterally resume testing in atmosphere. September, 1961. | Strong disapproval throughout government to Soviet action. Nixon, Rockefeller oppose, test ban partisan differences. |

34 Cf. Schramm, *op. cit.,* on rationalization, p. 326.

TABLE 6-1. *Public Opinion, Tension Levels, and Leadership Reaction to Events*

| Tension Level | State of Opinion * | Event | Leadership Reaction ** |
|---|---|---|---|
| Rising, High | Should U.S. test in the atmosphere. Yes. 45% November, 1961. | | |
| 1962 Steady | Favor test suspension. Yes. 44%. January, 1962. | Continued Soviet testing but no gross hostile moves. | |
| | Favor suspension. Yes. 25%. March, 1962. | Kennedy announces U.S. to test in atmosphere. March 3, 1962. | General support. Peace groups protest. |
| Period of decline | | No hostile moves from Soviets. | |
| Sharp Increase | | Cuban missile crisis. October, 1962. | Strong bipartisan support for removal of missiles, including the use of force |
| | | Removal of missiles. | Some Republicans ask for harder line against Cuba. |
| 1963 Period of decline | | Absence of overt hostile moves by the Soviet Union. Continuing military involvement of U.S. in Laos and South Vietnam. | |
| | Favor test ban? Yes. 52%, July, 1963 *** | Negotiation of hot line, June, 1963. | |
| | Yes. 63%, August, 1963. | Test ban negotiated. July, 1963. | Administration strongly supports. Bipartisan support slow but grows. |
| | Yes. 81%, September 1963 ***. | | |

* Based on American Institute of Public Opinion surveys unless otherwise noted.
** Based on accounts in the *New York Times*.
*** Based on Harris survey.

fallout among supporters of a test ban in 1963 [35] when this issue was pursued by the President and much of the press.

### *Public Opinion and the Test Ban Treaty*

Earlier chapters indicated the press and interest groups overwhelmingly supported the treaty. The executive branch was essentially united in publicly supporting the treaty, and the possible centers of opposition within the administration did not openly oppose the President. As later chapters will indicate, after initial uneasiness, Republican leaders in the Senate also supported the treaty, and much of the Senate opposition did not develop until September. In sum, the assessment of the treaty was generally favorable and the tone of the opinion-makers – in the government, interest groups, and mass media – indicated the treaty would bring positive advantages to the country and promote peace without endangering national security. Coincident with this favorable tone, no tension-provoking events had occurred between the Soviet Union and the United States for almost a year.

There was a progressive increase in support for an agreement throughout the summer of 1963. In early July, after the President's American University speech but before the negotiations began in Moscow, 52 per cent of the public gave unqualified support to a test ban. After the treaty had been negotiated, signed, and overwhelmingly supported by opinion-makers, 81 per cent of the public took this position.[36] In addition between July and September, Americans changed their reasons for favoring the test ban. While the reduction of atmospheric fallout was the second choice offered for supporting a test ban among the advocates who gave unqualified support to an agreement in July, Table 6-2 shows that it was the most often mentioned reason in September, although, as a later chapter will indicate, most Senators did not consider this an important reason for approving the treaty. If Senators reacted to public opinion, they accepted the general mood of the public and not its rationale. Fallout was an issue presented by the President, many of the editorial writers and several of the interest groups

[35] Louis Harris reported that 12 per cent of the public supported a test ban in July, 1963, because it would control fallout; but after the President and much of the press advanced this theme, 21 per cent of the public offered this reason for supporting the test ban two months later in September, 1963. *Washington Post,* September 16, 1963, p. 1.

[36] These results agree with the findings of other surveys normally considered reliable. For example, the Minnesota Poll released on September 1, 1963 reported that 77 per cent felt the treaty would strengthen world peace and that 84 per cent felt the Senate should approve the test ban. Only 7 per cent favored Senate rejection.

which endorsed the treaty. Nine per cent of the population supported the treaty in the September period because it represented a step toward world peace, but none had given this reason in July. As this theme and fallout were reiterated in the mass media, many people accepted them as meaningful reasons for supporting the agreement.

Those who gave qualified approval to the treaty also shifted in their rationale, notably on the matter of inspection. While 40 per cent who offered qualified approval wanted an inspection provision in early July, only nine per cent offered this qualification in September. The treaty contained no inspection provisions for manned or mobile teams on Soviet territory, but most of the supporters contended the United States could detect and identify any important tests which the Soviets conducted in contravention to the terms of the treaty. Although some opponents disputed this claim, it was not considered to be important by many Americans. This shift, along with the movements of opinion to the fallout and world peace themes, indicate the public was better informed about the specifics of the debate than some critics of public opinion in the foreign policy process would allow.[37]

The American Institute of Public Opinion conducted a survey shortly after the treaty had been signed; and opinion reflected reaction to the event itself as well as to the initial, favorable responses of the administration and other opinion-makers.[38] Of those who had some knowledge of the treaty, 63 per cent favored the test ban while 17 per cent opposed it, and 20 per cent had no opinion. As material on the test ban accumulated, as support from the opinion-makers mounted, and as the Senate hearings generally gave the treaty a favorable interpretation, the results of the September survey indicate sharply increased support over the August figures which, in turn, were higher than the July survey.

In the AIPO survey, only three groups supported the treaty below the fifty per cent level: Southerners, people living on farms, and households with an income under $ 3000. Supporters of Barry Goldwater for the Republican nomination for the presidency opposed the treaty more than any of the formal groups. Of those who expressed a preference for the Arizona

[37] Cf. Walter Lippmann, *Public Opinion* (New York: Penguin, 1946, originally 1922).

[38] AIPO, August, 1963. The AIPO data are used in the following analysis. Although the Survey Research Center had included a few items on the test ban treaty in an economic survey it conducted, it did not include several demographic questions such as party affiliation. For the sake of consistency, the AIPO data are emphasized.

TABLE 6-2. *Reasons for Favoring or Opposing a Test Ban Treaty*

| | Percent | |
|---|---|---|
| | July | September |
| Unqualified Approval | 52 | 81 |
| Cut fallout | 12 | 21 |
| Must end tests | 18 | 18 |
| End risk of atomic war | 12 | 15 |
| Stop world suicide | 6 | 13 |
| Step to world peace | 0 | 9 |
| Halt cost of testing | 4 | 5 |
| Qualified approval | 29 | 11 |
| If Russia keeps word | 12 | 8 |
| Only with inspection | 12 | 2 |
| If on our terms | 5 | 1 |
| Opposed | 19 | 8 |
| Russia will break it | 17 | 4 |
| Hurts U.S. defense | 2 | 4 |

Source: Harris Survey: *Washington Post,* September 16, 1963, p. 1.

Senator as the next President, 52 per cent voiced the opposition to the treaty, and 21 per cent supported the treaty, the lowest percentage of any group favoring it. Although lower income and lower educational groups generally supported the Democratic party in elections, they gave the administration less support on the treaty issue; but this is consistent with their previous patterns of foreign policy opinion, which demonstrated deep-seated suspicion of the Soviet Union.

### *The Structure of Opinion on Nuclear Testing*

Although support for nuclear arms control was unevenly distributed in the United States, there were no deep fissures in American society on this issue. While there were significant differences among groups in the magnitude of their support for the test ban, each group nevertheless supported the treaty. Popular lore has held that women are more concerned about fallout and therefore more opposed to nuclear testing; the Northeast is less inclined to rely on military solutions than the South and therefore more ready to support test suspensions; and the college-educated stratum of society is less hostile to other nations and more likely to support national leaders in reaching an agreement with other states than those with a grade school education. While some of these "common sense" approaches characterized opinion on the test ban treaty, others did not. An analysis of demographic groups in American society not only identifies the structure of opinion, it also enables us to study those groups which are more volatile in their support of arms control. The structural analysis will be used to reexamine the tension model and identify those sectors of the population which were most apt to follow national cues.

### *Age*

Although previous research indicated there were not appreciable differences in foreign policy attitudes by age, younger people supported arms control proposals more often than older citizens in each of the surveys studied. In the post World War II period, Gabriel Almond found there was a "substantial homogeneity in foreign policy attitudes" by age.[39] But this finding did not apply to arms control issues during the Kennedy administration. The manner in which age groupings are identified is crucial. Eugene Rosi wrote that the three age groups, 20–39, 40–59, 60 and over, "generally took similar stands on suspension."[40] But when age groups are identified as 20–29, 30–49, and 50 and over, there is a marked step-by-step progression of support for arms control, inversely related to age. Younger people had opinions more often than their elders about test suspension indicating greater saliency on this issue for those under thirty. See Table 6-3. When intensity of support is indicated by those who supported the treaty without qualification in the survey conducted by the Survey Research Center (SRC),[41] those over 45 showed intense opposition twice as often as those under 35. But there was no marked difference of intensity in support of the treaty, with each group clustering around 39 per cent in support without qualifications for the treaty.

Having come into the political system as voters after the bitter acrimony of the Stalin era, younger people were not as deeply affected by the early cold war as their elders and may have been prepared to take more chances. The older generation, however, remembered the hostilities of the Stalin era and the Korean conflict, which possibly made many of them less apt to accept proposals for limiting American military capability.[42] Another reason ac-

[39] Almond, *op. cit.*, pp. 117–119.

[40] Rosi, *op. cit.*, p. 285.

[41] SRC asked its respondents whether they supported or opposed the treaty with or without qualifications. Unqualified responses are considered to be reflective of more intense opinions than qualified responses.

[42] Cf. T. A. Steele, *The American People and China* (New York: McGraw Hill,

counting for the difference between the two groups was the greater idealism, optimism, and interest in world affairs of younger people compared to their elders who had experienced more disappointments and frustrations both in their private lives and in their expectations as citizens and consequently saw many arms control proposals as unachievable ideals.

*Social Class and Income*

Although there were some significant differences between occupations and between income levels, the cessation of testing was not an economic issue for most Americans. Some observers have suggested that arms control would lead to substantial economic relocations in society, possibly providing an opportunity to divert funds from military expenditure to more socially productive activity with continued high employment. Others have warned that because the economy was so closely tied to defense expenditures, any change of magnitude in military outlays would adversely affect the entire economy.[43] However, only sixteen per cent of those interviewed by SRC thought the test ban treaty would have any effect on business; ten per cent of the respondents expected it would be beneficial; three per cent thought it would have an adverse effect, and another three per cent suggested it would have an unpredictable impact. A decrease in government expenditures was the economic effect offered least often by the American public. Most thought consumer and business spending would increase following the reduction of tensions. A majority of those who expected the treaty would produce adverse economic effects nevertheless approved of the test ban, further indicating that the test ban was not interpreted as an economic issue. The higher income and occupational status groups favored the suspension of tests more often than middle income groups who, in turn, took a favorable position more often than lower income or occupational status groups.

Whether the national average ran high or low for testing during the Kennedy administration, class differences never were more than nine per cent from the national average. Generally, the professional classes tended to favor test suspensions more often than other occupational groups. In the summer of 1961, 33 per cent of the professional and managerial groups expressed their support for a continuation of the moratorium while only 21

1966), who finds that younger people are more flexible on the China question than older people. Pp. 103–104.

[43] For example, see Emile Benoit, *Economic Impacts of Disarmament,* U.S. Arms Control and Disarmament Agency, Publication 2, January, 1962.

TABLE 6-3. *Position on Treaty and Knowledge About Treaty*

| Population | For* | Against* | No* Opinion | Had Heard | Had Not Heard | No Opinion or Knowledge* |
|---|---|---|---|---|---|---|
| Total | 63 | 17 | 20 | 77 | 23 | 21 |
| Age | | | | | | |
| 20–29 | 72 | 16 | 12 | 83 | 17 | 26 |
| 30–49 | 60 | 19 | 21 | 76 | 24 | 37 |
| Over 50 | 55 | 19 | 26 | 65 | 25 | 45 |
| Occupation | | | | | | |
| Business and Professional | 70 | 15 | 15 | 93 | 7 | 21 |
| White Collar | 67 | 16 | 17 | 81 | 19 | 33 |
| Farmers | 61 | 29 | 10 | 68 | 32 | 39 |
| Skilled Labor | 61 | 18 | 21 | 80 | 20 | 36 |
| Unskilled Labor | 58 | 24 | 8 | 63 | 26 | 48 |
| Non-labor Force | 51 | 21 | 28 | 74 | 26 | 47 |
| Income | | | | | | |
| $ 7000 & over | 65 | 18 | 17 | 89 | 11 | 26 |
| $ 5000–$ 6999 | 62 | 19 | 19 | 82 | 18 | 34 |
| $ 3000–$ 4999 | 64 | 15 | 21 | 73 | 27 | 42 |
| Under $ 3000 | 48 | 21 | 31 | 57 | 43 | 61 |
| Party | | | | | | |
| Democrats | 67 | 13 | 20 | 74 | 26 | 41 |
| Republicans | 58 | 24 | 18 | 80 | 20 | 35 |
| Independents | 61 | 18 | 21 | 79 | 21 | 38 |
| Education | | | | | | |
| College | 72 | 18 | 10 | 93 | 7 | 17 |
| High School | 62 | 17 | 21 | 83 | 17 | 34 |
| Grade School | 50 | 23 | 27 | 59 | 14 | 57 |
| Community Size | | | | | | |
| 500,000 & over | 65 | 20 | 15 | 79 | 21 | 33 |
| 50,000–499,999 | 62 | 17 | 21 | 79 | 21 | 38 |
| 2,500–49,999 | 57 | 18 | 25 | 82 | 18 | 39 |
| Under 2,500 non-farm | 62 | 17 | 21 | 67 | 33 | 47 |
| Farm | 44 | 22 | 34 | 71 | 29 | 51 |
| N. | 1667 | 503 | 560 | 2730 | 830 | 1390 |

* Of those who had heard about the treaty (N=2730).
** Of the total sample of 3560.

Source, AIPO, August, 1963.

per cent of the unskilled and semi-skilled endorsed such a policy. Another pattern was the continued higher opinion apathy of the farmers and the unskilled laborers who consistently registered the highest rates of "no opinion" in the surveys.

### *Political Party Affiliation*

Since the Korean War, there had been no sharp partisan conflict about the general goals and direction of American foreign policy, although party leaders have debated about the timing and implementation of policy. When public officials disagreed about how energetically arms control should be pursued, there was generally a leadership consensus about its merits. After Governor Nelson Rockefeller and former Vice-President Richard Nixon opposed the prospect of a test ban in November 1961, there was a decline in Republican support for the test moratorium which the Democratic President supported.[44] In early 1962, five per cent more Democrats wished to continue the suspension of atmospheric tests than opposed such a policy while nine per cent more Republicans favored immediate tests above ground than supported the President's policy, a difference of fourteen per cent between the two parties. The party leadership was in basic harmony about the treaty in 1963 and party members generally followed their cues with disproportionate Democratic opposition coming from Southerners opposed to President Kennedy and Republican opposition to the treaty disproportionately based among supporters of Barry Goldwater's nomination for the presidency.

### *Education*

Where a person completed his formal education is one of the more important and persistent characteristics in the structure of opinion but not for the reasons generally assumed. Educational differences are important because they are closely related to a person's life style. People with a college background are not only earning more money and working in relatively higher status occupations than those with less education, they are more interested in politics, are more active politically, and are more alert to political information, particularly foreign policy issues. In 1950, Almond found that there were greater differences between the college educated and the grade-school educated than between upper income groups and lower income groups. He suggested the college trained individuals were "the most

[44] See *New York Times*, November, 15, 1963, p. 3.

alert, informed, interested, and discriminating audience for foreign policy decisions," while the grade school strata tended "to be inert and apathetic, a group which is most readily manipulated by organized bureaucracies such as church and trade-union leaderships."[45]

The observation of Almond and others that the college-educated group is more optimistic and internationally minded than those who never went to high school[46] appears to be superficially confirmed when the treaty is considered. The college group had fewer reservations and were more hopeful about the effects of the test ban than those with less education. Moreover, in July 1961, only 15 per cent of the college group feared the danger of a nuclear war compared to 27 per cent of the grade school population.[47] However, the reaction by the college group to the test ban was not typical of its earlier behavior in 1961 or 1962. On the issue of testing during the Kennedy administration, those with higher education were most characterized by opinion instability. They were more apt to support atmospheric testing by the United States in 1961 and 1962 than the grammar school group which showed a slow but steady increase in support for a test ban during this period even though they never reached the high levels of endorsement for the treaty in 1963 which the college group demonstrated. (See Table 6-4.)

TABLE 6-4. *Regional Support for Test Cessation in 1962 and 1963 by Education*

| | Per Cent College Against Tests | | | | Per Cent Grade School Against Tests | | | |
|---|---|---|---|---|---|---|---|---|
| | East | Mid. | South | West | East | Mid. | South | West |
| 1963 | 82.4 | 70.4 | 69.3 | 62.9 | 57.4 | 53.7 | 34.8 | 52.5 |
| 1962 | 30.7 | 51.6 | 24.6 | 57.5 | 41.5 | 33.1 | 52.5 | 53.7 |
| Difference | 51.7 | 18.8 | 44.7 | 5.4 | 15.9 | 20.6 | −17.7 | − 1.2 |

Source, AIPO, January 1962 and August 1963.

The most plausible explanation for the fluctuation of the college educated is that the cues they followed also fluctuated from skepticism to support for the treaty. This group tended to be Republican, and the leaders of the minority party opposed the test suspension in 1962 but

45 Almond, *op. cit.*, p. 127.
46 *Ibid.*, pp. 126–131 and Cohen, *op. cit.*, pp. 45–48.
47 AIPO, July, 1961.

largely favored it in 1963. The college group also consumed more news from the national printed media which portrayed the treaty as a reasonably beneficial agreement in 1963 but often argued for the need for testing in 1962. Almond's observations that the groups with less education and income are alienated and are manipulated by churches and trade unions must be seriously questioned, as well as his observations that the better-educated and affluent are independent-minded. One of the critical differences between the two groups is their information and recommending sources. Every citizen depends on others to supply him with information and evaluations about complex issues, and the college educated groups were disproportionately dependent on the national media and more alert to shifts in the tone of the mass media. Fluctuation may be an index of discrimination in following leaders rather than in understanding the inherent dangers involved in atmospheric testing. The college-educated primarily relied on the mass media for information and as the tone of the media shifted, so did the opinions of the college-educated. What is also arguable about Almond's analysis is that the lower income groups and grade school respondents were more apt to be manipulated by their unions or churches. But there were no startling shifts of opinion back and forth by those occupational and educational groups where the churches and unions might be expected to be most influential.

During the late 1950's and early 1960's, the better educated were more familiar with fallout but less worried about the issue than those with less formal education. While fallout was widely discussed during the Eisenhower administration, it declined as a matter of concern and lost its intensity during the Kennedy administration. As interest in fallout decreased throughout the nation, it nevertheless continued to have a disproportionate impact on the lower educational groups, while the higher education strata appeared to have accepted the arguments of the mass media that fallout was not a current threat, even with increased testing.[48]

### *Geographic Distribution*

Since World War II, regionalism has played relatively little importance in explaining American Foreign policy opinion differences. Prior to the war, the South and Midwest generally held antithetical opinions, with the old Confederacy supporting internationalism and the American heartland

[48] Cf. Rosi, *op. cit.*, p. 291.

favoring an isolationist position.[49] Writing in the early 1950's, Almond found that there was more cleavage by community size than by regions.

Although Table 6-5 reveals there were no sharp sectional cleavages on arms control during the Kennedy administration, there were several striking differences on foreign policy attitudes between the South and the rest of the country. When asked whether there would be an eventual war with the Soviet Union, 70 per cent of the Southerners took a dark view while 56 per cent of the rest of the country expected war in a 1960 survey.[50] In the same year, only 26 per cent of the South thought the United States would avoid another world war in the next five years compared to 44 per cent of the East, 40 per cent of the Midwest, and 42 per cent of the West.[51] When an identical question was asked after President Kennedy had been President for only a year, there was a decided increase in optimism throughout the country, but more Southerners (46 per cent) persisted in believing that war was likely in the next five years than the rest of the nation (27 per cent).[52] In 1963 fewer Southerners believed the United States should continue diplomatic relations with the Soviet Union than those in other parts of the country, although the difference between the South and West was not significant (65 to 69 in the West).[53] Southerners also tended to regard their region as a safe place to live in the event of a nuclear attack. Only 31 per cent of the Southerners believed they might be a nuclear target in a war with the Soviet Union compared to 59 per cent outside of the South.[54]

In spite of the absence of prior sharp regional cleavage on arms control questions prior to the test ban, there was almost a sixteen per cent spread between the South and non-South in their response to the treaty. This diversity may be partially explained by the greater opposition to the agreement from Southern Senators and other public officials as well as from the local press than was the case in the other areas of the country. The difference in 1963 may also be partially explained by the transformation of the test ban question from a possible policy to a committed program. When the previous surveys were conducted, there was no national movement mobilized demanding either to test or continue the moratorium and therefore fewer cues for Southerners and Northerners to follow. The crucial

[49] Cf. H. Bradford Westerfield, *Foreign Policy and Party Politics: Pearl Harbor to Korea* (New Haven: Yale University Press, 1955.)

[50] AIPO, June 24, 1960.

[51] AIPO, July 14, 1960.

[52] AIPO, March 8, 1961.

[53] AIPO, December 10, 1963. Cf. Alfred O. Hero, Jr., *The Southerners and World Affairs* (Baton Rouge: Louisiana State University Press, 1965), *passim.*

[54] AIPO, September 13, 1961.

TABLE 6-5. *Public Opinion and Arms Control by Region*

Should the U.S. continue moratorium with the Soviet Union? November, 1959 *

| | Yes | No | No Opinion |
|---|---|---|---|
| East | 80 | 11 | 9 |
| Midwest | 80 | 12 | 8 |
| South | 70 | 9 | 21 |
| West | 80 | 7 | 13 |

Should the U.S. resume tests at this time? June, 1961

| | Yes | No | No Opinion |
|---|---|---|---|
| East | 53 | 30 | 17 |
| Midwest | 59 | 26 | 15 |
| South | 50 | 25 | 25 |
| West | 55 | 27 | 18 |

In the event of an all-out nuclear war, do you think you live in a target area? September, 1961

| | Live in Safe Area | Live in Unsafe Area | No Opinion |
|---|---|---|---|
| East | 32 | 60 | 8 |
| Midwest | 36 | 59 | 5 |
| South | 54 | 31 | 15 |
| West | 28 | 67 | 5 |

Since the Soviets are testing in the atmosphere, should the U.S. expand from underground to atmospheric tests? November, 1961

| | Yes | No | No Opinion |
|---|---|---|---|
| East | 48 | 38 | 14 |
| Midwest | 46 | 44 | 10 |
| South | 40 | 38 | 22 |
| West | 41 | 47 | 12 |

Since the Soviets are testing in the atmosphere, should the U.S. expand from underground to atmospheric tests? January, 1692

| | Yes | No | No Opinion |
|---|---|---|---|
| East | 50 | 39 | 11 |
| Midwest | 49 | 41 | 10 |
| South | 38 | 48 | 14 |
| West | 41 | 52 | 7 |

Should the Senate ratify the test ban treaty? August, 1963

| | Yes | No | No Opinion |
|---|---|---|---|
| East | 73 | 15 | 12 |
| Midwest | 63 | 16 | 21 |
| South | 48 | 21 | 31 |
| West | 61 | 21 | 18 |

* All questions are adapted from questions asked in AIPO surveys.

difference between responses to the test ban and all other survey items on arms control during the Kennedy administration is that the test ban was a national issue while the others were not and received less media and leadership attention. Citizens marshall a different set of considerations to evaluate concrete issues than when they are asked to respond to relatively noncontroversial policy-oriented questions. Converting proposals to specific issues calls a host of new factors into play, including an increased number of messages concerning the proposal and the consideration of the reliability of the sponsors of the issue.

One of the reasons offered by many public officials and newspapers who reluctantly supported the treaty was that the country had been committed. If the test ban were rejected by the Senate, the nation's prestige would suffer immeasurably, and the President would lose his bargaining power in the international arena. Southerners were less apt to accept this reason than the rest of the country. In the early 1960's the South was experiencing mounting racial tension which it attributed to "outsiders". As sit-ins, marches, and boycotts increased, hostility to "outsiders" also mounted; and when the President used federal power to support court decisions, he became less popular. The Southerners were less apt to trust national leadership on civil rights, and those Southerners who disagreed with the President's civil rights program tended to distrust him on other issues including foreign policy proposals.[55]

In a continental country it is not surprising to find significant regional variations in national partisan opinion. Rosi and other observers indicated that party is not an important variable in the issue of test suspensions.[56] However, Democrats disproportionately supported the treaty in every region of the country and Republicans contributed a disproportionate share of the opposition. The South was the only region where more Republicans opposed the treaty than supported it.

Democratic opinion was relatively stable in the West and South when

[55] The South generally received more right-wing interpretative news than any other region of the country. In 1963, 60 per cent of the 289 "Life Line" daily broadcasts were in the South. In 1961, 121 of the 371 stations carrying the John Birch radio program "America's Future" were in the South. Rev. Carl McIntyre's "Twentieth Century Reformation Hour" was heard over 448 stations in 1964 of which 201 or 45 per cent were in the South. Reese Cleghorn found that the South carried a disproportionate share of right-wing broadcasts compared to other regions except for the "Dan Smott Report" which had a larger base in the North and West. *Radicalism: Southern Style* (Atlanta: The Southern Regional Council, 1968), pp. 19–21. For other regional differences in the mass media, see Charles Higbie, "Book Reviewing and Civil Rights: The Effect of Regional Opinion," *Journalism Quarterly*, 41 (Summer, 1964), pp. 385–94.

[56] Rosi, *op. cit.*, p. 283 and Almond, *op. cit.*, pp. 131–135.

responses collected in early 1962 are compared with those gathered in the summer of 1963. Southern Republicans were the only group which showed diminished support for a test suspension with 52.0 per cent taking this position in January, 1962, but only 37.7 per cent endorsing the treaty a year and a half later. In 1962, there was no clear partisan pattern. For example, slightly more Midwestern Republicans supported the President's position than Democrats but significantly more Democrats in the West desired to end testing. However, when a leading Republican presidential contender in 1963 opposed the treaty, there was a noticeable partisan difference of support for the treaty in every area of the country, ranging from 14.3 per cent in the South to 9.6 per cent in the West. Nonetheless, in every area except the South, Republicans registered an appreciable gain, particularly in the East and Midwest.

In every region of the country there was marked decline of treaty support with advancing age, but this was most pronounced in the South even though 24 per cent of the Southerners under 30 rejected the agreement compared to a national average of 14 per cent opposition by those in their twenties. Table 6-7 indicates that the age differences in the South are not due to disproportionately heavy endorsement for the treaty by younger people but the exceedingly weak support by older Southern citizens. In each region, there was a progressive rate of disinterest in the treaty with increasing age, but this was most pronounced in the South where those over 50 said they had no opinion about the issue 30 per cent more often than older citizens in the Midwest and West.

TABLE 6-6. *Treaty Support and Age by Region*

| | North | Midwest | South | West |
|---|---|---|---|---|
| Age | | | | |
| 20–29 | 80.1 | 72.8 | 63.0 | 68.5 |
| 50 and over | 63.8 | 59.2 | 38.4 | 52.1 |
| Difference | 16.3 | 13.6 | 24.6 | 16.4 |

Source, AIPO, January 1962 and August 1963.

The national economic pattern of support for the treaty showed favorable responses progressively increasing with income levels, but this did not hold in every area of the country. In the East and West, heaviest support came from those earning between $ 3000 and $ 5000 per year, income groups overrepresented by Democrats; in the Midwest all income groups above the

$ 3000 level supported the treaty by about the same margin; and in the South, support was bimodal, with greatest approval registered by those over $ 7000 and those between $ 3000 and $ 5000 respectively. In three regions – the East, South, and West – those earning between $ 3000 and $ 5000 and those earning more than $ 7000 showed greater similarity with one another than with the intervening income bracket. This is partially explained by the higher incidence of younger people and Kennedy supporters in the $ 3000 to $ 5000 bracket and the higher representation of college educated respondents in the higher income bracket, both of which disproportionately supported the treaty.[57] Because the individual sample sizes are often extremely small when the total population is broken down for analysis four times – by position on the treaty, by region, by income, and then by age or education – such conclusions must be tentative. The highest income respondents showed little opposition to the treaty, except in the West where those earning over $ 7000 opposed the treaty more than any other income group (24.9 per cent). In the other three areas, those earning less than $ 3000 ranked first or second in the region's opposition to the test ban.

Educational groups followed the same general pattern of increasing support for the treaty with higher education in each region. However, there was considerable regional variation separating those with a college education from those who terminated their formal education in grade school as seen in Table 6-7. This difference was most pronounced in the South where only 34.8 per cent of those with a grade school background endorsed the treaty while 69.3 per cent of those with a college background thought the treaty was a good idea. This range of 35 points is twice as great as the difference

TABLE 6-7. *Position on Test Suspension and Test Ban Treaty by Education and Region*

| | Per Cent Against Tests, 1962 | | | | Per Cent of Groups for Treaty, 1963 | | | |
|---|---|---|---|---|---|---|---|---|
| | East | Mid. | South | West | East | Mid. | South | West |
| Grade | 41.5 | 33.1 | 52.2 | 53.7 | 57.4 | 53.7 | 34.8 | 52.5 |
| College | 30.7 | 51.6 | 24.6 | 57.5 | 82.4 | 70.4 | 69.3 | 62.9 |
| Difference | 10.8 | –18.5 | 27.9 | – 3.8 | 25.0 | 16.7 | 34.5 | 10.4 |

Source, AIPO, January 1962, and August 1963.

[57] While there was no appreciable difference by race in response to the treaty, most Negroes had incomes of less than $ 5000 and added to favorable responses in those income categories while whites were distributed in each income bracket.

between those with the least education and those with the most education in the rest of the country.

In the West, however, there was relative stability in support for testing between 1962 and 1963, and this suggests there were previously developed evaluations about the importance of tests and test suspension. The variation in the South by the grade school group can partially be explained by their negative evaluation of national mass media which gave sympathetic treatment to the demands of Southern Negroes and their dislike of the President, whose image had been tarnished for Southern whites because of his civil rights activity.

There was no clear pattern of support or opposition by the size of the community. Although larger communities thought there was a greater danger of nuclear attack in their areas than in smaller communities, the difference was not nationally appreciable among the various sized communities on the test ban question in 1963.[58] The most persistent difference by community size was the high rate of disinterest in testing by people in smaller communities. Although Almond saw community size as a more important variable than region, in the case of the test ban, community differences were not the critical distinguishing variables. Community size, like some other variables, did not indicate a step-by-step progression with support increasing with the size of the community. In the South, communities with less than 2500 residents supported the treaty less often than members in any other community: in the West, communities between 2500 and 50,000 people fell into this category; in the North it was the cities between 50,000 and 500,000; while in the Midwest, least support came from areas with more than 500,000 people. (In every case, the differences are statistically significant.)

### *Sex*

Opponents of the test ban accused the administration and its allies of pandering to the fears of women, particularly mothers, in order to generate support for the treaty. The active participation of the Women's Strike for Peace and several other exclusively feminine organizations lent credence to the belief that the issue of nuclear testing had a special appeal to women. Public opinion surveys before and during the Kennedy administration consistently showed that women favored the suspension of nuclear testing more often than men, with a 1962 survey typically reporting a significant 15 per cent more women supported suspension than men. In June, 1961,

[58] Cf. AIPO, December 2, 1950, August 16, 1963, and April 25, 1954.

nine per cent more men than women wanted the United States to resume atmospheric testing, and by November a significant cleavage had developed between the sexes, with 51 per cent of the men and only 32 per cent of the women supporting that position.[59] This trend continued into 1962 when 53 per cent of the men and 38 per cent of the women wanted the administration to shift from underground to atmospheric tests while 50 per cent of the women and 37 per cent of the men opposed this position.[60] Their greater support for arms control was probably related to the greater concern of women over the possibility of nuclear war and the high danger levels of fallout. In July, 1961, almost twice as many women feared that war was likely as men did (27 per cent to 15 per cent.)[61] At the end of 1961, 24 per cent of the women expressed fear that fallout was at dangerous levels while 17 per cent of the men took this position.[62] The values of women, particularly mothers, and their life style were thought to be sufficiently different from men to explain these differences.

However, the earlier trend was reversed for the test ban in 1963 when 68 per cent of the males supported the agreement compared to only 54 per cent of the women. Before examining the reasons for this shift in opinion, one possible explanation for the reversal can be dismissed; there was no gross sampling error. The survey conducted by the American Institute of Public Opinion generally agreed with the results of the Survey Research Center of the University of Michigan on this item. It showed 55.9 per cent of its male sample favored the treaty while 40.2 per cent of the women endorsed it.

Treaty reaction by men and women was not related to either age or income. Support for the test ban increased with incomes among women, but men earning between $ 3000–$ 5000 as well as those over $ 7000 a year favored the treaty more than the other income categories. There was less of a cleavage between the sexes in the $ 5000 to $ 7000 range, where there was a dip in support from men and where most of the female opposition came. One of the factors which accounts for differences in support for the treaty by age groups was the disproportionately higher rate of support by men under 50 for the treaty. Men under thirty favored the treaty 82 per cent of the time and men between thirty and fifty endorsed it 71 per cent of the time compared to only 62 per cent of the women under thirty who favored the treaty.

59 AIPO, June, 1961 and November, 1961.
60 AIPO, January, 1962.
61 AIPO, July, 1961.
62 AIPO, December, 1961.

Educational and regional reactions are also related to the sex of the respondent. In every region but the West, men supported the treaty appreciably more often than women; while in the West, the two sexes registered approximately the same levels of support. Men with a grade school or high school background disproportionately supported the treaty over women in these categories; but both men and women with a college background registered approximately the same support, with less than one percentage point separating them. Almost all of the educational differences between high school and college respondents can be accounted for by the low rate of support by high school women. High school males (71.7 per cent) and college males (71.8 per cent) equally supported the treaty, indicating that appropriate distinguishing level of education for men was the eighth grade while the important breaking point for women was college.

A comparison between family size and support for the treaty reveals no clear pattern, discounting the argument that mothers were more affected by fallout arguments than women who had no children. In a survey conducted early in 1962, there was no appreciable difference by family size for support for nuclear testing, except those without any children were twice as often disposed to oppose atmospheric testing than families with children living at home. Table 6-8 indicates that respondents with no children and those with four or more children supported the treaty more often than middle-sized families when women were answering the questions but the reverse occurred when men answered the question. The differences are so great that the rationale that women were especially attracted to this issue because they had special interests as mothers in reducing fallout or lessening tensions must be rejected.

The analysis about group differences has been based on the responses of those who said they were familiar with the treaty in both the AIPO and SRC surveys and not every person interviewed. The change in the opinion pattern of women can partially be explained by the information question in 1963 but the absence of such a question in the earlier surveys. In the questions asked before 1963, the items customarily carried sufficient information to alert the respondent to the general outlines of the situation. In 1963, a disproportionate percentage of women were excluded from the sample because they were not familiar with the topic. Those who qualified less often than other women, namely Democrats and non-voters, had previously shown greater support for a test suspension than many of the groups who passed the information question. When the entire population is used, and not just those who answered the information question, both men and women opposed the treaty 14 per cent of the time, while men approved it

55 per cent and women 39 per cent of the time. The crucial difference between the sexes was in their interest in the treaty.[63]

TABLE 6-8. *Support for the Treaty by Family Size and Sex*

| Sex | No Children | | One Child | | 2-3 Children | | 4 Children | |
|---|---|---|---|---|---|---|---|---|
| | – Family Size – | | | | | | | |
| Male | 62.7% | (607) | 71.4% | (200) | 71.5% | (424) | 69.0% | (141) |
| Female | 55.4 | (577) | 44.7 | (180) | 53.7 | (397) | 68.3 | (186) |
| Difference | 7.3 | | 26.7 | | 17.8 | | 1.2 | |

AIPO, August, 1963. The SRC survey for the Summer 1963 has the figures reversed, showing more support by those with one or two children but less from those with three or more children or none. Nevertheless, the figures still reveal there is no clear pattern because of family size. The SRC data indicate that larger families tended to be somewhat more intense in their support of the treaty than smaller family respondents.

### *Interest and Apathy*

Considering the attention received by public officials and the mass media, it is reasonable to expect a substantial portion of the public would have been aware of the treaty and interested in it. It is difficult to arrive at an acceptable standard of what a satisfactory level of knowledge should be for this type of issue in a democratic society, and the fact that 77 per cent of the population had some acquaintance with the treaty indicates a high level of awareness by the public when compared to several other issues.[64] However, two troublesome features cloud this picture of awareness. Of those who had been exposed to the treaty in some fashion, twenty per cent had no opinion on the agreement, in spite of the publicity given it. The combined total of those who had not heard of the treaty and those who had no opinion is 40 per cent of the adult population.

The second problem is indicated in Table 6-3 which shows a considerable range of information and interest about the treaty. In some instances, the pattern is predictable because those with little education and income generally have had high levels of disinterest and low confidence levels in the efficacy of the political system. However, some of the groups which had

[63] The SRC survey indicated 13.6 per cent of the men and 12.5 per cent of the women opposed the treaty while 21.5 per cent of the men and 47.3 per cent of the women either had no opinion or had not heard about the treaty.

[64] Cf. Robert E. Lane and David Sears, *Public Opinion* (Englewood Cliffs, N. J.: Prentice Hall, 1964), p. 59.

previously shown considerable political interest were overrepresented by their lack of concern with the test ban. Women were unusually apathetic. Part of the behavior of older persons and Southerners can be explained not only by their disinterest and low efficacy but also by the presence of too many conflicting cues. Many of these people may have been suspicious of President Kennedy because of other policy stands he had taken, but were impressed with the importance of the treaty because of the tone conveyed in the mass media. While they could not bring themselves to support the agreement because of their distrust of the President, they did not feel they wished to attack the treaty either. The resolution of their dilemma took the form of not making any decision. The high rates of apathy in women may be explained by another, but related, phenomenon. Even as many Southerners and older people may have had mixed feelings about the President because of civil rights, many women who supported the administration were also preoccupied with this issue. There may be a maximum input level for the consumption of political information for different individuals; and to the extent some citizens are preoccupied with a particular issue, they may ignore other issues. While the test ban was being debated, Martin Luther King was planning his March on Washington; and this story received considerable attention in the national media. Many women, with limited interest in politics, may have devoted much of the time and attention they gave to news about public affairs to civil rights which seemed more salient to them.

In some instances, levels of awareness were overrepresented by supporters of the treaty, such as the college educated; while in other categories, supporters were underrepresented, such as Democrats. No clear pattern emerged which indicated that if those without information or opinions had offered opinions, the results would have changed substantially. Considering there was very little movement to the anti-treaty side of the continuum from the fluid population regardless of education, income, region, or occupation, it is not appropriate to assume that the opponents would have substantially increased with greater inclusion by the individuals who did not have an interest in the issue.

What separated groups in the structure of foreign policy opinion was not primarily their reaction to the treaty but their level of interest in the issue. As striking as the 17 per cent difference in opinion was between those under 30 supporting the treaty and those over 50 taking the same position, it is duplicated by the greater disinterest of older respondents. The 22 per cent difference in support for the test ban between college and grade school educated citizens is magnified to a 40 per cent difference in their levels of awareness. Because several groups which show high levels of apathy are declining as a percentage of the total population, it appears that political awareness of foreign policy problems may increase as fewer Americans live on farms, earn less than $3000, terminate their education in grade school, and remain outside of the labor force. The decline of many of these groups should also give the South a higher level of interest. However, to the extent that many Americans become preoccupied with domestic issues, several foreign policy questions, including arms control, will probably look marginal to those who find their lives are more intimately affected by the course of domestic policy. For all of the attention by public officials, the mass media, and interest groups, opinion apathy will probably decline for several groups only to the extent that other issues are not competing with the foreign policy issues and that issue is made salient to them.

CHAPTER VII

# THE SENATE: PRELIMINARY CONSIDERATIONS

The Senate considered arms control and disarmament on several occasions during the Kennedy administration. In 1961, it passed the bill to establish the Arms Control and Disarmament Agency by an impressive vote of 73 to 14. However, many members had been skeptical about the possibility or desirability of achieving arms control. For example, 33 members voted for a motion by Senator Everett M. Dirksen to refer the bill creating ACDA to the Committee on Armed Services, a move designed to weaken and probably kill the Agency. Doubts about disarmament were more forcibly expressed at that time when an amendment offered by Senator Barry Goldwater to limit the authority of the Agency was narrowly defeated by a vote of 43 to 46.[1] Authorization bills for ACDA always drew substantially more opposition than money bills for the Department of Defense.

Among several resolutions pertaining to arms control and disarmament introduced in 1963, one, co-sponsored by twenty Senators on February 20, urged "complete, on-the-spot" inspection of the Soviet Union and any other areas covered by the terms of the agreement, with members of Congress to serve on inspection teams. Designed to weaken the prospects for an arms control agreement, the resolution reflected the suspicions of many Senators who feared the administration would not diligently pursue inspection provisions with the Soviet Union.[2] In late May 1963, 32 Senators co-sponsored a resolution with Thomas Dodd and Hubert Humphrey which called for another attempt to seek a limited test ban with the Soviet Union.[3]

The Committees on Foreign Relations and Armed Services as well as the

1 *Congressional Record,* June 17, 1963, pp. 10958–10964. For a discussion of treaties and executive agreements, see Elmer Plischke, *Conduct of American Diplomacy* (2nd ed.; Princeton: D. Van Nostrand, 1961), pp. 370–442.

2 Senate Concurrent Resolution 21, February 20, 1963.

3 Senate Concurrent Resolution 148, May 27, 1963.

Joint Committee on Atomic Energy conducted seven sets of hearings or briefings between 1961 and 1963 on a limited test ban treaty. As it investigated the activities and proposals of the Arms Control and Disarmament Agency, each committee manifested its perspectives and experiences. Senator Humphrey's Disarmament Subcommittee of the Committee on Foreign Relations emphasized the diplomatic aspects of arms control, and he insisted that he would:

> not be satisfied unless we work for disarmament in fair weather and foul, unless we understand that disarmament is all the more urgent when the world teeters on the precipice of disaster. It is with the constituents of disarmament firmly in mind that we are conducting the present hearings.[4]

The chairman of the Preparedness Investigating Subcommittee of the Committee on Armed Services, John Stennis, insisted his subcommittee had:

> a direct and legitimate interest in any and all activities which affect or may affect the development and procurement of weapons and the size and quality of our fighting forces.[5]

He believed that proposals concerned with the limitation, control, reduction, or elimination of armed forces or armaments involved vital matters of national security and that they "should be subjected to scrutiny from a military point of view as well as from the standpoint of foreign policy."[6]

The Joint Committee on Atomic Energy was concerned about the technological effects of a test ban on nuclear development. Like the two subcommittees, it relied on its own information sources. The Joint Committee generally depended on the Atomic Energy Commission, Senator Humphrey's subcommittee on the Department of State and the Arms Control and Disarmament Agency and Senator Stennis's subcommittee on the military services,[7] Senator Joseph Clark, a strong advocate of arms control, found that there was little interest in the subject in the Senate, with six members occasionally attacking administration proposals, and five Senators

[4] Senate, Subcommittee of the Committee on Foreign Relations, *Hearings, Review of Operations of the Arms Control and Disarmament Agency*, 87th Cong., 2nd Sess., 1962, p. 3.

[5] Senate, Preparedness Investigating Subcommittee of the Committee on Armed Services, *Hearings, Arms Control and Disarmament*, 87th Cong., 2nd Sess., 1962, p. 1.

[6] *Ibid.*

[7] Harold Karen Jackobson and Eric Stein, *Diplomats, Scientists and Politicians: The United States and the Nuclear Test Ban Negotiations* (Ann Arbor: University of Michigan Press, 1966), p. 475.

supporting arms control proposals from time to time. He concluded that:

> members of both houses of Congress are so preoccupied with other matters which seem to them of more immediate importance that they have thought little, and presently care less, about the subject.[8]

Senator Clark's prognostication in evaluating the prospects of the test ban treaty was unnecessarily pessimistic. Much of his analysis concerned an agreement which was comprehensive, rather than limited, and which restricted and reduced the size of America's conventional and nuclear capability.

### *Initial Senatorial Reaction*

When the treaty was initialed in Moscow on July 25, several Senators immediately endorsed it, others called for a cautious, sober investigation, but there was little outright opposition. Senator Humphrey welcomed it as "the first significant breakthrough in the field of arms control since World War II."[9] Senate Majority Leader, Mike Mansfield thought it might serve as a brake on defense spending and appealed for Republican support.[10]

Senator Stephen Young, a junior member of the Committee on Armed Services, said the treaty was "designed to take some of the destructive sting out of the nuclear age," and that it was a "positive step toward limiting the spread of nuclear weapons, easing world tensions, and relieving anxiety of all Americans over nuclear fallout."[11]

Several Senators who were skeptical about arms control believed that little political benefit could be derived from opposing the treaty. Most expected the administration would not submit a treaty which could not elicit at least token endorsement from the Joint Chiefs of Staff.[12] If they and others in the Pentagon found the treaty compatible with national security requirements, opposition to the treaty would be politically difficult. The Republican leadership was accordingly circumspect. Senator Dirksen spoke of possible "gimmicks" and expressed doubt that the benefits of the treaty would outweigh the costs to national security. Among the problems

[8] Joseph Clark, "Congress and Disarmament," *Bulletin of the Atomic Scientists,* 19 (September, 1963), pp. 5–6.

[9] *Congressional Record,* July 25, 1963, p. 13396.

[10] *Washington Post,* July 28, 1963, p. A10.

[11] *Congressional Record,* July 30, 1963, p. 13667.

[12] Senator Dirksen, for example, said he believed the administration was "fully prepared through necessary witnesses to fortify the argument that our security, instead of being impaired, will be enhanced by the provisions of the treaty." *New York Herald Tribune,* August 10, 1963, p. 1.

he discovered were possible "backdoor recognition" of East Germany because the treaty was open to all nations for signature and possible "underground development of nuclear warheads by Cuba."[13] Many Senators feared that the administration might reach several agreements with the Soviet Union on a variety of fronts and ignore the Senate in the process. President Kennedy had characterized the treaty as a first step, and Senator Dirksen asked, ". . . if this is a first step, when does the second shoe drop? Khrushchev already speaks of a non-aggression pact and other matters. The treaty therefore must be examined against the opaque curtain of the future."[14]

The Senate-House Republican leadership released a statement in early August which was to serve as a guide for much of the treaty debate during the following month and a half. The leadership asked:

> Which will do most to preserve peace in the world:
> Ratification of a limited treaty placing selective restraints on development of nuclear weapons, or,
> A maximum up-to-the minute defense capability so destructive as to prohibit attack?
> This is the issue.[15]

By calling for military, scientific, and diplomatic experts to appear before "the appropriate committees" for a full evaluation of the effects of the test ban treaty, the Republican leaders indicated the treaty should not fall under the exclusive jurisdiction of the Committee on Foreign Relations.[16]

Sharing this prognosis, ranking members of the Committee on Armed Services said military considerations were the primary basis on which they would judge the treaty. If it did not jeopardize American national security, they would be more likely to vote for the treaty; but if the American military capacity were adversely affected, they would oppose it. From this perspective diplomatic and health considerations were secondary or immaterial. For example, Senator Richard Russell, chairman of the Committee on Armed Services, refused to commit himself in advance, although he said that he hoped to vote for the treaty and would if the Joint Chiefs of Staff and other specialists agreed the treaty would not adversely affect American defenses.[17]

13 *New York Herald Tribune,* July 31, 1963, p. 1.

14 "Press Release," July 28, 1963.

15 Joint Senate House Republican Leadership Statement. "Press Release", August 2, 1963.

16 *Ibid.*

17 "Meet the Press," National Broadcasting Company, August 11, 1963.

To a considerable extent, the character of the debate was determined by the underlying assumptions of some of the ranking members of the Senate who were skeptical of the President's diplomatic rationale of the treaty. If the supporters refused to consider the military aspects of the treaty, they faced the danger that some of the skeptics would not find its political or health ramifications sufficiently important to support the treaty. Consequently, the administration and most of its Senate allies shifted emphasis from political to military considerations in order to dispel some of the gnawing doubts of the skeptics.

### *Executive-Legislative Relations*

Through hearings, briefings, personal visits, written correspondence, telephone calls, and breakfast meetings, members of the executive branch attempted to inform concerned Senators of the objectives, content, and status of the proposed treaty.[18] In the year preceding the Moscow negotiations, Secretary of State Dean Rusk, Director William Foster, and Arthur Dean, United States Representative to the Geneva Disarmament Conference, appeared before various Senate committees to discuss the draft treaty and its progress. In addition, representatives of the Department of Defense, the Atomic Energy Commission, and other executive agencies appeared before the committees. A month before the United States and Great Britain presented their limited test ban proposal to the Geneva Eighteen Nation Disarmament Conference in 1962, Foster appeared before the Joint Committee on Atomic Energy and two days later told the Disarmament Subcommittee of the Committee on Foreign Relations:

> The purpose of this meeting with you, Mr. Chairman, is to put before you before the decision has been made some of the alternatives which are being considered for recommendation to the President for his decision. And that decision has not yet been taken.[19]

Accelerating its communications with the Senate in the closing days of the Moscow negotiations, the administration sent Rusk to meet with the Committee on Foreign Relations on July 23, 1963, two days before the treaty was initialed. At that time, he presented the text of the draft of the treaty and invited suggestions and comments from the Senators present.

[18] See *Congressional Record,* September 20, 1963, p. 16745.

[19] Senate Subcommittee of the Committee on Foreign Relations, *Hearings, Renewed Geneva Disarmament Negotiations,* 87th Cong., 2nd Sess., 1962, pp. 2–3.

One change was generated from this meeting: the instruments of ratification by the other countries adhering to the treaty could be deposited in all of the capitals of the three original parties of the treaty. Some Senators feared that implicit recognition might be extended to East Germany if its instrument of ratification were deposited in Washington. Consequently, under the terms of the senatorial suggestion, East Germany signed the treaty only in Moscow.[20]

The next day the Secretary of State briefed the Committee on Armed Services for two hours in the morning and devoted another two hours in the afternoon to the Joint Committee on Atomic Energy. Rusk continued his appearances in a closed door meeting before the House Committee on Foreign Affairs on July 29, while W. Averell Harriman briefed the Senate Committee on Foreign Relations the same morning.[21] On August 5, three Senate committees met with Harriman and Adrian Fisher, Deputy Director of ACDA.[22]

Harriman's remarks rankled several members who thought he was arrogant and intolerant of their questions. To those Senators who had difficulty understanding some features of the treaty, the Ambassador "showed great impatience" and "lectured them." He was not doing an effective job in convincing Senators they should support the treaty, and the administration did not send him to the open hearings.[23]

The administration believed the series of meetings of July 23 and 24 and of August 5 represented important advance consultation with the Senate on the treaty.[24] The meetings between the executive and the legislative branches, particularly in the days immediately preceding and following the initialing of the treaty in Moscow, provided each party with important information. The administration was apprised of senatorial sentiment and was able to incorporate at least one suggestion made by a Senator into the final draft of the treaty. Although it did not receive commitments from Senate leaders in support of the treaty, the administration partially involved several Senators by sharing information with them.

The lack of prior agreement between the President and leaders of the

[20] Senator Humphrey, in *Congressional Record,* September 13, 1963, p. 16127. Senator Aiken saw Dean Rusk's appearance as especially important because the Secretary of State "kept his promise to go over the draft before it would be initialed." *New York Times,* July 24, 1963, p. 1.

[21] *New York Times,* July 25, 1963, p. 1, and July 30, 1963, p. 2.

[22] *Ibid.,* August 6, 1963, p. 1.

[23] Interview, April, 1963. Several members in the State Department were reported to have been disturbed over Harriman's publicity which they believed was undeserved.

[24] *Congressional Record,* September 20, 1963, p. 16745.

minority party was most apparent when the administration attempted unsuccessfully to include Everett Dirksen and Bourke Hickenlooper, ranking Republican member of the Committee on Foreign Relations, in the American delegation to Moscow for the formal signing of the test ban treaty. Desiring to maintain their independence, both Senators refused to attend. However, the administration was able to persuade the second ranking Republican member of the Committee on Foreign Relations, George Aiken, and the ranking Republican member of the Committee on Armed Services, Leverett Saltonstall, to accompany the American delegation. They were joined by four Democrats, including the Chairman and two ranking majority members of the Committee on Foreign Relations, J. William Fulbright, Hubert Humphrey, and John Sparkman, and the Chairman of the Joint Committee on Atomic Energy, John Pastore.[25] No Democrats from the Committee on Armed Services attended. The senior members of the Committee had not yet declared a position, and in September the three ranking Democrats of the Committee voted against the treaty. The only Democratic members of the Committee who supported the test ban in early August were the two Senators with the least seniority on the Committee.[26]

The most publicized and important meeting between the President and members of the Senate occurred midway during the Senate debate. Senators Mansfield and Dirksen met the President to discuss the security aspects of the treaty. At Dirksen's suggestion, Kennedy sent letters to the majority and minority leaders assuring them of his determination to maintain and increase American nuclear strength.[27]

In another attempt to allay the concern of skeptics in the Senate, Roswell Gilpatrick, Assistant Secretary of Defense, wrote Senator Richard Russell that the United States would conduct a sharply expanded underground nuclear testing program.[28] Indeed, a week before the letter was sent, on the opening day of the hearings before the Committee on Foreign Relations, the Atomic Energy Commission announced that a low yield underground nuclear test had been conducted in Nevada.[29] This was the first nuclear test the United States conducted since the negotiation of the treaty; and whatever the scientific rationale for the test, the political message was clear,

[25] Also accompanying Secretary Rusk who signed the treaty on behalf of the United States were Arthur Dean, Dr. Glen Seaborg, William Foster, and Llewellyn Thompson.

[26] Senator Clair Engle also supported the treaty but was hospitalized at the time. The California Democrat ranked eighth in seniority among the Democrats on the Committee.

[27] *Congressional Record*, September 11, 1963, p. 15915.

[28] *New York Times*, August 25, 1963, p. 15.

[29] *Ibid.*, August 13, 1963, p. 1.

namely, that the administration would continue a vigorous underground testing program. It also lessened the apprehension of some that the President might engage in a unilateral moratorium in United States underground testing, pending further negotiations with the Soviet Union.[30] The President and his advisers accomodated themselves and their justification of the treaty to the diverse frames of reference and values exhibited by many Senators.

### *The Committee on Foreign Relations*

Ralph Huitt found that members of Congressional committees were not impartial arbiters, sitting as disinterested judges before witnesses. Rather than being removed from the struggle, the members were active participants in it. Huitt argued that the participants, both Senators and witnesses, were composed of "two loose groups of people who disagreed, not so much in their opinions upon what should be done about a known or ascertainable fact situation, as upon what the underlying facts themselves were."[31] The participants on both sides believed they were in possession of the facts, but their understanding of which data were relevant often differed radically in the hearings and debate on the treaty. This diversity was accentuated in the hearings conducted by the Committee on Foreign Relations. Members of the Committee on Armed Services and the Joint Committee on Atomic Energy as well as other interested Senators had been invited to participate in the proceedings. Their focus of attention often reflected their committee assignments.

In an earlier study of the Senate Foreign Relations Committee, David Farnsworth reported the major purpose of hearings was to reinforce and promote committee goals. He observed that the committee was not an unbiased arbiter of disputes between conflicting interests, but rather promoted its own interest.[32] This situation can occur only when there is general agreement among the leaders of the committee on the position they desire to take. While there was no avowed opposition from the committee members during the preparation of the hearings, a number of members, particularly Bourke Hickenlooper, ranking Republican on the committee, were skeptical of the treaty. Sharp partisan division within the committee would lessen the influence of the committee's majority on the floor of the Senate. In-

[30] Interviews, Washington, D.C., March and April, 1963.

[31] Ralph Huitt, "The Congressional Committee: A Case Study," *American Political Science Review*, XLVIII (1954), p. 363.

[32] David Farnsworth, *The Senate Committee on Foreign Relations* (Urbana: University of Illinois Press, 1961), p. 165.

tolerant tactics by the Democratic leaders would antagonize many Senators, and because a two-thirds vote was required, such dissatisfaction by important members of the committee could result in defeat for the treaty.

Senators Fulbright and Hickenlooper discussed the witnesses who were to be invited before the committee, and after the list was circulated to some other members of the committee, Dr. Robert Strausz-Hupe, Director of the Foreign Policy Research Institute of the University of Pennsylvania, was the only name added to the original roster.[33] Most of the witnesses who testified supported the treaty. Of the eleven government witnesses who appeared, none opposed the treaty, although two, General Curtis LeMay and Dr. John Foster, expressed considerable skepticism. Of the twelve non-governmental specialists, that is, nuclear scientists, science administrators, and political scientists, only three, Dr. Edward Teller, Lewis Strauss, the former Chairman of the Atomic Energy Commission, and Dr. Robert Strausz-Hupe, opposed the treaty. The same preponderance of supporters over opponents of the treaty was duplicated for those witnesses representing private organizations. Only three of the fourteen groups which appeared before the committee opposed the treaty, and each of them were of minor political importance.

Of the six witnesses who had held responsible positions in the Eisenhower administration, five supported the treaty.[34] Their appearances reinforced the contention of treaty supporters that the test ban was a logical outgrowth of the policies of President Dwight Eisenhower. However, Eisenhower's personal reaction was cautious. His written endorsement included the reservation that the United States should be "the sole judge of the kind and type of weaponry and equipment it would employ as well as the timing of their use," when American vital interests were threatened by armed aggression.[35]

He did not believe it was completely accurate to characterize the test ban

[33] Interview, Washington, D.C., April 1964. Senator Frank Lausche, eighth ranking Democrat on the Foreign Relations Committee, proposed on the floor of the Senate that the committee invite ten additional witnesses to appear. On the basis of their previous statements, these individuals generally were opposed to or were skeptical of arms control proposals as presented by the administration. Only Dr. Teller was invited, although Senator Humphrey, Majority Whip and third ranking Democrat on the Committee, promised that full consideration would be given to Senator Lausche's list. *Congressional Record,* July 31, 1963, p. 13758.

[34] George Kistiakowsky, Special Assistant to the President on Science and Technology, Willard Libby of the Atomic Energy Commission, Herbert York, Director of Defense Research and Engineering, Francis O. Wilcox, Assistant Secretary of State for International Affairs, and Harold Stassen, Special Assistant for Disarmament, supported the treaty. Lewis Strauss opposed it.

[35] Committee on Foreign Relations, *Hearings, op. cit.,* p. 846.

treaty negotiated in 1963 as a logical conclusion to his own policies in the 1950's. At the time the United States announced the suspension of tests, it was "equal to the Soviets in all branches of nuclear science and superior in most." However, the situation had changed, and the Soviet Union had conducted tests of much higher yield than the American series of atmospheric tests. The former President then observed that American "military authorities had never announced any military requirement for these specific tests." After that terse comment, he endorsed the treaty.[36]

Dr. Teller excited the unbounded good will of opponents and many of the skeptics of the treaty and thinly disguised malevolence of treaty supporters. In his six hours of testimony, he combined rhetorical skill, stricken moral outrage, and an impressive command of scientific, technological, and military data to give an "absolutely dazzling performance."[37] While treaty supporters suspected his motives and occasionally believed he was reactionary, treaty skeptics and opponents found him to be the incarnation of sobriety, reason, expertise, and political disinterest. Senator Wallace Bennett, who voted against the treaty, found Dr. Teller's credentials overwhelming. After the testimony of the Secretaries of State and Defense, the Joint Chiefs of Staff, and the Chairman of the Atomic Energy Commission, Bennett could say of Teller:

> (H)ere for the first time we hear a witness who has both the technical and scientific background to evaluate the dangers and suggest an alternative and the courage and freedom to give us this information, and I think, Dr. Teller, your contribution to this hearing is probably more important than any we have heard to date and I congratulate you on it.[38]

Teller was valued by the skeptics and opponents because of his previous work in the development of nuclear power. Supporters of the treaty emphasized other aspects of his background. Senator Fulbright observed:

> He was born in Hungary; I don't hold that against him. He has a great attachment to his home country; I don't hold that against him. He has had a very noted career in his well publicized attack upon Dr. Oppenheimer. This is not my affair, either. But I think all of these matters go into an evaluation of how sound his judgment it [sic].[39]

Fulbright implied that Teller was prejudiced and also a bit irrational.

[36] *Ibid.*, p. 848.
[37] Interview, Washington, D.C., April, 1964.
[38] Committee on Foreign Relations, *op. cit.*, p. 443.
[39] *Ibid.*, p. 772.

He claimed Teller believed that the hydrogen bomb was not "a weapon of devastation but a means of liberation, freedom, and justice."[40] Supporters of the treaty relied on the preponderance of scientists to question the reliability of Teller.[41]

Senator Hickenlooper, as others who tended to favor the treaty but who also had some doubts to overcome, insisted that scientific testimony was highly relevant, but that the scientist lost his credentials as an expert when he entered the political field.[42] He explained that he would cast his vote on the basis of:

> the composite testimony that comes in from men and women whose judgment I respect and whose particular knowledge and expertness I believe justify consideration of their testimony.[43]

Most Senators not only had an understanding of what areas were most germane in evaluating the treaty, but also believed they knew what sources of information were most helpful in supplying the necessary data and recommendations in their evaluation. To a considerable extent, these sources of information reinforced already established views on what was important and unimportant in the final consideration of the treaty. The topic of radioactive fallout was a subject which demonstrated the diverse ways in which Senators perceived and evaluated one particular issue. Skeptics and opponents generally found that fallout was not germane to treaty consideration. Senator Richard Russell characterized it as "captious and not genuine" and regarded it as an issue which was "cynically and irreverently" manipulated to influence "the mother vote."[44] Senator Hickenlooper attempted to dispose of fallout arguing that there had always been "abnormalities in birth, even before anybody heard of an atomic bomb." He believed an overdose of anything is harmful, but in moderation it could be helpful. Applying this to fish life he observed "a little stepped up radiation has actually increased the health of the recipient."[45] This was in sharp con-

[40] *Ibid.*, p. 766.

[41] Senator Fulbright asked Dr. Herbert York, who had served under President Eisenhower as Director of Defense Research and Engineering, whether "competent nuclear scientists" supported the views of Dr. Teller. Dr. York observed that most nuclear scientists favored the treaty and were prepared to proceed further in the control of nuclear weapons. *Ibid.*, p. 767.

[42] *Ibid.*, p. 772.

[43] *Ibid.*, p. 773.

[44] *Ibid.*, p. 214.

[45] *Ibid.*, p. 227.

trast with Senator Mansfield's observation that the question of fallout was "a vital matter which should be considered in relation to the welfare of our people."[46] Senator Albert Gore solicited from Dr. Seaborg the admission that most scientists would agree that radioactive fallout should be curbed because it was harmful.[47]

### *Topics Considered*

Eight major themes recurred during the questioning of witnessess by Senators during the hearings conducted by the Committee on Foreign Relations. Table 7-1 indicates that while 47.8 per cent of the questions and answers were devoted to scientific, technological, and military considerations, only 27.3 per cent dealt with international politics, including United States relations with the Soviet Union. The plans of the leadership to focus on the international ramifications of the treaty were thwarted, as topics related to its technological and military consequences represented a disproportionate ratio of committee consideration.[48]

TABLE 7-1. *Major Themes in the Committee on Foreign Relations Hearings*

| Topic | % of Total | | % of Total |
|---|---|---|---|
| | Voted For | Voted Against | |
| Tests and Technology | 29.0 | 37.7 | 31.1 |
| Soviet Union | 16.1 | 19.4 | 17.0 |
| Military Considerations | 10.9 | 17.3 | 12.5 |
| International Politics | 11.9 | 5.3 | 10.3 |
| Treaty Language | 9.0 | 7.8 | 8.7 |
| Fallout | 5.8 | 2.0 | 4.9 |
| Role of Science and Scientists | 4.9 | 2.3 | 4.2 |
| Peaceful Uses of the Atom | 4.1 | .6 | 3.2 |
| Other | 8.3 | 7.6 | 8.1 |
| | 100.0 | 100.0 | 100.0 |
| Contribution to Debate | 75.3 | 24.7 | 100.0 |
| No. Column Inches * | 2691 | 883 | 3574 |

* Column inches represents the questions and answers, but not the statements of witnesses. Each Senator was allocated 10 minutes, and Senators occasionally controlled answers either by requesting short answers or turning to other matters sooner than might have been the case had they been allotted more time.

[46] *Ibid.*, p. 489.

[47] *Ibid.*, p. 234.

[48] Senate Democratic leaders initially planned to emphasize the improvement in

While supporters devoted 39.9 per cent of their contribution to technological and military aspects of the treaty, opponents focused on these topics 55 per cent of the time. The anti-treaty Senators devoted only 7.3 per cent of their time to the diplomatic and health themes, while the pro-treaty Senators devoted 17.7 per cent of their contribution to these topics.

Table 7-2 reveals that committee membership is a more relevant criterion in explaining the type of questions asked than a Senator's vote on the treaty.[49] The members of the Committee on Armed Services ignored the political aspects of the treaty and were virtually unconcerned about the effects of the treaty on radioactive fallout and the future peaceful uses of nuclear energy. Members of the Committee on Foreign Relations were more interested in the role of science because of their unfamiliarity with

TABLE 7-2. *Differences among the Committees in the Hearings Before the Committee on Foreign Relations*

| | % of Total | | |
|---|---|---|---|
| Topic | Foreign Relations Committee | Armed Services Committee | Atomic Energy Committee |
| Tests and Technology | 27.5 | 39.5 | 35.0 |
| Soviet Union | 17.2 | 12.0 | 18.0 |
| Military Considerations | 10.7 | 25.9 | 13.6 |
| International Politics | 11.7 | 3.0 | 6.7 |
| Treaty Language | 7.5 | 7.6 | 9.2 |
| Fallout | 5.6 | 2.6 | 5.9 |
| Science and Scientists | 5.3 | 2.4 | 1.5 |
| Peaceful Uses of the Atom | 3.1 | 1.7 | 3.6 |
| Other | 11.4 | 5.2 | 6.5 |
| | 100.0 | 100.0 | 100.0 |
| No. Column Inches | 2587 | 575 | 1202 |

relations between East and West. Senator Humphrey, for example, hoped to see "a complete reassessment of our policy to Eastern Europe." *Congressional Record,* July 29, 1963, p. 13484.

49 There was overlapping membership on the committees. Rather than arbitrarily assign a particular member to one committee and remove him from another in order to eliminate counting the contribution of a member twice, each contribution was assigned to a member on the basis of his committee membership whether this was one or two. Democratic Senators Russell and Jackson were members of the Committee on Armed Services and the Joint Committee on Atomic Energy, Senator Gore was on Foreign Relations and Atomic Energy. Democratic Senator Symington was a member of Foreign Relations and Armed Services. Republican Senators Hickenlooper and Aiken were members of Foreign Relations and Atomic Energy.

applicability of science to government policy and their desire to acquaint themselves with unfamiliar scientific matters relating to the treaty. With greater experience in each of these areas, the members of the other two committees emphasized the applied, or technological, aspects of the treaty: the viability of safeguards, the limits of underground testing, and possible detection problems. When they discussed the Soviet Union, the Committee on Armed Services and the Joint Committee on Atomic Energy emphasized the probable nuclear position of the Soviet Union, while the Committee on Foreign Relations tended to probe the impact of the treaty on Sino-Soviet relations.

Members of the Committee on Armed Services were especially concerned with the degree of consultation by the administration with the military, particularly with the members of the Joint Chiefs of Staff. Senator Stennis could not understand how the American negotiators at Moscow could properly function without "first-hand military advice on the spot for interpretation of any points that might have arisen."[50] The first question asked of General Maxwell Taylor, Chairman of the Joint Chiefs of Staff, when he finished his testimony focused on the participation of the military during the course of the negotiations in Moscow.[51] Most of the members of the Armed Services Committee seemed to believe that military officers should not only advise the administration on arms control proposals but also have the opportunity to veto them anywhere during the decision-making and negotiating processes. The President welcomed military assessments in the early decision-making stages but believed that he must accept responsibility for the conduct of the negotiations and that the military officers could not offer any positive contribution to the negotiating process.

Supporters insisted that the military had been consulted on the treaty and that they testified without any restraint imposed by the administration. Senator Fulbright asked the members of the Joint Chiefs of Staff:

> Is it fair to say that you were aware of what was going on prior to the signing, and you were, as a body at least, not sufficiently alarmed by it to protest it, even before it was signed?[52]

[50] Committee on Foreign Relations, *op. cit.*, pp. 136–37. Senator Stennis told Secretary Rusk, "It is just unthinkable to me that you would undertake such a mission as this without having at least one of our top military advisers . . ."

[51] Question by Senator Russell, *Ibid.*, p. 280.

[52] *Ibid.*, p. 383.

Senator Fulbright was especially careful to obtain agreement from General Curtis LeMay, the most skeptical member of the Joint Chiefs. Implicitly rejecting the charge that consultation with the military had been too infrequent and too narrow, Senator Sparkman asked Secretary McNamara to discuss "the depth or the degree to which the military have been kept informed and consulted with reference to the treaty."[53]

The effects of the treaty on the development of an antiballistic missile was another major topic for the members of all three committees. Table 7-3 illustrates that this was the principal area of emphasis among the technological topics covered in the hearings. Anti-treaty Senators stressed the problems associated with testing the system under the provisions of the test ban treaty and insisted that without atmospheric testing complete confidence could not be placed in the finished product. Senator Stennis asked, "[H]ow can we know it will work or have the best information as to whether or not it is effective and workable if we cannot have atmospheric testing?"[54] Senator Goldwater questioned Secretary McNamara's statement that development of an antiballistic missile system could proceed without additional atmospheric testing. The Arizona Republican found the Defense Secretary's comments conflicted with the positions of several scientists. The Senator could not understand how it was possible to "say flatly something would work without testing it."[55]

TABLE 7-3. *Differences among the Committees in the Hearings: Major Themes as a Per Cent of the Technology Topic*

| | % of Topic | | |
|---|---|---|---|
| Theme | Foreign Relations Committee | Armed Services Committee | Atomic Energy Committee |
| Antiballistic Missile | 30.7 | 22.7 | 19.6 |
| Safeguards | 8.6 | 15.3 | 17.8 |
| High Yield Tests | 10.9 | 11.0 | 13.6 |
| Importance of Tests | 17.6 | 6.3 | 14.3 |
| Underground Tests | 4.9 | 12.7 | 9.8 |
| Detection | 4.7 | 12.0 | 8.1 |
| Cost of Treaty on Budget | 4.9 | 6.3 | 5.2 |
| Other | 17.7 | 13.7 | 11.6 |
| Total | 100.0 | 100.0 | 100.0 |

[53] *Ibid.*, p. 119.
[54] *Ibid.*, p. 138.
[55] *Ibid.*, p. 161.

Pro-treaty Senators insisted that there was no real problem associated with the development of the system. Senator Fulbright asked General Taylor whether laboratory work might not be sufficient for the development of the anti-missile missile, and received an affirmative reply.[56] Supporters argued the basic problem with an effective anti-ballistic missile system was the development of a guidance system which could discriminate nuclear warheads from decoys and it did not depend on atmospheric nuclear testing.[57]

### *The Role of the Leadership*

Chairman and Senators with the greatest seniority are generally the most influential members of committees. The chairman usually controls the agenda of his committee and is generally differential to the ranking members of both parties, particularly during the questioning of witnesses. It could be assumed that if there is leadership dominance, the chairman, the ranking majority member, and the two ranking minority members of the committee would rank in a 1-2-3-4 order as the members most active in committee questioning.[58] In the hearings conducted by the Committee on Foreign Relations, there were five ranking Democrats and four ranking Republicans for the three committees.[59] If formal leadership and seniority played no role, the leaders would cluster near an average score. With twenty Democrats the median average would be ten for the Democrats and 6.5 for the thirteen Republicans. The score for the Democratic leadership is 5.4, tending to the ranking score for leadership initiative, but the Republican leadership score of 6.0 is close to a random, rather than an active leadership pattern.

[56] *Ibid.*, p. 314.

[57] *Ibid.*, pp. 767–768.

[58] Contributions are calculated on the column inches of questions asked by a Senator *and* the column inches of the answer. Answers are included because the Senators were under ten minute time limitations and so if the witness spent too much time answering, he was sometimes cut off. Furthermore, Senator Fulbright, as chairman, was extremely cautious to give the ranking members of the Senate ample time and enforce the ten minute limit more often on junior members, a bias *in favor of high seniority members.* Furthermore, the combination gives an indication to what extent a Senator controlled the hearings.

[59] Overlapping membership is not counted here. Thus, one Democratic space was omitted because Senator Russell, Chairman of the Committee on Armed Services, was second ranking Democratic member of the Joint Committee on Atomic Energy. Senators Hickenlooper and Aiken, ranking Republicans on the Committee on Foreign Relations, held identical places on the Joint Committee on Atomic Energy, thereby reducing the number of leadership places attributed to the Republicans by two.

The pro-treaty leaders took greater initiative in the committee hearings, having an average ranking of 5.3 compared to a random score of 11.5. However, the leadership opposing the treaty showed the opposite tendency, having a 7.0 ranking which was above the random score of 5.0 for all opponents. The ranking committee members who voted against the treaty did not play the prominent role in opposing the treaty in the hearing of the Committee on Foreign Relations that committee leaders supporting the treaty did. Table 7-4 identifies the ranking of the formal committee leaders and their contributions.

Of the 33 Senators who participated, the nine chairmen and ranking members contributed 49.8 per cent to the hearings, a much higher proportion than might have been expected on a random basis. Ranking members who supported the treaty accounted for 59.2 per cent of the total pro-treaty contribution, but the leaders who opposed the treaty contributed only 18.3 per cent to the opposition total. Because all of the leaders who

TABLE 7-4. *Contributions to the Hearings by Rank Ordering for Committee Chairman, Ranking Democrat, and the two Ranking Republicans*

| Name and Committee * | Total | Democrat | Rank Republican | For | Against |
|---|---|---|---|---|---|
| Fulbright, FR | 1 | 1 | — | 1 | — |
| Sparkman, FR | 5 | 4 | — | 4 | — |
| Hickenlooper, FR, JCAE | 4 | — | 1 | 3 | — |
| Pastore, JCAE | 6 | 5 | — | 5 | — |
| Aiken, FR, JCAE | 8 | — | 3 | 7 | — |
| Russell, AS, JCAE | 9 | 6 | — | — | 2 |
| Saltonstall, AS | 19 | — | 7 | 12 | — |
| Stennis, AS | 25 | 13 | — | — | 9 |
| Smith, AS | 33 | — | 13 | — | 10 |
| No. Participating | 33 | 20 | 13 | 23 | 10 |

* Members of the Committee on Foreign Relations are designated FR; members of the Committee on Armed Services are designated AS, and members of the Joint Committee on Atomic Energy are designated JCAE. Those Senators who did not contribute at all in the hearings were not counted.

opposed the treaty were members of the Committee on Armed Services whose Preparedness Subcommittee conducted its own hearings on the treaty, it might be assumed that the ranking members of the Committee on Armed Services preferred to exercise their leadership at hearings of one of its subcommittees. However, Senator Russell, Chairman of the Committee, did not actively participate in the subcommittee hearing. Furthermore, the chairman and both ranking Republicans of the subcommittee each placed behind two junior members of the subcommittee, Senators Thurmond and Goldwater. While supporters of the treaty could expect active participation from sympathetic leaders during the hearings, opponents could not.

### *The Report of the Committee on Foreign Relations*

After twelve days of hearings, including executive sessions with the Director of the Central Intelligence Agency and the Joint Chiefs of Staff, the Committee on Foreign Relations met again with Secretary Rusk in closed session. The next day, the full committee discussed the treaty. The leadership was eager to bring the treaty to the floor of the Senate as soon as possible, without any reservations, but some members wanted to call more witnesses and wait for the report of the Preparedness Subcommittee.[60]

The Democratic leadership was able to counter a move by Senator Lausche calling for participation with the Committee on Armed Services and the Joint Committee on Atomic Energy before a Foreign Relations Committee vote was taken. It also defeated a motion by Senator Mundt to delay a vote for 48 hours after the printed record of the hearings were available. In each case, the minority consisted of Senators Lausche, Long, Hickenlooper, Mundt, and Williams. Senator Carlson, absent at the time, associated himself with this minority. A strong challenge to the Democratic leadership occurred when Senator Hickenlooper requested committee access to all of the correspondence on the treaty between Moscow and Washington, including the exchange of messages between the two heads of government. The proposal was defeated 7 to 10, with all of the Republicans and Democrats Lausche and Long supporting it.[61]

Senator Long was the only member to vote against the committee report. He argued that the committee had proceeded with unnecessary speed and observed that one-third of its members desired more time. He also insisted that other expert testimony should be heard and found that, as the treaty stood, it would "jeopardize our ability to defend the United States."[62]

The report was prepared by the committee staff which expected it to be a rationale for Senate approval. It reflected the chairman's position and contained a summary of the testimony heard. Military and political aspects were included by the staff because it believed the Senate expected both.

[60] *New York Times*, August 29, 1963, p. 5.
[61] *Ibid.*, August 30, 1963, p. 1.
[62] *Ibid.*

Senators Fulbright and Hickenlooper reviewed the report and suggested only minor changes. The proofs of the report were also circulated to the Arms Control and Disarmament Agency and to the Departments of State and Defense. No additional suggestions were made with the exception of a few alterations in language offered by the General Counsel of the Department of Defense, John McNaughton.[63]

Having given six pages to the political implications of the treaty and thirteen to the scientific and military questions raised by the test ban, the report concluded:

> A good part of the committee's time and attention during the hearings was devoted to military considerations. The treaty does bear, though perhaps not heavily, on the military balance. But its thrust is political. And among other things, it illustrates that military considerations cannot be divorced from political considerations; they are inseparable, especially in the nuclear age. The maintenance of a strong military position is clearly essential to the national security of the United States. But exclusive, or excessive reliance on military considerations could undermine national security by encouraging comparable military efforts by others, thereby strengthening the destabilizing forces adrift in the world, possibly creating new ones.
>
> This treaty offers the prospects of a gradual lessening of tensions, of a start toward the progressive elimination of the danger of nuclear war. Thus the committee (by a vote of 16 to 1) recommends that the Senate give its advice and consent to the ratification of the pending treaty.[64]

### *The Preparedness Investigating Subcommittee*

In late July Senator John Stennis, chairman of the Preparedness Investigating Subcommittee of the Committee on Armed Services, announced plans for the subcommittee to conduct hearings on the treaty. Hearings on the "Military Aspects and Implications of Nuclear Test Ban Proposals and Related Matters," had begun in May and were continued into June, after the President's American University speech. As seen in Table 7-5, the list of witnesses indicated the kind of facts the subcommittee considered most relevant. After the treaty was signed, scientific and military experts were called exclusively. The hearings of the subcommittee duplicated many of the scientific and military subjects covered in the hearings conducted by the Committee on Foreign Relations while ignoring others. When their interests overlapped, the two committees relied on different sources for reliable information.

[63] Interview, Washington, D.C., May, 1964.

[64] Senate, Committee on Foreign Relations, *Report, The Nuclear Test Ban Treaty*, 88th Cong., 1st Sess., September 3, 1963, p. 26.

Dr. Teller was accorded every courtesy by the members of the subcommittee. The questions were uniformly friendly and generally elicited answers damaging to the treaty. Just as this was in sharp contrast to his treatment before the Committee on Foreign Relations, so was the appearance of General Taylor. Although much of the questioning of the Chairman of the Joint Chiefs of Staff was designed to produce information on the military implications of the treaty and was presented in an amicable manner, Senator Thurmond asked the General whether he considered himself more of a political appointee than a military man. The General curtly replied that he "would not answer that question, because of the connotation involved in it."[65] The question was rhetorical for Senator Thurmond who considered that some officers were more political than others, that is, that some were more likely to support the President than others were.

TABLE 7-5. *Types of Witnesses Appearing before the Preparedness Subcommittee and the Committee on Foreign Relations* *

| Category | Preparedness Subcommittee May-June | Preparedness Subcommittee August | Committee on Foreign Relations August |
|---|---|---|---|
| Military | | | |
| Active | 4 | 6 | 5 |
| Retired | | 3 | |
| Scientists | | | |
| Government | | 3 | 3 |
| Non-Government | | 1 | 7 |
| Atomic Energy Commission | 1 | | 1 |
| Arms Control Agency | 1 | | |
| State Department | | | 1 |
| Defense Department | | | 1 |
| Individuals | | | 7 |
| Group Representatives | | | 16 |
| Total | | 19 | 41 |

* Individuals accompanying officials are not counted here.

When he opened his questioning of General LeMay, the service chief most skeptical of the treaty, Senator Goldwater attributed a level of confidence in the Air Force General which was generous in the extreme. He told LeMay, "It goes without my saying that your opinions in this field are

[65] Preparedness Subcommittee, 1963, *op. cit.*, p. 615.

more highly respected by the American people than all the rest of the Joint Chiefs put together, because you are the man charged with punching that red button and getting the weapons there when we have to."[66] When he referred to him as "*the* man responsible for the defense of this country," the Arizona Republican gave LeMay extraordinary power but also indicated his own faith in the reliability of information sources.[67]

The opponents of the treaty in the subcommittee often doubted the ability of the administration to protect and advance American security adequately. Senator Stennis feared that the President would not always act appropriately to protect national security because he did not have the necessary information.[68] However, Goldwater insisted it was not a problem of information flow. He suggested the administration was unwilling or unable to provide the safeguards requested by the Joint Chiefs of Staff and recalled the withdrawal of particular missile systems from production which had previously been promised by the administration.[69] He asked one witness whether the treaty prohibited the use of nuclear weapons in time of war. When he heard that the President, the Secretary of State, and the legal counsel of the witness all expressed the opinion that the treaty would not operate in time of war, Goldwater observed, "I don't take the word of the President or Mr. Rusk on this. I will take the word of a legal expert first."[70]

The report of the Preparedness Subcommittee reflected an uneasiness about the military ramifications of the treaty. It found that the treaty would "affect adversely the future quality of this Nation's arms, and that it will result in serious, perhaps formidable, military disadvantages." These disadvantages, however, would not affect the Soviet nuclear programs to the same degree.[71] The report admitted that "other important factors" were relevant to the overall assessment of the treaty and indicated that each Senator would have to reach his own decision on the "basis of personal philosophy, past experience, current knowledge, and the relative weight which he assigns to the various factors involved."[72] Senator Saltonstall dissented, and was the only committee member to vote against the report. He termed it "unduly pessimistic" and found its conclusions "overly adverse." He complained that the testimony of the Secretary of Defense and

66 *Ibid.*, p. 727.
67 *Ibid.*, p. 732. (Italics added).
68 *Ibid.*, p. 826.
69 *Ibid.*, p. 728.
70 *Ibid.*, p. 659.
71 *Congressional Record*, September 9, 1963, p. 16628.
72 *Ibid.*, p. 16629.

several leading scientists who appeared before the Committee on Foreign Relations was "not sufficiently emphasized in the report."[73]

When the Senate began to debate the treaty in September, it was confronted with two conflicting reports submitted by two separate committees, with minor divisions within the committees, and several Senate leaders who had not yet announced their position.

[73] *Ibid.*

CHAPTER VIII

# THE SENATE: THE DEBATE AND VOTE

On September 9, 1963, two weeks after the Committee on Foreign Relations concluded its hearings, the Senate began to debate the test ban treaty. Two weeks later the Senate gave its advice and consent to the nuclear test ban treaty by a vote of 80 to 19. During the intervening period, the Senate considered appropriation bills, had completed legislation on railroad strikes, and was confronted with a number of other pressing matters, including a proposed tax cut and a civil rights bill. In addition, politics remained an important preoccupation for many Senators. Meanwhile many groups, administration officials, scientists, and the public lobbied for the test ban. Several Senators, in turn, sought information and analysis from executive agencies, particularly the Departments of State and Defense, as well as nongovernmental scientists. Not every Senator received the same type or intensity of pressure or was concerned about the treaty to the same extent. Some were extremely interested in the treaty and sought out information while others had been preoccupied with domestic policy or were consistent supporters or opponents of arms control.

## *The Senate and Public Opinion*

Although public opinion polls, mail, and group activity had an apparent effect on some Senators, its demonstrated impact was missing or illusive for others.[1] Compared to other foreign policy issues, mail on the treaty was very heavy, although there were fewer letters than for several pending bills effecting the economy and civil rights. With few exceptions, Senators found the test ban stimulated more letters and telegrams from

[1] For a discussion of Senators and foreign policy lobbying see Lester Milbrath "Interest Groups and Foreign Policy" in James Rosenau (ed.), *Domestic Sources of Foreign Policy* (New York: Free Press, 1967), pp. 213–230.

constituents than any other foreign policy issue during the Kennedy administration, except for the Cuban missile crisis.[2]

Immediately after the initialing of the treaty in Moscow, the preponderance of mail favored the treaty, but this generally shifted to anti-treaty letters in early September. Senator Kenneth Keating, for example, said that his mail in late July ran 10 to 1 in favor of the treaty, although in the period immediately preceding the Senate vote, it favored the opposition. Cumulatively, he received 10,000 letters, with three-quarters of them favoring the treaty.[3]

Constituent mail was often defined to harmonize with the position of the Senator. Senator Strom Thurmond insisted that the published polls, which indicated public support for the treaty by a 4 to 1 margin, did not reflect his mail, which ran 30 to 1 against the treaty.[4] When Senators looked at their mail, they generally had it divided into in-state and out-of-state mail and rejected the latter. Senator Margaret Chase Smith, however, divided her in-state mail into pre-Labor Day and post-Labor Day categories and discounted some of the mail she received from her constituency prior to early September because "obviously a great deal of the Maine mail prior to Labor Day came from out-of-State summer visitors." Senator Smith, who opposed the treaty, reported that mail prior to Labor Day favored the treaty by a 3 to 1 margin, while there was a marked shift to the opposition after that day.[5] She reasoned that if the published polls reflected the position of the American public, it did not identify its intensity because those who supported the treaty did not have the enthusiasm to write, while those opposed to the treaty had "such a high degree of intensity" that they took "the time to write and express themselves."[6]

Senators often solicited mail in their newsletters to their constituents. Senator Harrison Williams not only requested the citizens of his state to inform him of their views on the treaty, but he also wrote several organi-

[2] Interviews, April and May, 1964, and *Congressional Record*, September 9–23, 1963, *passim*.

[3] *Ibid.*, September 20, 1963, p. 16731.

[4] *Ibid.*, September 17, 1963, p. 16245. However, another treaty opponent, Senator Willis Robertson reminded Senator Thurmond that the opposition represented the "unpopular side."

[5] *Ibid.*, September 24, 1963, p. 16909. Although the opposition mail peaked late, most of the Senators and their assistants interviewed believed it was artificially stimulated and did not pay attention to it.

[6] *Ibid.*

zations and requested the opinions of their members. After his request, his mail shifted from a 3 to 1 ratio to a 6 to 1 margin of support.[7]

However, not every Senator welcomed all of the letters. Senator Aiken complained that at no time in his "recollection has the mail on any issue before Congress contained so many threats and vituperations as that of the last few weeks." Identifying much of the opposition mail as organization inspired, he particularly took offense at opposition mail which identified treaty supporters "as Communists, or Communist sympathizers, dupes, dopes, renegades, and a few other things."[8] Treaty opponents were perturbed with mail which questioned their alleged moral unconcern about war and fallout. Senator Robertson regretted that "honored ministers of the gospel . . . seem to think we are dealing with a religious issue."[9]

The comments of Senators who discussed the treaty on the floor, as well as of those who were interviewed, indicated that mail did not have a conscious effect on their vote. Certainly they had no problem when the preponderance of mail coincided with their position. When it did not, the rationale for the rejection of the mail was varied, but it did contain the common theme that the treaty was a matter of such importance that Senators could not allow themselves to be affected by the reactions on a public which was not fully informed on the issue. One Senator found his mail ran heavily against the treaty, but insisted that the public could not be expected to understand the complex scientific, military, and diplomatic issues, and that some of the data available to him were classified. Consequently, his mail did not "interest" him. Furthermore, he believed that because there were some issues which were of such overriding importance, a Senator must be expected to base his final decision ultimately on his own experience, evaluation, and conscience.[10] Both the minority leader and the minority whip voted against the majority of letters sent to them.

## *The Senate Debate*

Three major topics occupied the Senate's plenary deliberations on the test ban treaty. Table 8-1 indicates that security considerations represented the primary concern of most of the Senators who discussed the treaty on the floor of the chamber, followed by the political and health ramifications of the treaty. None of the opponents of the treaty considered radioactive

[7] *Congressional Record,* September 17, 1963, p. 16295.
[8] *Ibid.,* September 18, 1963, p. 16506.
[9] *Ibid.,* September 20, 1963, p. 16713.
[10] Interview, Washington, D.C., April, 1964.

fallout as a primary factor in evaluating the treaty, all but one concentrating on its security aspects. Seventy per cent of the treaty supporters who participated in the Senate debate, however, emphasized nonsecurity matters in their addresses to the Senate, although they often discussed the military aspects as well.

The opponents who emphasized the security features of the treaty insisted that this goal could be achieved only through superior military power. The Senators who voted for the treaty and accepted the thesis that superior nuclear weapons were necessary for the continuance of the existing relative status of American power were among the most reluctant supporters of the treaty. Most of the proponents who discussed the military aspects insisted that security could be maintained through the safeguards President Kennedy promised to implement. Many of them tended to equate security with a parity of power *vis-à-vis* the Soviet Union. As Table 8-2 indicates, only a handful of Senators held that the United States had an excess of power and categorized the American arsenal as having an overkill potentiality.

TABLE 8-1. *Priorities in the Senate Debate* *

| Priority | For | Against | Total |
|---|---|---|---|
| Military | 16 | 15 | 31 |
| Political | 20 | 1 | 21 |
| Fallout | 10 | 0 | 10 |
| Unidentifiable | 2 | 0 | 2 |
| | — | — | — |
| Total | 48 | 16 | 64 |

* Forty of the Senate speeches were examined by the author and an independent reader, and the remaining 24 were analyzed by the author alone. In the assignment of priorities to speeches, the independent reader differed with the author once. The independent reader assigned a political priority to one short speech which the author designated as unidentifiable. It is listed in the latter category in the Table.

When opponents examined the relationship of peace to the treaty, they continued to reason that a superiority of military power was an essential element of the American policy to deter Soviet aggression. However, a large bloc of treaty proponents felt assured that a parity of power was sufficient, and that a spiraling arms race would promote tension. Only a small minority believed that peace should be examined in a moral context, or that the treaty should be considered as a worthwhile step to future disarmament measures. When security was the major goal of a Senator, and when he believed that this could be achieved only through superior military power, he tended to find that the effects of the treaty were detrimental to the national interest.

Opponents and proponents of the treaty viewed the Soviet Union's moti-

TABLE 8-2. *Perception of Senators and the Treaty Vote*

| Theme | Treaty Vote Yes | Treaty Vote No |
|---|---|---|
| Security | | |
| Achieved only through superior power | 5 | 15 |
| Achieved through a parity of power | 4 | 1 |
| Safeguard will maintain security | 16 | 0 |
| We have more power than we need, overkill | 5 | 0 |
| Peace | | |
| Assured only through superior U.S. power | 4 | 11 |
| Assured through parity of U.S. power | 2 | 0 |
| Must reduce tensions | 5 | 0 |
| Must control arms race | 12 | 0 |
| Must work for more arms control, disarmament | 5 | 0 |
| A moral issue | 2 | 0 |
| Fallout | | |
| No problem at all | 1 | 2 |
| Cannot be a factor in judgment, not enough information | 5 | 4 |
| Cannot be a factor in judgment, other factors are more important, especially security | 4 | 4 |
| One of the reasons for voting for the treaty | 14 | 0 |
| Major reason for voting for the treaty | 10 | 0 |
| Effects on Future Policy | | |
| Disadvantageous, Soviets will benefit | 0 | 11 |
| Risky, uncertain, must be cautious | 9 | 3 |
| A small first step, but important | 17 | 0 |
| Very important beneficial step | 7 | 0 |
| Trusting the Soviet Union | | |
| Can never trust the Soviets | 9 | 14 |
| Treaty not based on trust, U.S. protected by safeguards, detection methods | 11 | 0 |
| Behaves like other countries | 2 | 0 |
| Motivation of the Soviet Union | | |
| To improve its defenses *vis-à-vis U.S.* | 2 | 13 |
| To stop Communist China from acquiring the nuclear bomb, or factors related to China | 7 | 0 |
| To cut its arms costs | 5 | 0 |
| To reduce fallout | 5 | 0 |
| It knows nuclear war is no longer a rational policy | 10 | 0 |

vation in signing the treaty much differently. Opponents credited the Soviets with devious motives, while treaty supporters looked to a variety of reasons, many of which concerned mutual interests shared by the two great powers. The two sides also evaluated the domestic actors much differently. As seen in Table 8-3, opponents placed more confidence in the military leaders and less in the President.

TABLE 8-3. *Perception of Domestic Actors and Treaty Vote*

| Category | Treaty Vote | |
|---|---|---|
| | Yes | No |
| Military | | |
| Knows better than anyone else, primary source | 4 | 7 |
| One of the major experts, attach considerable weight to them, important source | 14 | 4 |
| If it were not for administration pressure the military would attack the treaty | 0 | 3 |
| Skeptical, often seen in comments on too much money for the military | 4 | 0 |
| Outright rejection | 1 | 0 |
| Scientists | | |
| Primary source | 7 | 3 |
| One of the major experts | 15 | 6 |
| Lose their specialization when they enter political realm | 4 | 0 |
| Contradict themselves too much | 4 | 0 |
| President | | |
| Cannot trust because he does not realize the real dangers | 0 | 7 |
| Needs Senate approval if he is to be an effective leader of the free world | 13 | 0 |
| Most knowledgeable on the subject | 4 | 0 |
| He will do what is necessary for national security | 5 | 0 |
| Public Opinion | | |
| Favors treaty | 14 | 4 |
| Mail indicates U.S. public uneasy or against treaty | 2 | 4 |
| Public, in whole or in part, too emotional | 9 | 5 |

Although most of the treaty supporters listened carefully to the military leaders and attached considerable importance to their arguments, a few believed that military considerations were irrelevant and were skeptical of the recommendations of the military officers. Even though both sides viewed scientists as important recommending sources, they hardly agreed about which scientists were pertinent to the issue and which were superfluous. Opponents concentrated on Edward Teller while the treaty supporters generally emphasized Herbert York and George Kistiakowsky.

*Three Senatorial Approaches to Arms Control*

Three basic approaches to arms control characterized the ratification debate in the Senate. They are identified as the anti-war maximizers, the power maximizers, and the security optimizers. It is convenient to view the approaches as a continuum with the maximizers at each pole and the optimizers at the center. In their evaluations of policy, optimizers are concerned with several conflicting variables which affect policy outcomes and find it necessary to weigh their importance and interaction. Optimizers have security as a primary goal, but find that any solution to a given security problem must be flexible when the variables fluctuate in direction or intensity.[11] Maximizers, however, look "for policies which provide the highest fulfillment of a relatively small number of noncompeting values."[12] Maximizers tend to have one overriding goal which, if realized, will affect the other variables in the system beneficially.

Before examining the approaches as distinct types, it is appropriate to note their common features. All other things being equal, each prefers peace over war, none believes it is desirable for the Soviet Union to possess overwhelming nuclear superiority, each perceives the introduction of nuclear weapons as profoundly affecting national power, and each values national security, although it is defined differently.

The anti-war maximizers did not ask for immediate unilateral disarmament by the United States. Rather, they hoped that the test ban treaty would be the beginning of a systematic process of multilateral disarmament which would greatly diminish the dangers of nuclear war. Depreciating military considerations in the conduct of American foreign policy, they recognized its necessity for national security at the time but believed it should be subordinate in foreign policy-making.

The power maximizers insisted that only by superior military power, generally nuclear power, could the United States maintain its security. In the acquisition and application of power, political and economic considerations were generally secondary. The power maximizers argued that the

[11] The terms used here are suggested in Robert A. Levine, *The Arms Debate* (Cambridge, Harvard University Press, 1963), pp. 33–40. Levine uses five categories for analysis, the anti-war and anti-Communist systemists, and the anti-war, anti-Communist, and middle marginalists. However, the Senate does not contain all of his five types, or if it does, not every type has articulated its position, e.g., unilateral disarmament as proposed by Levine's anti-war systemists.

[12] *Ibid.*, p. 36.

military variable was primary, and only by concentrating on it, could the United States maintain its independence. They generally rejected any possible areas of mutual interest between the United States and the Soviet Union. Not only was the military variable considered to be the most important one, but, according to this approach, it should be perfected to the greatest possible extent. Any restriction on the development or application of military weapons was viewed as fundamentally disadvantageous to the United States. They believed that national power was primarily military power and insisted that the United States should not compromise its control of the military variable.

The security optimizers shared some of the positions of each of the two maximizers. They believed that military considerations constituted a vital component in the maintenance of American security but rejected the idea that it was radically more important than political and economic considerations. Because they believed that military power had been transformed by the atom in such a way as to pose serious hazards for national security, they were prepared to impose some restraints on the development of new weapons. Unlike the peace maximizers, the security optimizers believed it was impossible to achieve a concrete solution to the Cold War through widespread disarmament.

There was a tendency for Senators to fall into the optimizer position, rather than either of the maximizer categories. Based on the discussion of Table 8-2, the power maximizers were more numerous than the anti-war maximizers. However, three precautionary comments are in order. A particular Senator may be a member of one school for some issues but move to another school on other issues. This shifting occurred between a maximizer type and an optimizer, but not from one of the maximizers to another. In addition, the Table records only those comments made during the Senate debate. Often Senators concentrated on only one or two topics at the time and left the others untouched. Many other senators did not participate in the debate at all. Finally, the remarks in the Senate were addressed to a public audience and may not in each case reflect the same emphasis with which the Senator evaluated the issue.[13]

The positions of three Senators will be used to illustrate these three

[13] One Senator who discussed the military aspects of the treaty at great length, but who had been expected to emphasize its political ramifications, took this course of action in order to establish his credentials as a person who was concerned with aspects of the treaty which preoccupied many undecided Senators. Interview, Washington, D.C., March, 1964.

approaches in the debate. Senators Wayne Morse, J. William Fulbright, and Strom Thurmond represented the anti-war maximizers, security optimizers, and power maximizers, respectively.

Senator Morse identified the retardation of future radioactive pollution of the atmosphere as the central purpose of the treaty. Those who denied the relevancy of fallout as a vital issue were seeking to deceive the American public that no harm would come to future generations. He regretted that there was not more substance to the treaty, particularly provisions which would ban all nuclear testing, place real restraints on the armament race, and call "for disarmament of the kind that would permit substantial cuts in our defense budget."[14]

Nuclear weapons had profoundly changed the nature of security, and they had to be brought under control, not only for national survival, but because of the moral imperatives involved. Senator Morse told his colleagues that he had been concerned with nuclear weapons,

> ever since the sinful nature of this arms race became crystal clear to me and ever since I became convinced of the inevitable destruction of a large part of civilization if we do not live up to our military responsibilities and start doing the things necessary to be done in order to bring to an end the immoral, nuclear armaments race.[15]

He vigorously rejected the primacy of military considerations in foreign policy and warned the public to keep itself on guard "against the growing and dangerous power of American military minds over public policy."[16] National security would be destroyed the moment nuclear weapons were used, for their implementation would mean "the destruction of the lives, property, and freedom of millions upon millions of Americans," and the probable destruction of the democratic way of life.[17] Consequently, he believed that increased funds for armaments and the development of new weapons would add little to national security. Senator Morse and other anti-war maximizers de-emphasized the military aspects of the treaty and highly valued the health benefits. They believed that future arms control agreements were essential if humanity were to be spared the terrors of nuclear war.

For Senator Fulbright and other security optimizers, the test ban treaty

[14] *Congressional Record,* September 18, 1963, p. 16487.
[15] *Ibid.,* p. 16488.
[16] *Ibid.*
[17] *Ibid.*

was not a moral issue. Although it was tentative, the treaty's essential purpose was important because it attempted "to bring an element of sanity and restraint into the relations of the great nations." No technical solution could solve the problems of national security. "It is," the Chairman of the Committee on Foreign Relations insisted, "a dangerous oversimplification to regard national security solely in terms of weapons systems and military systems and military technology."[18] He perceived security to be a function of a country's political and economic resources as well as its military strength.

Senator Fulbright held that although military power was an essential ingredient of national power, armaments were "a cause as well as result of world tensions." Granting the seriousness of the conflict between the United States and the Soviet Union, he maintained that it was neither total nor absolute. Both of these great powers had a mutual interest in the avoidance of nuclear war. For Senator Fulbright, the cold war would continue after the test ban treaty, but the treaty did aim at "attaining a measure of stability and moderation in the military confrontation between two great powers."[19]

Many of the security optimizers viewed the Soviet Union as an antagonist of the United States, not simply because it was Communist, but because it was a powerful state whose interests conflicted with those of this country. The struggle remained, but it was perceived less in the ideological context, and more in the *realpolitik* school. In discussing the probable motivations of the leaders of the Soviet Union in signing the treaty, Senator Fulbright identified three overriding factors. The Soviet leaders hoped the treaty would lessen the prospects of nuclear war, assist the Soviet Union in its conflict with the Chinese Communists, and divert needed funds for the construction of a sound domestic economy.[20] The tentative nature of the treaty for the security optimizers was reflected in Senator Fulbright's observation that:

> The purpose of the nuclear test ban treaty is not to end the cold war but to modify it, not to resolve the conflict between communism and freedom – a goal which is almost certainly beyond the reach of the present generation – but only to remove some of the terror and passion from it.[21]

Strom Thurmond placed his confidence completely in American nuclear

[18] *Ibid.*, September 9, 1963, p. 15669.
[19] *Ibid.*, p. 15673.
[20] *Ibid.*, p. 15677.
[21] *Ibid.*

power to achieve national security. He was most suspicious of political leadership which did not accept the military variable as paramount. His remarks indicated considerable confidence in the potentiality of American power to achieve its objectives, provided no restrictions were imposed on it. For example, the South Carolinian contended that American scientists, laboratories, and military planners were superior to their Soviet counterparts, but that American political leadership had not supplied the requisite will and policy for the maximum utilization of these superior resources.[22]

Senator Thurmond ignored any areas of mutual interest between the two great powers, and held that the Soviet Union had signed the treaty solely because it wished to destroy the United States. He reasoned that the Soviets had collected valuable data from their high megaton tests in the atmosphere and required time to perfect and manufacture weapons based on the knowledge gained from these tests. Once these new weapons were operational, the Soviet Union would issue an ultimatum to the United States: "Either surrender or be destroyed."[23] Viewed from this perspective, it was imperative that the United States reject the treaty and immediately resume testing in order to protect its national security. He questioned the idea that new nuclear weapons systems could be developed without atmospheric testing. Just as the United States must be certain that it was militarily superior, so it must be absolutely satisfied that its arsenal was completely reliable. In fact, the two were intimately related, for the first requirement flowed from the latter.[24]

Senator Thurmond believed the military power was concrete and was the primary variable in international relations. He told the Senate that the military disadvantages of the treaty "are specific and quantitative. They can be numbered and weighed. They are real, practical, and when understood, awesome." The political considerations were, "at most, vague generalizations." He asked proponents to explain how the political ramifications of the treaty would prevent nuclear war "in the absence of an overwhelming superiority of strategic power in the United States."[25] Certainty was characteristic of the power maximizer approach. This not only included confidence in weapons systems; but the probability that the Soviets would clandestinely test in violation of the treaty. Senator Thurmond suggested that the Soviets might choose to locate their testing facilities in Communist China, or move them to the Chinese border, in which case American instru-

[22] *Ibid.*, September 11, 1963, p. 15927.
[23] *Ibid.*, p. 15924.
[24] *Ibid.*, p. 15929.
[25] *Ibid.*, p. 15931.

ments would not be able to identify whether the tests were Soviet or Chinese. Because China was not a party to the treaty, no international law would be broken if that country tested.[26]

Senators who were members of either of the maximizer categories tended to have fewer doubts about their positions on the treaty than many of the optimizers, particularly those who shared some common features with the power maximizers. Senators Bourke Hickenlooper and Henry Jackson, who are examples of this latter position, were security optimizers, but tended to evaluate the military variable as more important than other members sharing this approach. Senator Fulbright, who was in the middle of the optimizer position, had less trouble in deciding the issue than some Senators, but even he had some questions in the early stages of consideration of the treaty, particularly concerning its scientific aspects.

Extrapolating from Table 8-2, it is possible to categorize the reaction of Senators to the treaty in accordance with the three approaches discussed above. These breakdowns, based on Senate speeches, are found in Table 8-4.

TABLE 8-4. *Themes and Senatorial Approaches to Arms Control*

| Approach | Perception or Recommendation | No. Senators |
|---|---|---|
| Peace | Disarmament as a goal | 7 |
| Security | Arms control as a goal | 19 |
| Power | Disarmament or arms control as a threat | 15 |
| Total | | 41 |
| Peace | Suspicion of military power | 5 |
| Security | Military parity is necessary | 21 |
| Power | Military superiority is essential | 20 |
| Total | | 46 |
| Peace | Fallout the major concern | 10 |
| Security | Fallout important but not determining factor | 14 |
| Power | Fallout not important | 19 |
| Total | | 43 |

## *The Administration and the Senate*

Interaction between the legislative and executive branches continued throughout the Senate debate. At times this was prompted by requests from

[26] *Ibid.*, p. 15923.

Senators for information, counsel, or assistance, while on other occasions the administration initiated direct contacts with Senators. The most notable exchange between the administration and the Senate was the meeting between the President and the majority and minority leaders.

On the day the Senate opened its debate on the treaty, Majority Leader Mike Mansfield and Minority Leader Everett Dirksen conferred with the President at the White House. The minority leader presented some of his doubts about the treaty which were resolved by the President. The Senator believed that the President's assurances that national security would not be endangered would influence undecided Senators if a letter were sent to the two Senate leaders.[27]

Two days after his meeting with the President, Senator Dirksen addressed the Senate and supported the treaty without qualification or hesitation. His endorsement added impetus to broad Republican support, as well as minimized the effectiveness of the adverse report released by the Preparedness Investigation Subcommittee that day.

The minority leader informed the Senate that he was supporting the treaty in spite of heavy mail from his state which opposed the test ban. He had received 40,000 letters on the treaty and a petition with 10,000 signatures asking him to vote against it. Yet, he insisted, he would betray his conscience and do a disservice to his constituents and his country if he failed to exercise his independent judgment.[28] Senator Dirksen further reported that he had discussed the treaty not only with the President, but also with Dr. Edward Teller in a private conversation, and then asked, "Where do we turn in our difficulty, if it is not to our leaders"?[29]

The Senator said that he saw no need for treaty reservations, and, in response to a question by Senator Fulbright, he expanded this to include the stipulation that had been suggested by former President Dwight D. Eisenhower. The minority leader asserted that the Eisenhower letter to the Committee on Foreign Relations indicated that it was desirable to stipulate that the United States would use nuclear weapons if armed aggression endangered an American vital interest. The minority leader believed the President's letter cleared all doubts on that question.[30] Senator Dirksen expected that if the treaty failed, the United States would continue to be militarily strong. "We have not forfeited caution. We have forfeited nothing. The President has given us assurances."[31]

[27] *New York Times,* September 8, pp. 1–9, and September 10, pp. 1–14.
[28] *Congressional Record,* September 11, 1963, p. 15912.
[29] *Ibid.*, p. 15913.
[30] *Ibid.*, p. 15919.
[31] *Ibid.*, p. 15915.

Prior to his meeting with the President, he and four other Republican Senators met with Secretary of Defense Robert McNamara, Undersecretary of State Averell Harriman, Disarmament Agency Director William Foster, and the Director of Defense Research Harold Brown. With the exception of Senator Dirksen, all of the other Senators were members of the Committees on Foreign Relations or Armed Services and were respected as specialists in their respective areas. All but one voted for the treaty.[32]

The amendment to the preamble of the resolution authorizing ratification offered by Richard Russell also prompted considerable executive-legislative consultation. Senator Russell asked that in the future all amendments to the treaty be submitted to the Senate for the advice and consent of two-thirds of its members. Initially, treaty supporters argued that this was unnecessary because it was guaranteed in the Constitution. Senator Mansfield had consulted earlier with the Secretary of State on this matter; and, in a letter written by Dean Rusk on the same day Senator Russell introduced his amendment, the Secretary of State characterized the proposal as constitutionally unnecessary.[33] Senator Fulbright also submitted a letter written by Secretary Rusk on this matter, and the Chairman of the Committee on Foreign Relations consulted the legal adviser of the Department of State.[34] However, by September 18, the leaders decided to approve the Russell amendment and requested other Senators to vote for it.[35] In part this was based on a consideration that a fight with Senator Russell on his amendment might only increase his opposition to the treaty. The Chairman of the Committee on Armed Services had been relatively inactive in opposition to the treaty. However, a few Senators refused to accomodate either their leaders or Senator Russell. For example, Senator Morse announced that he wished to inform the leadership that he was "not interested in placating anyone by agreeing that unessential language be added to this treaty or to its resolution of acceptance."[36]

During the debate, representatives from the Department of State and the Arms Control and Disarmament Agency were in the Senate gallery and were often waved down to the cloakroom when Senators had questions which the staff of the Committee on Foreign Relations could not answer.[37] Representatives of these executive agencies also made themselves available

[32] *New York Times,* September 5, 1963, p. 19.
[33] *Congressional Record,* September 12, 1963, p. 15969.
[34] *Ibid.,* p. 16003.
[35] *Ibid.,* September 18, 1963, p. 16489.
[36] *Ibid.*
[37] Interview, Washington, D.C., May, 1963.

to Senators in their offices to answer questions or supply information for speeches, newsletters, or letters.

The fact that the United States had signed the treaty imposed indirect pressures on the Senate. Rather than debating a proposed policy, the Senate was considering a treaty which involved considerations of presidential leadership in the world and the prestige of the United States. Before the treaty had been successfully negotiated, the Senate could debate the effects of a test ban without devoting much attention to public opinion as a central factor. Several Senators, including Bourke Hickenlooper, ranking Republican on the Committee on Foreign Relations, expressed their annoyance that the Senate had lost some of its independence once the treaty had been initialed.[38] Many believed it was necessary for them to consider the reactions of other nations to the treatment of the treaty by the Senate. Sam J. Ervin reflected the sentiments of several other Senators when he announced that he would reluctantly vote for the treaty because it was the lesser of two evils. Actually, it should never have been signed but to reject it after it had been signed, Senator Ervin believed, "would . . . irretrievably, if not absolutely, destroy any opportunity for the United States to furnish the free world any effective leadership during the foreseeable future."[39]

Those who voted against the treaty argued that world reaction should not be the primary concern. Senator Russell told the Senate that he would prefer other nations "to like us," but this goal had been extended beyond rational limits, according to him. He feared that American preoccupation with world opinion had "become almost a national disease."[40]

The relationship between the executive and legislative branches was not only one of direct interaction, such as consultations and letters, but also included perceptions by the Senate of the past performance of the administration and the future role of the Senate in the treaty making process. The discussion of Table 8-3 identified some of these perceptions by Senators of the President. Those who were satisfied with past administration behavior were more apt to trust and support the President than the skeptics.

[38] *Congressional Record,* September 20, 1963, p. 16742.
[39] *Ibid.,* September 17, 1963, p. 16243.
[40] *Ibid.,* September 19, 1963, p. 16615.

### *The Senate Vote*

The vote on the treaty was a function of a number of factors, although party membership was not one of them. Senators who were liberal on domestic matters were most likely to support the treaty, while those who opposed conservative proposals less than 10 per cent of the time were most apt to oppose the treaty. Committee membership also was a factor. Table 8-5 indicates that members of the Committee on Foreign Relations were least likely to oppose the treaty, and that other Senators, excluding those on the Committee on Armed Services, followed the recommendations of the Committee on Foreign Relations rather than the Committee on Armed Services.

Previous votes on arms control measures and opposition to administration foreign policy explains much of the vote. Most of those who had previously supported measures affecting arms control and had voted for the administration's recommendations on foreign policy voted for the treaty, while those who normally voted against such measures opposed the treaty. The next most significant factor was the conservatism of the Senators; the more conservative a Senator was, the more apt he was to oppose the treaty.

One of the votes cast against the treaty by a member of the Committee on Foreign Relations can, in part, be attributed to conservatism. Senator Frank Lausche supported the conservative coalition 84 per cent of the time, which was the highest level of support for the coalition for all of the northern Democrats. Russell Long, the other committee member opposed to the treaty, had supported the conservative coalition 28 per cent of the time. In addition, both Senators tended to the power maximizer approach while most of the other members of the committee tended to an optimizer position.

The three Senators voting against the treaty who had the highest scores of opposition to the conservative coalition were Robert Byrd, Russell Long, and Margaret Chase Smith. Senators Byrd and Smith were both members of the Committee on Armed Services and attended most of the hearings conducted by its Preparedness Subcommittee.

Four reservations were introduced and were defeated before the Senate agreed to the treaty. By a vote of 33 to 61, the Senate defeated a resolution by Russell Long which would have permitted the use of nuclear weapons in an armed conflict. John Tower's proposed reservation was to postpone the effectiveness of the treaty until the United Kingdom, the Soviet Union,

TABLE 8-5. *Selected Characteristics and the Treaty Vote* [a]

| Characteristic | No. Voting | | % of Category | |
|---|---|---|---|---|
| | Yes | No | Yes | No |
| Party | | | | |
| Democrat | 56 | 11 | 83.6 | 16.4 |
| Republican | 25 | 8 | 75.8 | 24.2 |
| Committee Membership [b] | | | | |
| Foreign Relations | 15 | 2 | 88.3 | 11.7 |
| Atomic Energy | 6 | 3 | 66.7 | 33.3 |
| Armed Services | 10 | 7 | 58.8 | 41.2 |
| All others | 54 | 9 | 84.0 | 16.0 |
| Region | | | | |
| East | 21 | 1 | 5.4 | 4.6 |
| Midwest | 25 | 3 | 89.3 | 10.7 |
| West | 21 | 5 | 80.8 | 19.2 |
| South | 14 | 10 | 58.3 | 41.7 |
| Seniority | | | | |
| Freshman | 13 | 3 | 81.2 | 18.8 |
| 2 to 6 years | 24 | 2 | 92.3 | 7.7 |
| More than 6 years | 44 | 14 | 75.8 | 24.2 |
| Disarmament Score [c] | | | | |
| 0 (Low) | 1 | 11 | 8.3 | 91.7 |
| 1-3 (Medium low) | 6 | 4 | 60.0 | 40.0 |
| 4-5 (Medium high) | 18 | 3 | 85.7 | 14.3 |
| 6-7 (High) | 56 | 1 | 98.2 | 1.8 |
| Oppose Administration Foreign Policy [d] | | | | |
| 50% or more of the time | 11 | 13 | 45.8 | 54.2 |
| 20 to 49% of the time | 19 | 5 | 79.2 | 20.8 |
| 0 to 19% of the time | 51 | 1 | 98.1 | 1.9 |
| Oppose Conservative Coalition [e] | | | | |
| 0 to 9% of the time | 14 | 15 | 48.3 | 51.7 |
| 10 to 49% of the time | 24 | 3 | 88.9 | 11.1 |
| 50 to 79% of the time | 31 | 1 | 96.9 | 3.1 |
| 80 to 100% of the time | 12 | 0 | 100.0 | 0.0 |

[a] This Table is based on the total votes cast as well as the one vote which was announced for the treaty.

[b] Overlapping membership brings the total to more than 100.

[c] The Disarmament Score is based on the percentage of vote or announced positions of Senators on seven disarmament measures. If a Senator did not vote or announce a position on every issue, his score was computed on the basis of the ratio of pro-arms control positions to his total vote on these issues.

[d] Based on scores computed by *Congressional Quarterly* on 40 roll calls for 1963. *Congressional Quarterly Almanac,* 1963, p. 716.

[e] Based on scores computed by *Congressional Quarterly* on 43 roll calls for 1963. *Ibid.,* p. 746.

and the United States agreed to on-site inspections, and it was defeated by a vote of 16 to 76. Another reservation introduced by John Tower was defeated 11 to 82. Under its terms, the treaty would not become effective until the Soviets had fully paid all of their assessments due the United Nations for its peacekeeping operations. Barry Goldwater introduced a reservation which would have delayed the effectiveness of the treaty until the Soviet Union removed all of its nuclear weapons and missiles from Cuba. The Senate rejected the reservation by a vote of 17 to 75. An amendment to the preamble of the Senate resolution of ratification was offered by Richard Russell, and, as noted, it was reluctantly supported by the Senate leadership. Approved 79 to 9, it called for the President to submit all future amendments to the test ban treaty to the Senate for its advice and consent.

With the exception of the Long reservation and the Russell amendment, none of these proposals received much support. The Tower and Goldwater reservations reflected an uneasiness bothering many of the power maximizers that the United States had made dangerous concessions affecting American military power when it negotiated the treaty, but had received no military or political compensation from the Soviet Union. They argued that the Soviet Union wanted the treaty because it would benefit them disproportionately, and consequently the Soviets would accept the reservations.

The Long reservation represented the most serious challenge to the leadership, and received the support of most of the power maximizers as well as many security optimizers who leaned to the power maximizer position on some matters. In his letter to Senator Dirksen, President Kennedy pledged that he would not interpret the treaty in any way which might endanger American security and assured the country that the treaty would not be operative in time of war. However, as Table 8-6 indicates, 35 Senators, or one-third of the legislative chamber, supported the Long reservation, and a disproportionate number of them were Republicans. Four factors help to explain why a majority of the Republicans supported the reservation: (1) It incorporated the essence of the stipulation suggested by former President Dwight D. Eisenhower in his letter to the Committee on Foreign Relations. (2) There was a tendency for conservative Senators, as identified by the *Congressional Quarterly* score, to oppose disarmament, and more Republicans were conservative than liberal. (3) The members of the non-administration party were less susceptible to arguments concerning loyalty to the President. (4) The ranking Republican member of the Committee on Foreign Relations supported the proposal and exercised greater influence on this issue than did the minority leader who opposed the reservation.

Most of the support for the reservation came from conservatives, South-

TABLE 8-6. *Selected Characteristics and the Vote on the Long Reservation* [a]

| Characteristic | Number Against | Number For | % of Category Against | % of Category For |
|---|---|---|---|---|
| Party | | | | |
| Democrat | 51 | 16 | 76.1 | 23.9 |
| Republican | 14 | 19 | 42.4 | 57.6 |
| Committee Membership [b] | | | | |
| Foreign Relations | 12 | 5 | 70.6 | 29.4 |
| Atomic Energy | 5 | 4 | 55.6 | 44.4 |
| Armed Services | 8 | 9 | 47.1 | 52.9 |
| All Others | 44 | 19 | 72.4 | 27.6 |
| Region | | | | |
| East | 18 | 4 | 81.8 | 18.2 |
| Midwest | 21 | 7 | 75.0 | 25.0 |
| West | 17 | 9 | 65.4 | 34.6 |
| South | 9 | 15 | 37.5 | 62.5 |
| Seniority | | | | |
| Freshman | 12 | 4 | 75.0 | 25.0 |
| 2 to 6 years | 22 | 4 | 84.6 | 15.4 |
| More than 6 years | 31 | 27 | 53.5 | 46.5 |
| Disarmament Score | | | | |
| 0 (Low) | 1 | 11 | 8.3 | 91.7 |
| 1-3 (Medium Low) | 1 | 9 | 10.0 | 90.0 |
| 4-5 (Medium High) | 9 | 12 | 42.9 | 57.1 |
| 6-7 (High) | 54 | 3 | 94.6 | 5.4 |
| Oppose Administration Foreign Policy | | | | |
| 50% or more of the time | 4 | 20 | 16.7 | 83.3 |
| 20 to 49% of the time | 13 | 11 | 54.2 | 45.8 |
| 0 to 19% of the time | 48 | 4 | 92.4 | 7.6 |
| Oppose Conservative Coalition | | | | |
| 0 to 9% of the time | 3 | 26 | 10.3 | 89.7 |
| 10 to 49% of the time | 20 | 7 | 74.1 | 25.9 |
| 50 to 79% of the time | 30 | 2 | 93.8 | 6.2 |
| 80 to 100% of the time | 12 | 0 | 100.0 | 0.0 |

a The formal vote was 61 to 33 to table the Long reservation. Each of the Senators not voting announced a position, and is included in this table. The ratio is then 65 to 35.

b Overlapping membership brings the total to more than 100.

erners, and previous opponents of disarmament in particular and administration foreign policy in general. Of the 57 Senators who had a 6 or 7 score for previous disarmament measures, that is, high scores, only 5.3 per cent voted for the Long reservation, while 90.9 per cent of the members with a score ranging from 0 to 3 supported it.

Table 8-7 accentuates the characteristics of treaty opposition already discussed. It constitutes a profile of support which was constructed by assigning one point for a vote for the treaty and one point for each vote against a proposed reservation.[41] Including pairs and announced votes, 64 Senators had scores of 5, and 11 had a profile of 0. Conservatives were the Senators who most likely had low scores, as were Southerners and members of the Committee on Armed Services. There is no serious difference by party, except for the vote on the Long reservation. Of the Senators who voted against the treaty, Senators Smith and Lausche had scores of three, and Senator Byrd of West Virginia had a score of four, voting only against the treaty. All other treaty opponents had profiles ranging from 0 to 3.

## *Conclusions*

The vote in the Senate represented the apogee of the test ban treaty-making process.[42] The hearings and the debate demonstrated considerable concern over the matter of future steps in arms control agreements with the Soviet Union, particularly those which required inspection. Given Soviet reluctance to accept widescale inspection on its territory and given the hesitancy of many Senators to accept any treaty which was based on trusting the good intentions of the Soviet Union or which did not have inspection provisions for underground tests, it appears that any future arms control proposal would not necessarily fare as well as the limited test ban treaty. A considerable proportion of the members of the Senate belonged to the power maximizer group or leaned to this position in some respects. These Senators were likely to be most impressed with arguments about inadequate inspection and the possibility that American security could be critically endangered.

[41] The Russell amendment is not included in the profile.

[42] The President signed the instrument of ratification in the treaty room of the White House on October 8, 1963, formally completing the process. Copies were sent to Moscow and London, another was deposited with the Department of State, while the fourth was given to the National Archives. *Washington Post*, October 8, 1963, p. A2.

TABLE 8-7. *Selected Characteristics and Profile of Support for the Treaty without Reservations or Amendments*

| | Profile [a] | | | | | |
|---|---|---|---|---|---|---|
| Characteristic | 0 | 1 | 2 | 3 | 4 | 5 |
| Party | | | | | | |
| Democrat | 5 | 2 | 2 | 1 | 7 | 50 |
| Republican | 6 | 0 | 4 | 2 | 7 | 14 |
| Committee Membership [b] | | | | | | |
| Foreign Relations | 1 | 0 | 2 | 1 | 1 | 12 |
| Atomic Energy | 2 | 0 | 1 | 0 | 1 | 5 |
| Armed Services | 4 | 1 | 0 | 1 | 4 | 7 |
| All Others | 5 | 1 | 3 | 1 | 9 | 44 |
| Region | | | | | | |
| East | 0 | 0 | 1 | 1 | 2 | 18 |
| Midwest | 0 | 0 | 2 | 2 | 4 | 20 |
| West | 5 | 0 | 1 | 0 | 3 | 17 |
| South | 6 | 2 | 2 | 0 | 5 | 9 |
| Oppose Administration Foreign Policy | | | | | | |
| 50% or more of the time | 10 | 1 | 4 | 1 | 4 | 4 |
| 20 to 49% of the time | 1 | 1 | 2 | 2 | 5 | 13 |
| 0 to 19% of the time | 0 | 0 | 0 | 0 | 5 | 47 |
| Oppose Conservative Coalition | | | | | | |
| 0 to 9% of the time | 10 | 2 | 6 | 1 | 7 | 3 |
| 10 to 49% of the time | 1 | 0 | 0 | 2 | 4 | 20 |
| 50 to 79% of the time | 0 | 0 | 0 | 0 | 3 | 29 |
| 80 to 100% of the time | 0 | 0 | 0 | 0 | 0 | 12 |

[a] A zero score indicates the Senator voted against the treaty and supported all reservations and amendments to the treaty; that is, he voted against the administration position each time. A score of one indicates he voted with the administration once, although the table does not indicate whether he voted for the treaty or against an amendment or reservation.

[b] Overlapping membership brings the total to more than 100.

Should the ratio of Senate conservatives to liberals change, support for arms control proposals would decrease. This is not to suggest that every conservative is opposed to any arms control measures or that every liberal will automatically support this type of proposal, but the figures consistently indicated that the most effective index for accounting for a Senator's position is his ranking with respect to opposition to the conservative coalition as well as his level of previous support for an internationally minded President's foreign policy.

Opposition to arms control by members with greater senatorial seniority appeared to be a reflection of their conservatism rather than their tenure in the Senate. Those elected between 1958 and 1962 had a tendency to be more liberal than were Senators who had been elected at an earlier date. Conservatism also helps to explain the high ranking of opposition among Southerners, inasmuch as this region had a high proportion of conservative Senators. The Southerners who voted for the treaty also tended to vote against the pattern set by a majority of Southern Democrats on other issues. Senators Mike Monroney, Albert Gore, Olin Johnston, Ralph Yarborough, and J. William Fulbright, in that order, had the highest opposition scores to the conservative coalition among Southern Democrats.

CHAPTER IX

# CONCLUSIONS

Neither of the two dominant models purporting to explain policy-making in the United States is applicable to the test ban treaty or to similar types of foreign and national security issues which are highly technical but which also stimulate considerable political activity.[1] The pluralist model emphasizes group activity and the dispersal of power while the elite model focuses on the concentration of power in the hands of an interlocking clique who are not accountable to the public.[2] Activity by individuals, groups, and the mass media does not indicate that the pluralist model is operating because these non-governmental participants may not penetrate the decision-making system. Nevertheless because linkages between non-governmental participants and official decision-makers are difficult to locate, it is not logical to conclude that an elite necessarily decides all major issues.[3]

C. Wright Mills argued that the United States is essentially ruled by an

[1] The test ban differed from those types of foreign policy issues which were intimately related to specific economic interests in the United States such as the reciprocal trade bills. It also differed from programs to which a considerable amount of money was associated such as foreign aid bills. Foreign aid has been debated not only on the basis of diplomatic, strategic, and humanitarian considerations but also around the money used to finance the program. Higher taxes and the need for a balanced budget were arguments the opponents of foreign aid often invoked against the proposal. On the test ban issue, there was no strong interest in the outcome from an economic perspective as would be the case with tariffs or a large reservoir of illwill because of the program's effects on the budget as was the case with foreign aid.

[2] C. Wright Mills, *The Power Elite* (New York: Oxford University Press, Galaxy Edition, 1959), for the elitist approach and Robert A. Dahl, *Who Governs?* (New Haven: Yale University Press, 1961) for the pluralist approach.

[3] David Easton has discussed the importance of inputs penetrating the political system. Without demands crossing over the boundaries of the system, either because they are not strong enough to compete with other demands or because they are blocked by 'gatekeepers,' there is no system response. For a comprehensive treatment of this problem, see his *A System Analysis of Political Life* (New York: John Wiley, 1965), pp. 117–149.

industrial-military-political complex which makes important decisions without regard to the electorate. The overlapping interests of the highest strata of the corporations, the military services, and the bureaucracy propelled them to cooperate. They established a consensus about what must be done and how to do it, and when disagreements arose, the elite settled its problems in private. Mills insisted that the absence of conflict about consequential decisions, such as multibillion dollar budgets of the Department of Defense effecting national security, indicates the presence of a power elite. He rejected the group-theory hypothesis, finding that the interests represented in Congress were so parochial that they do not impinge on really vital national concerns such as the issues of war and peace.[4]

Mills' approach is often unrewarding as an explanatory tool because agreements among diverse decision-makers often stem from several causes, and an elite conspiracy does not account for every accord. His analysis is more applicable to other types of decisions than the test ban, namely, for crisis situations in which a few individuals make important decisions without consulting the public or for problems which are considered to be technical rather than political. Furthermore, Mills does not account for marginal or partial losses by his military-industrial complex. Moreover, his approach does not adequately account for the influence of the scientists in the decision-making process. The conflict that has been identified in the case of the test ban can be explained by the elite model only by suggesting that the treaty was not really important and therefore the elite was uninterested in the outcome or that the opponents of the treaty were not part of the power elite. The first objection begs the question for if this issue were unimportant, why did senior members of the Senate and the military services oppose the test ban?[5] Furthermore, the test ban accords with Mill's identification of the issues which interest the military-industrial-

[4] "More and more of the fundamental issues never come to any point of decision before Congress, or before its most powerful committees, much less before the electorate in campaigns. The entrance of the United States into World War II, for example, in so far as it involved the American decision, by-passed the Congress quite completely. It was never a clearly debated issue clearly focused for a public decision." Mills, *op. cit.*, p. 255. For his discussion of Congress, see pp. 250 and 256, and *passim*. Mills contends that Congressmen more often consider local interests than international issues. Other social scientists have accepted this conclusion but for reasons which differ from Mills. For example, see Anthony Downs, *An Economic Theory of Democracy* (New York: Harper, 1957).

[5] Mills argues that "the chairman [sic] of the major committees are the elite members of Congress. In their hands rest the key powers of Congress, both legislative and investigative." *Op. cit.*, p. 252.

complex.[6] The second qualification contradicts the meaning of an elite; for if the generals and admirals are part of the elite only when they succeed, then the elite is transistory, but Mills accorded the ruling elite some measure of permanence.

Robert Dahl does not attempt to prove that the general public is directly or intimately involved in decision-making. But denying the notion of dominance by any one group, he holds several groups participate in the examination and resolution of political issues.[7] He believes that when a group finds that an issue is important to it, the organization mobilizes its resources to compete with groups with opposing interests. Because it has limited resources, an organization only participates in those areas which will affect it in a consequential way. Therefore, issues such as beautification projects which are peripheral to most of the members will receive only passing attention for most groups. Whatever the strengths of the Dahl model to explain many areas in domestic politics, it is not convincing when transferred to most national security and foreign policy questions. Groups, including mass membership groups, are not very important in foreign policy and national security matters except for issues like the tariff which have a direct and tangible effect on the interests of their members.[8] By their own admission, most of the mass membership groups identified in Chapter 5 did not believe they were instrumental in influencing votes in the Senate.

In contrast to Mills, Dahl insisted that the presence of elites could be proven only in conflict situations when one group, the elite, was continuously victorious over its opponents.[9] Exclusive reliance on either approach is often unrewarding. To exclude all nonconflict situations leads to such unlikely conclusions as James Payne's that there are no oligarchies in Latin America because there is no measurable conflict between the rulers and the people.[10] But Mills would have an elite operating whenever an important policy was settled without conflict. In several respects, Dahl's approach reflects the reluctance of many political scientists to study situations which

[6] For Mill's discussion of the military services, see *Ibid.*, pp. 171–224.

[7] For a contrast between populism and pluralism, see Robert Dahl, *A Preface to Democratic Theory* (Chicago: University of Chicago Press, 1956).

[8] Cf. Raymond A. Bauer, Ithiel de Sola Pool, and Lewis Anthony Dexter, *American Business and Public Policy: The Politics of Foreign Trade* (New York: Atherton Press, 1963). The intense public political activity on behalf of the tariff should be compared with the intense restricted activity in the matter of military research and development. See Robert J. Art, *The TFX Decision: McNamara and the Military* (Boston: Little, Brown, and Co., 1968).

[9] Dahl, *Who Governs? op. cit.* Also see Nelson Polsby, *Community Power and Political Theory* (New Haven: Yale University Press, 1963), p. 119.

[10] James L. Payne, "The Oligarchy Muddle," *World Politics,* XX (April, 1968), pp. 439–453, particularly p. 449.

are not easily managed methodologically. To the extent that we have attempted to become scientific, we have often ignored certain political problems because they could not be subjected to the scrutiny we thought was used in the natural sciences. Some of Dahl's students have intimated that his model is the method scientifically best suited for examining decision-making,[11] but not only are there other models which can be used, Dahl's contributions present some serious shortcomings in their own right. Some of the factors ignored by Dahl are the control of information, latent power, access to the system, the distinction between technical problems and political issues, and management of the agenda and the options available to other participants.

Decision-makers, the mass media, groups, and the public are all dependent on others for information, so that strategically located individuals can withhold information from other participants, including uninterested bystanders who might otherwise have acted if the information were available. The withholding of information is designed to avoid conflict, and when individuals or agencies can route messages, allowing some to travel through public or permeable channels but restricting others to private channels, then power is in fact being exercised, and indeed the purpose of using this power is to preclude a conflict situation. In the case of foreign policy and national security, the channels are relatively impermeable, reducing the number of participants and possible sources of criticism of the policy. During the period when the administration was formulating its position on the test ban and while the agreement was being negotiated at Moscow, the White House exercised close supervision over the cables exchanged between Washington and Moscow, reducing the possibility of premature opposition developing. Furthermore, the information supplied Congress from the agencies was often coordinated with the White House.[12] By controlling information, the White House, in the early stages of the treaty-making process at least, was able to limit the number and types of participants and forestall opposition.

However, no participant is guaranteed control over information without challenge. Senators opposed to the treaty tried to collect their own data and make the control of information by the executive branch an issue itself.[13] Both strategies were employed by the Preparedness Subcommittee

[11] Polsby, *op. cit.*, Chapter 6.

[12] Cf. Theodore Sorensen, *Kennedy* (New York: Harper and Row, 1965), p. 738.

[13] This appears to have become a pattern as Senators who do not have access to expert supporting testimony within the government sponsor their own research outside or call on scientists outside of government to support their position. Senator Edward

which relied on its own independent information source, Dr. Edward Teller, to supply alternative interpretations and information. The committee also hammered away at administration witnesses about the extent of consultation between the White House and Joint Chiefs of Staff prior to and during the Moscow negotiations.

Latent power has often been confused with potential power, which simply refers to the resources which provide the basis of power for a participant but which he is not currently using. The observer who assigns power to a participant simply because he has resources available to him is constructing causal connections which cannot be justified. Latent power, however, refers to the real expectations of one of the participants about the future application of power by another participant. The discussion of the armed services in Chapter 3 showed that latent power can be used to explain the public restraint of some officers.

Even if there is considerable discussion among the public as well as intense activity by some groups, there is no guarantee that they have reached decision-makers. Activity might occur only at the periphery of the political system and not enter the decision-making system itself. Access does not mean every participant makes decisions but does mean that the demands of citizens or groups enter the system and are given attention by decision-makers. They gain access because decision-makers believe that their position is relevant to the issue or because they have convinced a decision-maker they either may be able to help or hinder his continuation in office or may be able to assist or retard him in reaching other policy goals. Technical, not political, considerations determine who has access under the first condition, but politics or power are central in the second. Both trade unions and management groups have access to the political decision-making system when a labor law is under consideration because each side has expressed its interest in the subject and has indicated it will use its resources to effect a favorable decision. In such a case, legislators as well as administrators do not substitute the advice of specialists in place of the interest groups but take into account the interests and power of the groups. Access, in such cases, does not guarantee success but does assure a hearing because decision-makers who ignore the groups endanger their own tenure in office and their other political goals.

In national security matters, the mass membership groups are not customarily considered relevant to the problem because they do not possess

Kennedy called on several eminent scientists to evaluate the anti-ballistic missile in 1969. Cf. *Washington Post,* May 7, 1969, p. 1.

the expertise which interests most decision-makers and because they cannot demonstrate the intense, salient interests of their members in this issue. If a group cannot activate its members and sustain their interest in the issue, the organization possesses no realistic political threat to decision-makers.[14] During the test ban hearings, the Senators were interested in 'experts' and the committee concentrated on technical specialists. Attendance precipitously fell when private witnesses testified before the Committee on Foreign Relations following the testimony of military officers and scientists.[15] The Preparedness Subcommittee notably excluded all representation by private groups because they were considered to be ill-equipped to contribute to the military and technical evaluation of the treaty. When fallout, for example, was considered irrelevant to the examination of the treaty, then experts on this issue had no worthwhile contribution to make. That someone is given a platform, such as fifteen minutes before a Senate committee, does not mean he has gained access to the decision-making system. The pattern of themes in the hearings and the debate, the attendance of Senators for different types of witnesses, and the preponderance of specialists concerned with the military implications of the treaty who appeared at the hearings all reinforce the observation that the specialists had access to the decision-making system while the public and organizations did not.[16]

It might be assumed there was access because of the close similarity between the Senate vote on the one hand and the public and media reaction on the other. Table 9-1 shows a high level of correspondence for most regional and partisan comparisons, but Table 9-2 demonstrates there was relatively little congruency on the issue. Correspondence refers to a similarity of behavior while congruency refers to a similarity of perceptions and

[14] Of course the members of peace groups felt intensely about arms control; but the size of these groups was so small they were largely ignored.

[15] Two measures of access by groups into the senatorial decision-making system are (a) the number of representatives of organizations called to testify and (b) the number of Senators in attendance to hear the groups compared to Senatorial attention to other witnesses, particularly administration witnesses and specialists. The Preparedness Subcommittee called no witnesses from organizations although several military officers were invited to testify. The Committee on Foreign Relations heard from 18 witnesses representing groups. When the Secretaries of State and Defense appeared, over thirty Senators were in attendance, a few more than heard from scientists like Drs. Teller, Foster, and Brown. When private and organizational witnesses testified, between five and eleven Senators were present.

[16] For the themes discussed, see Tables 8-2 and 8-3.

TABLE 9-1. *Correspondence of Support for the Treaty by the Public, Press, and Senate according to Selected Characteristics*

| Area | Public | | | Press | | | Senate | | |
|---|---|---|---|---|---|---|---|---|---|
| | | Party | | | Party | | | Party | |
| | Total | Rep. | Dem. | Total | Rep. | Dem. | Total | Rep. | Dem. |
| East | 73 | 67 | 75 | 86% | 84% | 100% | 95% | 94% | 100% |
| Midwest | 63 | 61 | 69 | 80 | 76 | 100 | 89 | 91 | 88 |
| South | 48 | 37 | 52 | 58 | 56 | 100 | 58 | 0 | 70 |
| West | 61 | 55 | 69 | 60 | 46 | 100 | 81 | 50 | 100 |
| Total | 63 | 58 | 67 | 73 | 70 | 100 | 81 | 84 | 76 |

Sources: Public Opinion, AIPO, Aug. 1963; Press: Sample from Table 4-2, with Republican papers identified as those which supported Richard Nixon for the Presidency in 1960 and the Democratic papers identified as those which endorsed John Kennedy. Clair Engle's announced support for the treaty is included as a vote although the California Democrat was hospitalized at the time and did not vote.

evaluations. Even though the Senate, public, and press showed the same levels of support for the treaty, they did so for substantially different reasons. The public was particularly concerned with health, diplomatic, and humanitarian factors while the Senate highlighted military considerations, almost to the exclusion of such topics as fallout or the state of the world following a nuclear exchange. The press was closer to the Senate than to the general public.

If there is a correspondence and not a congruency among the three participants when considerable pressure is exerted, it seems likely that the concerns of the public and groups are not apt to become important when they do not actively press their position. When the Senate vote on the treaty is compared not only with the themes in the Senate debate but also the vote on the Long reservation to permit the United States to use nuclear weapons during time of war, it is even more apparent that there was little congruency between many senators and most of the public.

### *Public Opinion and Foreign Policy: Burke Revisited*

Edmund Burke maintained that the public representative must follow his conscience and intelligence when he voted, mindful of what was best

TABLE 9-2. *Rationale for Favoring or Opposing the Test Ban for the Public, Press, and the Senate*

| Theme | Public | Press | Senate |
|---|---|---|---|
| Fallout & Humanitarian | 81 | 15 | 16 |
| Diplomatic | | 45 | 33 |
| Military | 19 | 31 | 48 |
| Total | 100 | 91 | 97 |

Sources, Tables 4-2, 6-2, and 8-1.

for his constituents. The representative does not measure public opinion or the goals of a few groups, but asks what would objectively best serve the well-being of the entire community in the present and the future. Burke's approach assumes that what is truly good for the community can be discovered by the representative who would consult groups or individuals not to determine their narrow interest in the matter but to use their expertise in helping him identify whether a proposal is beneficial or detrimental to the entire community. Elected officials have generally taken Burke's advice concerning the role of the public on national security and foreign policy matters, excluding issues like the tariff. However, they have not always dismissed the importance of public support for their position. Contending sides often work to build a public following for their position because majorities legitimize the decision within the democratic framework. Public officials also try to build a consensus about the merits of foreign and military policy, thereby removing the matter from popular debate and, where there is disagreement, charging the opposition with unpatriotic or parochial perspectives. Some officials who are discontent with a proposal may promote discussion to transform it from a technical problem or a consensus policy to a political issue, that is, a debatable, disputable public issue, thereby injecting new considerations, such as public opinion, for policy makers.

One way to consider the role of public opinion is to compare decision-making with electronic message transmission. In such a transmission, a sender attempts to pass a message to a receiver; or in the political system, one participant attempts to influence another. However, in both instances, the background setting is important. Static, noise, or distortion may arise in the electronic transmission, altering the meaning of the message or possibly even prohibiting its reception. In the political system, public opinion is one of the factors which affects the clarity, integrity, and intensity of a message. Through its attention, the public may alter a problem which is considered to be a specialized diplomatic, scientific, or military problem to a political issue. In the case of the test ban the public, groups, and media recommendations were not decisive in determining Senate approval but were influential in altering the parameters of debate. The President relied on the groups to demonstrate increasing interest in arms control to the Senate, reinforcing the political elements in his agenda. Even though most Senators were probably not affected by these considerations, some from marginal states were under a variety of constraints which they could ignore only at considerable expense.[17]

The President and his supporters in the Senate used the public opinion surveys, press, and group support to legitimize their position as reflecting the will of the people. Senate supporters were busy building their case, as Hubert Humphrey inserted scores of editorials in the *Congressional Record* and J. William Fulbright reported the latest Harris survey to the Senate. The Senate opposition also insisted that it had public support. Margaret Chase Smith's ingenious division of mail into pre-Labor Day and post-Labor Day letters to load response in her favor, A. Willis Robertson's contention that the polls were incorrect, and Strom Thurmond's report of a flood of mail against the treaty suggests that the opposition found it necessary to justify its position in the face of strong support for the other side. For all of this, during the hearings and the debate, most attention was given to highly specialized matters which did not primarily interest most of the public or the groups which supported the treaty.

The public did not have effective access to many Senators during this period although scientists and military officers did. The scientists were expected to provide insight on technical features and not examine the social or political ramifications of the test ban. However, experts are sometimes selected because they are expected to endorse a position, discredit other specialists, or nurture suspicions about proposed policies. Nevertheless, they can also present new information or interpretations which enlighten decision-makers not strongly committed to a position, particularly Senators who are not intimately concerned with an issue but are nevertheless called upon to vote on several hundred unfamiliar issues each year.

Mills argued that the elite are responsible to one another but not to the general public and that a substantial number of decision-makers were not restrained by even marginal checks of accountability to the public. Mills'

[17] In interviews conducted a year after the vote, I found that only two Senators appeared to have been primarily influenced by pressures within their home states.

observations seem appropriate to many national security questions and reinforce the conclusion that decision-makers follow Burke's advice regarding the role of public opinion on these matters. Nonetheless, Mills asked the wrong question about responsibility in a mass society when he linked it with accountability to the public, that is to the voters. There are a myriad number of complex decisions facing the voter who selects among candidates who often follow his wishes on some matters but not on others. From a policy-making perspective, responsibility may be concerned with assuring the representation of diverse viewpoints early in the decision-making process and providing alternatives throughout the process. The problem with Dahl's pluralist community power model for national security and foreign policy is not that it shortcuts democracy as some of its critics have charged but that it simply does not operate at this level.[18]

## *Option Management*

Not only are those who can control information important in decision-making, but those who can otherwise contract or enlarge the parameters of debate are also crucial, particularly those who can determine or influence the format of the agenda, who are instrumental in identifying the relevant questions to be solved or who are responsible for the collection, interpretation, and distribution of relevant data. Although the President could not ignore information collected by strategically located agencies without running the possible risk of opposition from some agency personnel and their supporters in Congress, he had greater flexibility than most other government officials in selecting the information he wished to use, partly because he had more sources of competing information and related recommendations. Moreover, he had superior claims to legitimacy than any of the other participants and could use his claims as protector of the national interest to advance his position. He could claim he considered all of the ramifications of conflicting proposals; and, in selecting some, he transcended the possibly narrow perspectives of agencies. When there was public disagreement between the agencies and the President, he generally had greater access to the public, mass media, interest groups, and others to present his position than his opponents.

One of the strategies the President used to facilitate his flexibility was

[18] See Charles McCoy and John Playford (eds.), *Apolitical Politics* (New York: Crowell, 1967).

to submit a signed treaty to the decision-making process. His potential opposition and uncommitted Senators, government scientists, and military officers had to consider the effects of the treaty not only on national security but also on the possible detrimental effects on American leadership in the international community if the treaty were rejected in the Senate. Because national security is partially related to the support of American policy by foreign governments and publics, rejection of the treaty by the Senate could seriously endanger American interests.[19] The effects of changing the agenda are illustrated in Senator Ervin's remark that he would have opposed the test ban had he been consulted before it had been signed. These new factors also account for the shifting position of the Joint Chiefs of Staff from opposition to a test ban in June to support in August after the treaty had been negotiated in Moscow.[20] Changes in the format can introduce new considerations which cause some of the participants to shift positions. Dahl's observation that only conflict situations can be studied ignores the effects on behavior of altering the agenda. Changing the nature of the proposal introduces new options, including the addition of costs which might be so considerable for some potential opponents that they forego earlier plans to oppose the proposal.

The President also changed the agenda by making the test ban a public issue and removing it from exclusively technical and military considerations. In problem-solving situations, specialists almost exclusively had access to the decision-making system and the public was considered an unwelcome and uninformed intruder.[21] The President publicized the treaty in order to stimulate public opinion, the press, and groups to take an active

[19] The same observations apply to Lyndon Johnson's conduct of the Vietnam war. He was able to introduce such factors as the projected adverse consequences on American prestige if the United States withdrew its forces; the effects of withdrawal on other Southeast Asian countries; that opposition at home gave aid and comfort to the enemy, and that we needed to support the boys in the field and not engage in divisive debate at home. Obviously, there are important differences in the two cases, including the length of time involved in the two processes, the inability of President Johnson to deliver his promises, the growing cost of American lives and dollars, and the increased distaste for the war as it became a salient issue for a large segment of the general public. Nevertheless, President Johnson effectively controlled the parameters of debate for many of the participants until the last 18 months of his administration. It was at his time that the costs increased and the issue became increasingly salient to the public.

[20] U.S. Senate, Preparedness Subcommittee, *Military Aspects and Implications of Nuclear Test Ban Proposals and Related Matters*. 88th Cong., 1st Sess., 1963, pp. 355 and 589–90.

[21] However, the Preparedness Subcommittee never accepted the changes and declined to hear from health or arms control witnesses.

interest in the agreement, but he took care to avoid transforming the test ban into a partisan issue. This change helps to explain the coincidence between the reactions of the public, the media, and the Senate even though the Senate examined the treaty from a more technical perspective than did the public or media.

The integrity of individuals, groups, or agencies submitting alternatives for consideration also affects the viability of the pluralist approach. In the Dahl model, each participant articulates his own interests as he sees them, and if he moderates his claims it is because he believes it is politically prudent to do so. However, this was not always the case with government agencies in the test ban case. In the armed services, those with lower ranks had to consider the preferences of those in higher authority. Many officers and scientists opposed the treaty and although they advanced their objections within the service, they were precluded from debating the matter publicly and were expected to follow the lead of the service chiefs. Loyalty, discipline, and consideration for the future of the service were relevant factors which they had to consider in taking a public stand. Even though some Air Force officers worked through the Air Force Association, they did not take a public position themselves but left vocal, public opposition to the civilians. This covert opposition, along with news leaks, did not prove effective in this issue because only widespread, visible opposition by the military to the President's contention that national security was not seriously endangered could have added credibility to the opposition. Occasional anonymous attacks coupled with the public disagreements of a few retired officers and the head of the Strategic Air Command did not excite widespread opposition.

The independence of the Arms Control and Disarmament Agency can also be questioned because of personnel from the military services included in its research and policy-proposing activities. Whether this enlarged staff affected the recommendations of the Agency is not known, but such an arrangement opens questions about the degree to which arms control proposals were muted or rewritten to conform to the expectations and evaluations of military officers associated with the Agency. Such an arrangement did not work totally to the disadvantage of the Agency because its proposals, having been formulated with military considerations in mind, anticipated some of the misgivings of those who believed that disarmament was potentially a dangerous venture.[22]

[22] Joseph H. Monane suggests this type of enhancement is common in system interaction and refers to enhanced power or access as "gilt by association." *A Sociology of Human Systems* (New York: Appleton-Century, 1967), pp. 35–41.

*Feedback: The Options of the Opposition*

If the President changed the context of the Senate deliberations by introducing a signed treaty, those who had been skeptical about arms control altered his intentions of treating the agreement primarily as a diplomatic document. The President had to consider the early reactions of the Republican leadership who announced that it would study the military implications of the test ban before it decided whether to support or oppose the treaty. Furthermore, the chairman of the Armed Services Committee announced he would withhold judgement, and the chairman of the Preparedness Subcommittee reported he would take the unusual step of conducting hearings on the treaty to consider its national security consequences. By satisfying some skeptics that there was no military danger, the President reduced the chance of defeat but in the process accepted the misgivings of his opponents as relevant. If the President refused to recognize their preoccupations, he risked losing the necessary two-thirds majority needed in the Senate.

The object of some of the skeptics was not to vote down the treaty which was becoming increasingly difficult to do as an overwhelming majority in the public and press supported the treaty. In the face of this developing consensus, the skeptics worked to change the direction of policy and warn the President that there was a residue of suspicion in the Senate about further arms control pacts. The activity of the skeptics in part helps to explain the President's quick acceptance of the safeguards proposed by the Joint Chiefs of Staff.

The President had not asked the Chiefs to draw up safeguards, although he quietly accepted them. Even though he might have elicited an endorsement without accepting their demands for underground tests, he increased the credibility of his military witnesses by accepting the safeguards. Without some consideration for national security, the changed position of the Chiefs from opposition to support would have seemed too sudden and contradictory to have been acceptable to some of the marginal skeptics and might have introduced the charge that the President had forced the chiefs into endorsing his treaty.[23] Although a majority of the Senate was not skep-

[23] The two major biographers of Kennedy disagree on this point. Arthur Schlesinger writes that the Chiefs "attached 'safeguards' to their support." This led to an immediate increase in underground testing. "The President was prepared to pay this price to commit the nation to a treaty outlawing atmospheric tests." *A Thousand Days* (Boston: Houghton Mifflin Co., 1965), pp. 912–913. However, Theodore Sorensen intimates that the President and Secretary of Defense simply "reassured" the Chiefs that there would

tical, enough Senators were undecided about the military ramifications that the President had to cater to their misgivings, and they, in effect, set the terms of the Senate debate. To have avoided any concern about the military considerations in the debate, as he had in his television speech when he announced the treaty had been signed, would have given the opposition party sufficient cause to make the treaty a partisan issue, accusing the administration of laxity with national security. Had the treaty become a partisan issue the treaty would probably not have received the necessary two-third approval of the Senate.

The President also had to consider that most of the groups which had assisted him on other issues were indifferent to the test ban. Several of them were preoccupied with the impending civil rights issue while others simply did not wish to become involved in foreign policy issues. Even some of the mass-membership organizations which endorsed the treaty were not enthusiastic. George Meany, President of the AFL-CIO, was reluctant to support the agreement even though several of the leaders of the industrial unions were vigorously working for its ratification. The President called Meany and asked him to endorse the treaty, not because the labor leader's support was essential for success but because it would add to the tone of overwhelming acceptance of the test ban which the President wished to create.[24] When Meany finally endorsed the treaty, he paralleled the skeptics and not the supporters of arms control. The President could not count on some of his earlier reliable group supporters to assist him on the treaty if he ignored the military issues, and he consequently had to consider their hesitancy when he dealt with the demands of the military services for safeguards and the misgivings of the skeptics in the Senate.

The extent of Senate suspicion can be seen in the vote on the Long reservation to the treaty which would have permitted the use of nuclear weapons in an armed conflict. Although it failed, it was supported by 35 Senators, two more than needed to defeat the treaty if every Senator were voting. Defections from votes for the treaty to the reservation were most pronounced among Republicans and conservative Senators on whom the President had less influence than among liberal Democrats. While 75 per

be continued underground testing, *op. cit.* p. 738. Several of the opponents of the treaty charged that the military had not been sufficiently consulted and that their endorsement was a proof of duress brought by the White House. However, these accusations did not excite much attention in the floor debate or in most newspapers.

[24] Interviews, Washington, May, 1964.

cent of the Republicans voted for the treaty, 58 per cent of them voted for the reservation; 48 per cent of those who generally voted with the conservative coalition supported the treaty, but only 10 per cent of these same Senators voted against the reservation.[25] To have ignored the military implications of the treaty might have induced some of the liberal power maximizers to oppose the treaty. In other words, the substantial vote for the treaty conceals considerable skepticism about arms control in the Senate.

The President was not alone in adjusting his priorities to accord with the preoccupation of the skeptics. Most of the attention of Senator J. William Fulbright and the staff of the Committee on Foreign Relations was devoted to dismissing the argument that the treaty endangered national security and to insisting that neither American security nor nuclear research would be compromised by the test ban. Yet Fulbright believed that the importance of the treaty lay in its diplomatic ramifications and the staff was impressed by the political priorities of the President when he initially presented the agreement. But both of them had other objectives than simply supporting the treaty on the grounds they thought were important. Fulbright believed that he would have more credibility with the skeptics if he displayed familiarity, concern, and optimism about the military implications of the treaty. Because Senator Bourke Hickenlooper's support was considered necessary, the staff had to adjust to his priorities when it arranged the witnesses, including the large representation of scientists, and when it wrote the committee report.

## *Summary and Conclusions*

The treaty did not become the first step that President Kennedy envisioned or that Senator Dirksen and other skeptics feared. During the period following ratification, little attention was devoted to arms control, and there was no effective pressure to retard demands for a growing nuclear testing program. It was not until 1967 that Senator John Pastore introduced his resolution calling for a nonproliferation treaty, a year later the proposal was successfully negotiated with the Soviet Union, and still a year later, after it became a campaign issue, the Senate gave its advice and consent to the treaty. The test ban had been seen by the administration as

[25] A majority of the Senators voting was needed to approve a reservation or amendment to the treaty while a two-thirds vote of those Senators voting was required for the approval of the treaty.

a means of controlling the arms race and as a commitment to achieving national security by moving away from military superiority and toward diplomatic solutions. However, the treaty proved to be a step to the most expensive series of nuclear tests the United States had attempted. While the treaty was still before the Senate, the Kennedy administration embarked on underground tests in Nevada. In fiscal 1963, the Atomic Energy Commission spent $ 133,150,591 on testing, in fiscal 1967 the figure climbed to $ 193,181,782, and in fiscal 1969, $ 314,600,000 was requested for testing.[26] Moreover, the increasing commitment of the United States in Vietnam indicated that military priorities were still paramount over other criteria to define and advance American security.[27]

Between 1964 and 1967, national security again became a problem to be solved by experts and not an issue subject to public debate and decision. During this period, there was considerable public apathy about national security as the groups and media turned to domestic problems or ratified the President's behavior in Vietnam. National security was seen as an administrative, technical problem which specialists ought to solve and was not considered fit for citizen review.[28] As is usually the case when technical considerations are paramount, the evaluation of the effects of military solutions and increased nuclear testing focused on only selected implications. Several other related questions were ignored such as whether there might be adverse consequences for the domestic economy, whether increased testing by the United States might prompt the Soviet Union to take countermeasures, and whether development and procurement of military materials was not creating a constituency which had an interest in the continuation of large-scale military spending. Within the milieu of public, press, and group indifference, the administration was able to move unhindered until its claims that the policy was technical no longer seemed

[26] U.S. Congress, Joint Committee on Atomic Energy, *AEC Authorizing Legislation, Fiscal Year, 1965, Hearings,* 88th Cong., 2nd Sess., 1964, Part I, p. 279 and *AEC Authorizing Legislation, Fiscal Year, 1969, Hearings,* Part II, 90th Cong., 2nd Sess., 1968, p. 2088. Interestingly, only $ 5,500,000 was requested for detection activities in fiscal 1969, p. 2089.

[27] The Johnson administration offered several reasons for the American commitment in Vietnam, but one of the recurring ones was the national security argument that by meeting the communist threat in Vietnam, the United States would be able to protect herself from her enemies better in the future or possibly even avoid a larger war.

[28] One of the interesting features of the period was the decline of diplomacy and the increasing importance of military experts in the Southeast Asia area. Diplomacy was often seen as an adjunct of national security policy which was primarily based on strategic military considerations.

credible and the consensus for its national security collapsed as the costs rose disproportionately to any anticipated benefits.

American politics has been seen more concerned with bargaining than with debates or fights and open bargaining is the basis of democratic politics.[29] But when certain matters become the exclusive domain of specialists with little or no access provided to public agencies, we move from politics and issues to administration and problem-solving.[30] One of the challenges for American leadership in the 1970's is whether it will move to make arms control a debatable issue while the challenge facing members of the articulate public, including the groups, mass media, and professions, is whether it will move to stimulate popular interest in the issues of national security and arms control, making them appropriate matters for public review and debate rather than delegating the powers of decision to specialists who have much to contribute but who are neither omniscient nor above criticism.

[29] Anatol Rapport, *Fights, Games and Debates* (Ann Arbor: University of Michigan Press, 1960).

[30] Of course, administration is infused with politics, but by making a problem administrative rather than political, the parameters of participants is generally closed and access into the problem-solving system is less permeable to those who do not have the credentials of experts.

## APPENDIX I

### Comparison Between Texts of Treaty Tabled at the Geneva Disarmament Conference on August 27, 1962, and That Signed at Moscow on August 5, 1963[1]

#### TITLE

Draft Treaty Banning Nuclear Weapon Tests in ~~the~~ Atmosphere, *in* Outer Space~~-~~, and Underwater

#### PREAMBLE

The Governments of the ~~Union of Soviet Socialist Republics~~ *United States of America*, the United Kingdom of Great Britain and Northern Ireland, and the ~~United States of America~~ *Union of Soviet Socialist Republics*, hereinafter referred to as the "*O*riginal Parties",

*Proclaiming as their principal aim the speediest possible achievement of an agreement on general and complete disarmament under strict international control in accordance with the objectives of the United Nations which would put an end to the armaments race and eliminate the incentive to the production and testing of all kinds of weapons, including nuclear weapons.*

~~Desirous of bringing about~~ *Seeking to achieve* the ~~permanent~~ discontinuance of all ~~nuclear weapon~~ test explosions *of nuclear weapons for all time*, ~~and~~ determined to continue negotiations to this end, *and desiring to put an end to the contamination* ~~on man's environment by radioactive substances,~~

~~Confident that immediate discontinuance of nuclear weapon test explosions in the atmosphere, in outer space, and in the oceans will facilitate progress toward the early agreement providing for the permanent and verified discontinuance of nuclear weapon test explosions in all environments,~~

Have agreed as follows:

[1] Senate, Committee on Foreign Relations. *Nuclear Test Ban Treaty, Hearings.* 88th Cong., 1st Sess., 1963; pp. 814–816. Deletion – elimination of material from August 1962 text; italic – addition of new material in August 1963 text.

## ARTICLE I

~~OBLIGATIONS~~

1. Each of the Parties to this Treaty undertakes to prohibit, *to* ~~and~~ prevent ~~the carrying out of~~, *and not to carry out* any nuclear weapon test explosion, *or any other nuclear explosion* at any place under its jurisdiction or control:

(a) in the atmosphere, ~~above the atmosphere;~~ *beyond its limits, including outer space,* or in *underwater, including* territorial *waters* or high seas; or

(b) in any other environment if such explosion causes radioactive debris to be present outside the territorial limits of the State under whose jurisdiction or control such explosion is conducted. *It is understood in this connection that the provisions of this subparagraph are without prejudice to the conclusion of a treaty resulting in the permanent banning of all nuclear test explosions, including all such explosions underground, the conclusions of which, as the Parties have stated in the preamble to this Treaty, they seek to achieve.*

2. Each of the Parties to this Treaty undertakes furthermore to refrain from causing, encouraging, or in any way participating in, the carrying out of any nuclear weapon test explosion, *or any other nuclear explosion*, anywhere which would take place in any of the environments described, or have the effect ~~prescribed,~~ *referred* to in paragraph 1 of this Article.

~~ARTICLE II~~

~~EXPLOSIONS FOR PEACEFUL PURPOSES~~

~~The explosion of any nuclear device for peaceful purposes which would take place in any of the environments described, or would have the effect prescribed, in paragraph 1 of Article I may be conducted only:~~

~~(1) if unanimously agreed to by the original Parties; or~~

~~(2) if carried out in accordance with an Annex hereto, which Annex shall constitute an integral part of this Treaty.~~

~~ARTICLE III~~

~~WITHDRAWAL~~

~~1. If any Party to this Treaty determines~~

~~(a) that any other Party has not fulfilled its obligations under this Treaty,~~

~~(b) that nuclear explosions have been conducted by a State not a Party to this Treaty under circumstances which might jeopardize the determining Party's national security, or~~

~~(c) that nuclear explosions have occurred under circumstances in which it is not possible to identify the State conducting the explosions and that such explosions, if conducted by a Party to this Treaty, would violate the Treaty or, if not conducted by a Party, might jeopardize the determining Party's national security,~~

~~it may submit to the Depositary Government a request for the convening of a conference to which all the Parties to this Treaty shall be invited, and the~~

~~Depositary Government shall convene such a conference as soon after its receipt of the request as may be practicable. The request from the determining Party to the Depositary Government shall be accompanied by a statement of the evidence on which the determination was based.~~

~~2. The conference shall, taking into account the statement of evidence provided by the determining Party, and any other relevant information, examine the facts and assess the significance of the situation.~~

~~3. After the conclusion of the conference or after the expiration of a period of sixty days from the date of the receipt of the request for the conference by the Depositary Government, whichever is the earlier, any Party to this Treaty may, if it deems withdrawal from the Treaty neccessary for its national security, give notice of such withdrawal to the Depositary Government. Such withdrawal shall take effect on the date specified in the notice, which shall in no event be earlier than sixty days from receipt of the notice by the Depositary Government. The notice shall be accompanied by a detailed statement of the reasons for the withdrawal.~~

## ARTICLE ~~IV~~ *II*

### ~~AMENDMENTS~~

1. Any Party may propose amendments to this Treaty. The text of any proposed amendment shall be submitted to the Depositary Governments which shall circulate it to all Parties *to this Treaty*. Thereafter, if requested to do so by one-third or more of the Parties, the Depositary Governments shall convene a conference, to which ~~it~~ *they* shall invite all the Parties, to consider such amendment.

2. Any amendment to this Treaty ~~or its Annex~~ must be approved by a ~~vote of two thirds of the Parties~~ *majority of the votes of all the Parties to this Treaty*, including *the votes of* all of the original Parties ~~to this Treaty. It~~ *The amendment* shall enter into force for all Parties upon the deposit of *instruments of* ratification by ~~two thirds of the Parties~~ *a majority of all the Parties*, including *the instrumentals of* ratification ~~by~~ *of all of* the original Parties.

## ARTICLE ~~V~~ *III*

### ~~SIGNATURE, RATIFICATION, ACCESSION, ENTRY INTO FORCE AND REGISTRATION~~

1. This Treaty shall be open ~~until~~ ———————— to all States for signature. Any state which does not sign this Treaty *before its entry into force in accordance with paragraph 3 of this article* may accede to it at any time.

2. This Treaty shall be subject to ratification by signatory States. Instruments of ratification and instruments of accession shall be deposited with the ~~Government of~~ ————————, ~~which is hereby designated the Depositary Government~~ *Governments of the original Parties—the United States of America, the United Kingdom of Great Britain and Northern Ireland, and the Union of Soviet Republics—which are hereby designated the Depositary Governments.*

3. This Treaty shall enter into force ~~on~~ ———————— ~~for States which have deposited instruments of ratification of accession on or before that date, pro-~~

~~vided that the ratifications deposited include those of the original Parties. If ratifications by all three original Parties are not deposited on or before ———, this Treaty shall enter into force on the date on which ratifications by all of them have been deposited~~ *after its ratification by all the original Parties and the deposit of their instruments of ratification.*

4. *For States whose* instruments of ratification or accession *are* deposited subsequent to the entry into force of this Treaty ~~shall become binding,~~ *it shall enter into force* on the date of *the* deposit *of their instruments of ratification or accession.*

5. The Depositary Governments shall promptly inform all signatory and acceding States of the date of each signature, the date of deposit of each *instrument of* ratification of and accession to this Treaty, the date of its entry into force, and the date of receipt of any requests for conferences or ~~other~~ notices ~~of withdrawals.~~

6. This Treaty shall be registered by the Depositary Governments pursuant to Article 102 of the Charter of the United Nations.

### *ARTICLE IV*

*This Treaty shall be of unlimited duration. Each Party shall in exercising its national sovereignty have the right to withdraw from the Treaty if it decides that extraordinary events, related to the subject matter of this Treaty, have jeopardized the supreme interests of its country. It shall give notice of such withdrawal to all other Parties to the treaty three months in advance.*

### ARTICLE ~~VI~~ *V*

~~AUTHENTIC TEXTS~~

This Treaty, of which the English and Russian texts are equally authentic, shall be deposited in the archives of the Depositary Governments. Duly certified copies of this Treaty shall be transmitted by the Depositary Governments to the Governments of the signatory and acceding States.

IN WITNESS WHEREOF the undersigned, duly authorized, have signed this Treaty,

DONE *in triplicate* ~~AT~~ *at* ——————— *Moscow*, this *fifth* day of *August*, one thousand nine hundred and ~~sixty-two~~ *sixty-three.*

APPENDIX II

## SELECTED SENATE ROLL CALL VOTES *

| *Senator* | *1* | *2* | *3* | *4* | *5* | *6* | *7* | *8* | *9* | *10* |
|---|---|---|---|---|---|---|---|---|---|---|
| Aiken | x | x | x | x | x | x | x | x | x | x |
| Anderson | x | x | x | x | x | x | x | x | x | x |
| Batlett | x | x | x | x | x | x | x | x | x | x |
| Bible | x | x | x | x | x | x | x | x | x | x |
| Byrd (W. Va.) | x | x | x | x | x | x | x | x | – | x |
| Case | x | x | x | x | x | x | x | x | x | x |
| Church | x | x | x | x | x | x | x | x | x | x |
| Clark | x | x | x | x | x | x | x | x | x | x |
| Cooper | x | x | x | x | x | x | x | x | x | x |
| Douglas | x | x | x | x | x | x | x | x | x | x |
| Engle | x | x | x | x | x | x | x | x | x | x |
| Fulbright | x | x | x | x | x | x | x | x | x | x |
| Gore | x | x | x | x | x | x | x | x | x | x |
| Gruening | x | x | x | x | x | x | x | x | x | x |
| Hart | x | x | x | x | x | x | x | x | x | x |
| Hartke | x | x | x | x | x | x | x | x | x | x |
| Hayden | x | x | x | x | x | x | x | x | x | x |
| Hill | x | x | x | x | x | x | x | x | x | – |
| Humphrey | x | x | x | x | x | x | x | x | x | x |
| Javits | x | x | x | x | x | x | x | x | x | x |
| Keating | x | x | x | x | x | x | x | x | x | x |
| Long (La.) | x | x | x | x | x | – | – | – | – | – |
| Long (Mo.) | x | x | x | x | x | x | x | x | x | x |
| McGee | x | x | x | x | x | x | x | x | x | x |
| McNamara | x | x | x | x | x | x | x | x | x | x |
| Mansfield | x | x | x | x | x | x | x | x | x | x |
| Metcalf | x | x | x | x | x | x | x | x | x | x |
| Monroney | x | x | x | x | x | x | x | x | x | x |
| Morse | x | x | x | x | x | x | x | x | x | x |
| Moss | x | x | x | x | x | x | x | x | x | x |

* Selected Votes on Foreign Policy Measures, 1961–1963, and Votes on the Test Ban Treaty and Reservations

| *Senator* | *1* | *2* | *3* | *4* | *5* | *6* | *7* | *8* | *9* | *10* |
|---|---|---|---|---|---|---|---|---|---|---|
| Muski | x | x | x | x | x | x | x | x | x | x |
| Neuberger | x | x | x | x | x | x | x | x | x | x |
| Pastore | x | x | x | x | x | x | x | x | x | x |
| Pell | x | x | x | x | x | x | x | x | x | x |
| Proxmire | x | x | x | x | x | x | x | x | x | x |
| Randolph | x | x | x | x | x | x | x | x | x | x |
| Sparkman | x | x | x | x | x | x | x | x | x | x |
| Symington | x | x | x | x | x | x | x | x | x | x |
| Williams (N. J.) | x | x | x | x | x | x | x | x | x | x |
| Yarborough | x | x | x | x | x | x | x | x | x | x |
| Young (Ohio) | x | x | x | x | x | x | x | x | x | x |
| Bayh | 0 | 0 | 0 | 0 | x | x | x | x | x | x |
| Brewster | 0 | 0 | 0 | 0 | x | x | x | x | x | x |
| Burdick | 0 | 0 | 0 | 0 | x | x | x | x | x | x |
| Edmondson | 0 | 0 | 0 | 0 | x | x | x | x | x | x |
| Inouye | 0 | 0 | 0 | 0 | x | x | x | x | x | x |
| Kennedy | 0 | 0 | 0 | 0 | x | x | x | x | x | x |
| McGovern | 0 | 0 | 0 | 0 | x | x | x | x | x | x |
| McIntyre | 0 | 0 | 0 | 0 | x | x | x | x | x | x |
| Nelson | 0 | 0 | 0 | 0 | x | x | x | x | x | x |
| Ribercoff | 0 | 0 | 0 | 0 | x | x | x | x | x | x |
| Carlson | 0 | 0 | x | x | x | x | x | x | x | x |
| Walters | 0 | 0 | 0 | 0 | 0 | x | x | x | x | – |
| Pearsons | 0 | 0 | x | x | 0 | x | x | x | x | x |
| Fong | x | – | x | x | x | x | x | x | x | x |
| Hickenlooper | x | – | x | x | x | x | x | x | x | – |
| Johnston | x | x | – | x | x | x | x | x | x | x |
| Williams (Del.) | x | – | x | x | x | x | – | – | x | – |
| Boggs | – | x | x | x | x | x | x | x | x | x |
| Dodd | – | x | x | x | x | x | x | x | x | x |
| Ervin | – | x | x | 0 | x | x | x | x | x | – |
| Jackson | – | x | x | x | x | x | x | x | x | x |
| Jordon (N. C.) | – | x | x | x | x | x | x | x | x | x |
| McCarthy | – | x | x | x | x | x | x | x | x | x |
| Magneson | – | x | x | x | x | x | x | x | x | x |
| Morton | – | x | x | x | x | x | x | x | x | x |
| Scott | – | x | x | x | x | x | x | x | x | x |
| Miller | – | x | – | x | x | x | x | x | x | – |
| Smathers | – | x | x | x | – | x | x | x | x | x |
| Beall | – | – | x | x | x | x | x | x | x | – |
| Cannon | – | – | x | x | x | x | x | x | x | – |
| Dirksen | – | – | x | x | x | x | x | x | x | x |
| Holland | – | – | x | x | x | x | x | x | x | – |
| Kuchel | – | – | x | x | x | x | x | x | x | x |
| Lausche | – | – | x | x | x | x | x | x | – | – |
| Prouty | – | – | x | x | x | x | x | x | x | x |
| Saltonstall | – | – | x | x | x | x | x | x | x | x |

| *Senator* | *1* | *2* | *3* | *4* | *5* | *6* | *7* | *8* | *9* | *10* |
|---|---|---|---|---|---|---|---|---|---|---|
| Allott | – | – | x | x | – | x | x | x | x | – |
| Cotton | – | – | – | x | x | x | x | x | x | – |
| Smith | – | – | – | x | x | x | x | x | – | – |
| McClellan | – | – | – | x | – | x | – | x | – | – |
| Mundt | – | – | – | x | – | x | – | – | x | – |
| Stennis | – | – | – | x | – | x | – | – | – | – |
| Young (N. D.) | 0 | 0 | – | x | 0 | x | x | x | x | – |
| Eastland | – | – | – | 0 | – | x | x | – | x | – |
| Dominick | 0 | 0 | 0 | 0 | – | – | x | – | x | – |
| Jordan (Id.) | 0 | 0 | 0 | 0 | – | – | – | – | – | – |
| Mechem | 0 | 0 | 0 | 0 | – | – | – | – | – | – |
| Simpson | 0 | 0 | 0 | 0 | – | – | – | – | – | – |
| Bennett | – | – | – | – | – | – | – | – | – | – |
| Byrd (Va.) | – | – | – | – | – | – | – | – | – | – |
| Curtis | – | – | – | – | – | – | – | – | – | – |
| Ellender | – | – | – | – | – | x | x | x | x | – |
| Goldwater | – | – | – | – | – | – | – | – | – | – |
| Hruska | – | – | – | – | – | x | x | – | x | – |
| Robertson | – | – | – | – | – | – | – | – | – | – |
| Russell | – | – | – | – | – | – | – | – | – | – |
| Talmadge | – | – | – | – | – | x | – | – | – | – |
| Thurmond | – | – | – | – | – | – | – | – | – | – |
| Tower | – | – | – | – | – | – | – | – | – | – |
| *Senator* | *1* | *2* | *3* | *4* | *5* | *6* | *7* | *8* | *9* | *10* |

x indicates a vote favoring arms control and related measures. – indicates a vote against arms control and related measures. 0 indicates the Senator did not vote, was not paired, or did not have a position on the particular vote.

1. The Goldwater amendment to limit the authority of the Arms Control and Disarmament Agency. Rejected, 43 to 46, September 8, 1961.
2. Dirksen amendment to refer the bill creating the Arms Control and Disarmament Agency to the Committee on Armed Services. Rejected, 33 to 54, September 8, 1961.
3. Final vote authorizing purchase of up to $ 100 million in United Nations bonds. Accepted, 70 to 22, April 5, 1962.
4. Appropriations for the Arms Control and Disarmament Agency. Passed, 59 to 14, June 17, 1963.
5. Final vote to create the Arms Control and Disarmament Agency. Passed, 73 to 14, September 8, 1961.
6. Tower reservation which would require payment of United Nations peace-keeping debts accumulated by the Soviet Union before the treaty became operative. Defeated, 11 to 82, September 23, 1963.
7. Tower reservation requiring on-site inspections before treaty became operative. Defeated, 16 to 76, September 23, 1963.
8. Goldwater reservation requiring the Soviet Union to remove its forces from Cuba before the treaty became operative. Defeated, 17 to 75, September 23, 1963.
9. The test ban treaty. Approved, 80 to 19, September 24, 1963.
10. Long Reservation allowing the use of nuclear weapons in an armed conflict. Tabled, 61 to 33, September 23, 1963.

# INDEX